ANCESTORS AND DESCENDANTS OF
CHARLES HUMPHRIES
(d. 1837)
OF
UNION DISTRICT, SOUTH CAROLINA
1677-1984

Including Records from
Virginia, North Carolina, South Carolina,
Mississippi, and Other States

BY

Brent Howard Holcomb
Certified Genealogist

HERITAGE BOOKS
2025

HERITAGE BOOKS

AN IMPRINT OF HERITAGE BOOKS, INC.

Books, CDs, and more—Worldwide

For our listing of thousands of titles see our website
at
www.HeritageBooks.com

Published 2025 by
HERITAGE BOOKS, INC.
Publishing Division
5810 Ruatan Street
Berwyn Heights, MD 20740

Library of Congress Catalog Card Number: 84-52535

International Standard Book Number
Paperbound: 978-1-68034-679-4

ABOUT THE AUTHOR

Brent Howard Holcomb is a professional genealogist residing in Columbia, South Carolina. He is a Certified Genealogist, author or co-author of over fifty books of genealogical material including several family histories, and has been editor of The South Carolina Magazine of Ancestral Research since 1977. He is also a descendant of Charles Humphries (see page 127).

TABLE OF CONTENTS

ANCESTORS AND DESCENDANTS OF CHARLES HUMPHRIES (d. 1837) OF UNION DISTRICT, SOUTH CAROLINA 1677-1984

INTRODUCTION

The author has been aware practically all of his life that he was an Humphries descendant. [Note that the "h" has not been pronounced in the name within the memory of any living member of the family, and that the name is pronounced as if it were spelled "Umphries."] Almost any descendant is aware of his Humphries heritage, and distant relationships are recognized and acknowledged among members of this family. When the author was about thirteen years old, he went with a friend, Lee Benjamin, to visit the grandmother of the latter, Mrs. Will Rice. The author noticed the name Humphries in the home, and a conversation with Mrs. Rice was commenced. The connection was immediately recognized, and the sleeping interest in the family on the part of the author was awakened. A good friend and neighbor, Mrs. Roy Workman, in Clinton, South Carolina, was also aware of the connection. The author attended the Humphries Reunion in 1967, and found that considerable information had been compiled. In fact, a chart which stretched the width of Sardis Methodist Church was available, and had been in progress for over twenty years. The information thereon was copied by the author, and it became the nucleus of this volume. The information concerned the descendants of Charles Humphries (d. 1837), and though undocumented, was of utmost help in beginning.

Incidentally, the Humphries Reunion is still held annually, as it has been since 1931. In the early years, it was a rather large gathering, sometimes as many as three hundred fifty people attending. Many Humphries descendants who had moved away from Union County made an annual journey back to the Reunion, from Greenville, Walhalla, Darlington, and other places. Some were descendants of people who had moved away as long as eighty years before, particularly those of Darlington County. They were known as the "down the county Humphrieses."

Although not a pioneer family of Union County, South Carolina, (moving there after the Revolutionary War), the Humphries family has made a significant contribution to the history and development of that county. Members of the Humphries family have been ministers, doctors, county officials, and have been active in church and civic affairs. The names of Rev. Thomas Young, Billy Humphries, Dr. Christopher Young, and "Polly" Young are still familiar to many Union County residents. Hardly a child in the school system of Union in the twentieth century exists who has not been taught by a member of this family.

Of course, this is not a complete genealogy. Information on some descendants has not been available. An effort has been made to contact every family group, but this is not possible, and some have not responded for one reason or another. However, cooperation has been very good, and the author thanks every person who has contributed, especially the following: Mrs. Leon (Mannie Lee Edwards) Mabry, Mrs. Hay Fant (Vivian) Bradburn, Mrs. Sims (Betty

Keisler) Johns, Mr. T. H. (Hop) Peake, Mr. Franklin Lambert, all descendants of Charles Humphries, and Mrs. J. B. Christopher, a connection of the family. My thanks especially to Mrs. Stahle (Jo White) Linn, Jr., for her support, encouragement, and helpful suggestions in writing this genealogy. Also, Union County Cemeteries by Mrs. E. D. Whaley, Sr., published by A Press, Inc., Greenville, South Carolina, has been invaluable in locating graves of many persons in this volume.

The format of this volume is roughly that of the New England Register Method. It is organized by generations. The Arabic numbers are only reference points, and have no signficance to generations. The superscript numbers show the generation of the person, and the lineage of the person being discussed is given in parenthesis after his or her name. This system has worked fairly well, except the author has not found anything in this system to deal with persons who have more than one Humphries line. The author has done this as best he can. Because of rather heavy intermarriage, some persons are actually of more than one generation in descent from Charles^1 Humphries or John^1 Humphries. Therefore, a person will appear in the earliest generation to which belongs. The Arabic numbers are useful to direct the reader to other lines. The author has two Humphries lines himself, and there are several persons in this volume who have four Humphries lines. This is the only family known to the author wherein a person might address his or her mother-in-law as "Cousin Sallie" or "Cousin Lucy."

A plus sign before the Arabic number in the listing of children indicates that there will be more information on that person later in the volume and/or his descent is continued. Documentation for the early generations of this family is found in notes at the end of each generation. Information on living persons or given by living persons within their memories has been accepted, if no conflicting information has been found. Some persons have requested that information on them found in this volume not be repeated in other genealogies without their consent. Therefore, readers are advised not to include information contained in this volume for other works without contacting the persons concerned.

The author hopes that this will be a beginning for many readers to research their own lineages further, both in the Humphries lineage and others that they may have. Additions and corrections to the information in this volume are welcomed by the author.

Brent Howard Holcomb
November 26, 1984

ANCESTORS OF CHARLES HUMPHRIES (d. 1837)

Although there is no absolute proof of descent from any generation prior to John Humphries, who left a will in Brunswick County, Virginia, in 1738 (see below), the earliest person of this surname in the same area was one Evan Humphreys. Several researchers, working independently of one another, have reached the same conclusion: Evan Humphreys is the progenitor of the Humphries family of Brunswick County, Virginia. The circumstantial evidence for this statement follows.

Evan Humphreys (Humphry, Humphrey) was imported to Virginia by 1677. The deposition of Rowland Davies, "aged 24 or thereabouts... touching his tithables...he hath 4 men servants, called James Johnson, Jno Collins, Evan Humphreys, and Jno Esquire," dated 4 September 1677.[1] Evan Humphreys appears on the 1678 list of tithables in Surry County, Virginia, as "Van Humphry," and on the 1679 list as "Evan Humphreys."[2] Mr. Richard Slatten of Ashland, Virginia, has kindly searched the Surry County, Virginia, tithable lists (which will be published in future articles) and reports that Evan Humphreys appears on the list for 1680 as a title of Walter Tayler. He appears on the lists of 1681, 1682, 1683, 1684, 1685, 1687, 1690, and 1691 as head of his own household, listing only one tithable. On the 1692, 1693, 1694, and 1698 lists he appears with Richd. Stringefellow (probably his step-son) listed as one of his tithables. In 1701, Evan Humphreys is listed as head of household with only one tithable (presumably himself). In 1702, "Evens Humphrey & Evens Humphrey Junr." are listed; in 1703, "Evens Humphrey & Robt. Humphrey" are listed. In general, a male became a tithable at age sixteen. Therefore, the conclusion is that Evan Humphreys Junr. and Robert Humphreys were sons of Evan, and that they were probably born about 1684-1685. On 3 December 1705, Evan Humphrey and wife Jane, "in ye lower parish of Surrey County, planter," sold to Richard Stringfellow, for 1000 pounds of tobacco, a tract of land given to Jane by her father's will of April 1679, "on Lawnes Creek in ye county above, laid out 12 February 1679, 145 acres." Both Evan and Jane signed by mark, and the deed was witnessed by Robert Crafford, John Shugars, and Arch. Griffin. It was proved 18 November 1707.[3] Although the deed states that Jane inherited the land from her father, the father's name is not mentioned. A page-by-page search of the Surry County will books revealed a will of that date. The will of Richard Harris, dated 18 April 1679, left land to his son-in-law Walter Tayler [note above that Evan Humphreys was a tithable of Walter Tayler in 1680], and the remainder to his daughter Jane Stringfellow and heirs; his wife, Jane Harris, and son Walter were named executors. This will was proved 16 June 1679.[4] The interpretation of the documents indicates that Jane was a Harris by birth, and a widow Stringfellow when she married Evan Humphreys and that the marriage of Evan Humphreys to Jane Stringfellow took place after 18 April 1679. Another item of interest regarding Evan Humphrey is a certificate granted to him 7 November 1710 for fifty acres of land for importation of himself "into this Colony, having been in 30 years and was a servant when he came in."[5] By simple arithmetic, there is a three year discrepancy in the year of his arrival. However, the record contemporary with or closer to the event of his arrival is the deposition of Rowland Davies. The number of years mentioned in the certificate might be interpreted to mean at least thirty years, rather than exactly thirty years.

The next generation provides one John Humphries. He left a will dated 19 April 1738, in which he left an entry on Allen's Creek of 400 acres to his four sons William, John, Thomas, and Charles, to be equally divided, reserving 100 acres to his wife Mary; he left to his son Richard Humphries a young grey mare. Also the will states that his children may live with his loving wife until they arrive at the age of eighteen years. Mary is named executrix, and the will is signed by mark. The witnesses were Wm. Hagood, Mary Hagood, and Clemt. Read. The will was proved 1 March 1738/9.[6] If it can be assumed that the oldest of the five named sons was approaching the age of eighteen at the time of the writing of the will, John Humphries may have been about thirty-eight years old at the time of the will. If we assume that the oldest child was only ten, John Humphries may have been about thirty-one at the time he wrote the will. Of course, this assumes that John married and fathered the first child at age twenty-one. He may have been quite a bit older. From the tithable lists mentioned above, John does not appear as a tithable on any of the lists. He would probably be in the household of his father and still under age sixteen as late as 1703. The point of this exercise is to determine if there could be a generation between John Humphries and Evan Humphrey. There was a Robert Humphreys, who died by 1714 in this area, and was probably a son of Evan Humphrey, as stated above. The inventory of Robert Humphreys was made 17 June 1714. [7] However, since Robert Humphries died intestate, no real property is listed. Primogeniture was in effect in Virginia at this time: that is, the eldest son inherited all real property in the case of intestacy. Nothing in the inventory gives any clues about heirs. If Robert were the father of John, several things must have happened: (1) Evan Humphrey married the widow Jane Stringfellow in 1679 or 1680 and had a child (Robert) immediately. (2) Robert married at a young age and had a child (John) immediately. The implications of the tithable lists, as stated above, make this scenario impossible.

No land descended from Robert Humphries to John Humphries, nor are both names found on any one document. Since there is no proof at all that Robert Humphries was closely connected with John Humphries, and the given name Robert is not used among the descendants of Charles Humphries with any great degree, this writer is forced to assume that John was a son of Evan Humphries and wife Jane, rather than a grandson through Robert Humphries.

John Humphries (d. 1738/9) married Mary White. The will of John White, dated 14 March 1727/8, names his "cozen John Humphry son of sister Mary."[8] Also, this would lead us to believe that John Humphries was the oldest son of John and Mary Humphries, and therefore, John Humphries (d. 1738/9) was probably born 1700 or before. After the death of John Humphries in 1738/9, Mary married William White, as they conveyed land to Charles "Humphreyes" of Brunswick County, 26 March 1751, one hundred twenty-four acres of land patented to John Humphreys decd., in 1736, and devised to said Mary relict of John Humphries by will.[9] The children of John Humphries and wife Mary were as follows:

3

i. John Humphries.
ii. Thomas Humphries.
iii. William Humphries.
iv. Richard Humphries.
+ v. Charles Humphries.

Charles Humphries Senr. (son of John d. 1738/9) was born ca. 1725. His son John was born 27 December 1749 (see data on him further). He conveyed land on 22 May 1753, to John Pilkinton, 150 acres, part of 324 acres, granted to John Humphries, and which his mother Mary and step-father William White had conveyed to him (see above). Mary, wife of Charles, relinquished her dower interest in the property.[10] Therefore, they were married prior to that date. The land entry which was left to Charles and his brothers in the will of their father John lay in the area that became Lunenburg County, Virginia. All four of them (John, William, Thomas and Charles) of Lunenburg County, sold a portion of this land on Allens Creek on 1 January 1749, to Lewis Delony.[11] They sold the remainder to James Tucker of Amelia County on 1 October 1750.[12] Allen's Creek is in present Mecklenburg and Halifax counties, Virginia.

Charles's wife is said to have been Mary Bennett, but no actual proof of her maiden name has been found. The fact that a son was named Bennett offers some evidence, but certainly is not conclusive. Charles Humphries and wife Mary sold 200 acres in Lunenburg County to Thomas Cadet Young of Brunswick County on 26 July 1762.[13]

Charles Humphries moved to Johnston County, North Carolina, prior to 3 May 1765, when he purchased from Wm. Humphries and wife Mary land there, on the west side of upper Bartons Creek, it being "the land whereon the said Charles Humphreys now liveth."[14] (This William Humphries is probably the brother of Charles Humphries. On 15 July 1766 both William and Charles Humphres [sic] served on a grand jury for the Johnston County, North Carolina, Court of Pleas and Quarter Sessions.[15] Also living in the same county was John Humphries, probably also his brother, who served in the North Carolina legislature.) The land mentioned later fell into Wake County, North Carolina, and Charles Humphries obtained additional land there: a grant for 200 acres, surveyed 17 November 1778 and granted 9 August 1779,[16] and a grant for 595 acres on Lick Creek, surveyed 18 November 1778, and also granted 9 August 1779.[17] Charles Humphries did not remain in North Carolina long but moved to South Carolina in March or April of 1779. An entry in the court minutes of Wake County, North Carolina, on the first Monday in March 1779, "Ordered that a Commission issue to Joseph Davis, Esq., to take the deposition of Charles Humphries who is about to remove himself out of the State...."[18]

Charles purchased land on a branch of Sandy River (in present Chester County, South Carolina), from William Roden and wife Margaret of Camden District, South Carolina, on 10 April 1779, 100 acres. Witnesses were James Tims, Amy Tims, and John Humphreys. The deed was proved the same day before Amos Tims, J. P.[19] On 17 February 1783, Charles Humphries "of the State of South Carolina" sold 295 acres on the south side of Great Lick Creek, granted to sd. Humphries 9 August 1779, to Jesse Lumbly of Wake County, North Carolina.[20] Because of his advancing age, Charles Humphries did not have any military service in the Revolution. However, he was paid for supplying beef for the Continental Army in 1781.[21] Charles Humphries, apparently, was married a second time to Sarah, whose maiden name is not known. Charles Humphries, Senr., died in Chester District, South Carolina, before 3 April 1803, when the citation on his estate was read, the administrators being Thomas Humphries and Sarah Humphries. The inventory total was $840.38, not the inventory of a very wealthy nor an extremely poor person. The legatees listed in the estates papers are Sarah Humphries for herself and three children [not named], Absolom, John, Bennet, and Charles Humphries, Robt Smith for his wife's part, Thos Reney for his part, Richard Humphries, and Jeremiah Kingsley.[22]

The children of Charles Humphries and wife Mary (not necessarily in order of birth):

+ 1   i.   John[1] Humphries, b. 27 Dec 1749, in VA.
       ii. Bennet Humphries, b. _____, d. 1836, Chester District, SC.[23]

  iii. (dau.), m. Robert Smith.
  iv. (dau., Charlotte?), m. Jeremiah Kingsley.
   v. (dau.), m. Thomas Reney or Rainey.
  vi. Thomas Humphries.
 vii. Richard Humphries, b. _____, d. 1820, Union District, SC.[24]
viii. Absalom Humphries, b. Aug 1760, d. Dec 1834, Trigg Co., KY., m. 31 Mar 1791 to Barthenia Wall.[25]
+ 2 ix. Charles[1] Humphries, b. ca. 1762, probably in VA.

The names of the three children of Sarah are unknown.

NOTES AND REFERENCES

1. Surry Co., VA, Deeds, Wills, No. 2, 1671-1684, p. 144.

2. Edgar MacDonald and Richard Slatten, "Surry County Tithables 1677, 1678, 1679," Magazine of Virginia Genealogy, Vol. 22, No. 3, August, 1984, pp. 55-68.

3. Surry Co., VA, Deed Book 5, p. 379.

4. Surry Co., VA, Deeds, Wills & Orders, 1671-1684(transcript), pp. 323-324.

5. Surry Co., VA, Order Book, p. 353.

6. Brunswick Co., VA, Will Book 2, pp. 2-3.

7. Surry Co., VA, Book G, p. 196.

8. Surry Co., VA, Will Book 7, pp. 800-801.

9. Brunswick Co., VA, Deed Book 5, p. 66.

10. Brunswick Co., VA, Deed Book 5, p. 406.

11. Lunenburg Co., VA, Deed Book 2, p. 47.

12. Ibid., pp. 167-8.

13. Brunswick Co., VA, Deed Book 7, p. 149.

14. Johnston Co., NC, Deed Book E-1, p. 25. The deed was proved at October Court, 1765.

15. Minutes of that date, p. 121.

16. NC Land Grant Office, Raleigh, NC, Book No. 38, p. 129, File #596.

17. Ibid., p. 176, File #645.

18. Weynette Parks Haun, Wake County, North Carolina, County Court Minutes, 1777 thru 1784, Book I, p. 35.

19. Charleston, SC, Deed Book C-5, pp. 91-2.

20. Wake Co., NC, Deed Book H, p. 258.

named in the suit carried the surname Palmer.[2] The question lies unresolved.

Charles Humphries received a deed of gift dated 13 March 1798 from his father to sons Bennet Humphries "of Chester County" and Charles Humphries "of Union County" negroes Jack and Jud, horse, stills and vessels, etc.[3] Charles Humphries made a will 24 September 1837, in which he is styled "Charles Humphries Sen." to distinguish himself from his nephew Charles Humphries. He bequeathed to his daughter Polly Young wife of Christopher Young Sen., one negro man Stephen and a horse and saddle (known as Stephens), one bed and furniture. He bequeathed to "the children of Jared Young by his wife Sarah deceased my daughter" $550 to be equally divided between them. He left in trust to his friends John Rogers Esq. and Dr. Christopher Young, for the benefit and support of his son William and his family, a tract of land on which the said William Humphries "now resides, 162 acres, and one negro Jack, and $250 to pay the debts of the said William Humphries." He also mentioned Mary, the daughter of his son William Humphries; a son Ahsalom Humphries; a daughter Elizabeth Johnson; a daughter Patsey Gregory; daughter Aggatha Young, wife of Geo. Young; son Thomas Humphries; daughter Charlotte Humphries; wife Elizabeth; and named as executors his son Thomas Humphries and his son-in-law Christopher Young, Sen.[4]

The children of Charles[2] Humphries and his first wife Elizabeth (not necessarily in order of birth):

+ 12   i. Sarah[2] Humphries, b. ca. 1782.
  13   ii. Absalom[2] Humphries.
+ 14   iii. Mary (Polly)[2] Humphries, b. 18 March 1786.
+ 15   iv. William (Billy)[2] Humphries, b. 1788.
  16   v. Elizabeth[2] Humphries, m. _____ Johnson.
+ 17   vi. Martha (Patsey)[2] Humphries.
+ 18   vii. Aggatha (or Agnes)[2] Humphries, b. 1796.
+ 19   viii. Thomas[2] Humphries, b. 11 Apr 1799.
+ 20   ix. Charlotte (Lottie)[2] Humphries, b. 11 July 1806.

NOTES AND REFERENCES

1. Union Co, SC, Deed Book T, p. 217.

2. Union Co, SC, Equity Records, Bill #148, originals at South Carolina Archives.

3. Union Co, SC, Deed Book E, pp. 235-236.

4. Union Co, SC, Probate Records, Box 23, Package 25.

SECOND GENERATION

4. Charles[2] Humphries Junr. (John[1]) was born 7 August 1777, married on 9 July 1801 Sarah Gregory, and died 10 November 1829 in Union District, South Carolina. Sarah was born 11 November 1780, and died 10 August 1866 in Union District. The burial place of Charles is unknown. Sarah is buried at the "Polly Young" Graveyard, in the Sardis community in Union County. The data on them is also taken from the Humphries Bible at the Union County Historical Foundation (see John[1] Humphries). Also, a petition of Sarah Humphries, dated 3 September 1844, for a division of the estate of her deceased son Charles, shows the names and residences of his surviving siblings.[1] The children of Charles[2] Humphries and wife Sarah Gregory:

21	i.	Mary (Polly)[3] Humphries, b. 6 Sept 1802, m. 18 July 1822 Hobson Thompson, and d. 13 May 1880. In 1844, she was living in AL.
22	ii.	Cassandra (Cassy)[3] Humphries, b. 27 Nov 1803, m. 9 June 1831 John Eison, and d. 19 Nov 1878. Bur. at Sardis United Methodist Church, Union Co, SC.
23	iii.	Elizabeth G.[3] Humphries, b. 15 Sept 1805, m. 11 Jan 1825 to Edward A. Jackson. In 1844, they were living in AL.
24	iv.	Sarah T.[3] Humphries, b. 29 Dec 1807, m. 23 Dec 1828 to Miles Malone. They were living out of state in 1844.
25	v.	Caty[3] Humphries, b. 6 Apr 1810. She was still single in 1844.
26	vi.	Charles[3] Humphries III, b. 2 July 1802, d. 11 Sept 1843, Union Dist, SC, unm.[2]
27	vii.	Lettie G.[3] Humphries, b. 27 July 1814, m. 25 Dec 1834 to her second cousin George McCrary[3] Young. (See #36 below for descendants.)
+ 28	viii.	John[3] Humphries, b. 1 Mar 1817.
29	ix.	Emmaline D.[3] Humphries, b. 3 Dec 1819, m. Ezekiel Gross, 1 Aug 1839, and d. 6 May 1886 at Rehoboth, AL.

12. Sarah[2] Humphries (Charles[1]) born ca. 1782, married Jared Young (ca. 1780-1840), and died before 22 July 1834, when Jared made a marriage agreement with Nancy Holder, his second wife.[3] The children of Sarah Young are mentioned, but not named, in the will of her father, Charles Humphries. Her husband, Jared Young, left a will dated December 1839, and proved 30 July 1840, in which he named the five children listed below. The will was witnessed by P.

W. Skelton, Thomas Humphries, and George Spencer.[4] The children of Sarah[2] and her husband Jared Young:

30   i.   Eleanor[3] Young, b. _____, m. Samuel Martin.
+ 31   ii.   Christopher[3] Young (Dr.), b. 23 Oct 1806.
+ 32   iii. Mary[3] Young, b. 1811.
+ 33   iv. Thomas[3] Young (Rev.), b. 1812.
+ 34   v.   Charles[3] Young, b. 1814.

14. Mary (Polly)[2] Humphries (Charles[1]) born 18 March 1786, died 8 September 1870 in Union County, South Carolina, married 7 January 1806,[5] Christopher C. Young Sr., who was born 14 August 1772, and died 28 February 1849 in Union District. Both are buried in the "Polly Young" Graveyard. This cemetery, though vandalized, can still be found off the "Deep Water" Road in the Sardis community, five miles south of Union.

Polly Young is one of the ancestors who has never been forgotten. Her name is well known in Union County, as the family cemetery bears her name. Hardly a family gathering goes by that someone does not relate a story of Polly Young. Tradition has it that she ran the farm after the death of her husband, and she always had a small sack of gold coins on a string around her neck. It is told that she was so stingy that she kept honey in the safe [pie safe] until it turned dark with age.

The children of Mary (Polly)[2] Humphries and her husband Christopher Young:

+ 35   i.   Thomas[3] Young,[3] b. 1807.
+ 36   ii.   George McCrary[3] Young, b. 14 Sept 1815.
37   iii. John B.[3] Young, b. 6 Nov 1817, d. of typhoid fever in hospital, Richmond, VA., 5 Nov 1862, buried at the "Polly Young" Graveyard.[6] He was a private in Co. A, 18th Regiment, S. C. Infantry. He made a will dated 7 Apr 1862, proved 1 Dec 1862, naming his mother Mary, and brother C. C. Young, and mentioning his interest in an undivided tract of which his mother still owned one third. He was not married.[7]
+ 38   iv. Sarah (Sallie)[3] Young, b. 10 Apr 1821(?).
+ 39   v.   Catherine Brandon[3] Young, b. 12 Oct 1825.
40   vi. Christopher C.[3] Young Jr., b. 1 Jan 1830, d. 6 Feb 1865, "at home in South Carolina," per his military record. He was a Sergeant in Co. A, 18th Regiment, S. C. Infantry, the same unit

as his brother John Young.[8] He m. his second cousin once removed, Lettie A.[4] Humphries, #69, dau. of John[4] Humphries, #28, and niece of Lettie G.[3] Humphries, wife of his brother George McCrary[3] Young. Lettie was b. 27 Aug 1847, and d. 11 Feb 1865, said to have died of a broken heart over the death of her husband. Both are bur. at the "Polly Young" Graveyard. His estate was administered by his mother Mary (Polly) Young. The estates papers state that there were no children.[9]

15. William (Billy)[2] Humphries (Charles[1]) was born in 1788, and died 6 March 1876. He married Katherine Troutman, who was born in 1792, and died 5 May 1856. William is buried at Sardis United Methodist Church in Union County, South Carolina. Katherine is buried at the "Polly Young" Graveyard. A photograph of William Humphries, the only such photograph of any child of Charles[1] Humphries known to exist, is reproduced on the page following. He appears on the 1850 census with Catharine, Absolam, Louisa, Wallace, and Frances A. still in the household. His property was valued at $1620.[10] A clipping of his obituary notice is preserved by descendants, though undated. For the year 1876, many Union newspapers are not extant, and no issue was located in any extant file containing this obituary. Therefore, it is quoted in its entirety:

"We are called upon to announce the death of Mr. William Humphries, one of the oldest and much respected citizens of this County, which occurred at his residence on Monday night last. He had reached the ripe old age of 87 years, and was one of the few connecting links that remained to bind the present generation with the patriots of the past. Although nearly blind and very feeble, he felt it to be his duty, at the last election, to travel five miles and cast in the ballot box his mite for reform in the government of his loved native State, telling us soon afterward that he had [torn]_____ the last vote he would give_[torn]."

He survived several of his children. The heirs are listed in his estates papers.[11] The children of William (Billy)[2] Humphries and wife Katherine Troutman:

+ 41   i. John Thomas[3] Humphries, b. 20 Jan 1821.
+ 42   ii. Absalom B.[3] Humphries, b. 22 Oct 1824.
+ 43   iii. Mary E.[3] Humphries, b. 2 Mar 1826.
+ 44   iv. Charles H.[3] Humphries, b. 1828.
  45   v. Louisa[3] Humphries, b. 1830, m. Reason Crocker
        as his second wife. No issue.
+ 46   vi. Katherine[3] Humphries, b. 1832.
  47   vii. Wallace[3] Humphries, b. 1833, said to have been killed

William Humphries

1788-1876

In the Confederate Service in 1864. Although no service record for him has been found, he is not mentioned in the estates papers of his father, and is presumed to have pre-deceased his father, without heirs.

+ 48   viii. Frances Ann[3] Humphries, b. 1835.

17. Martha (Patsey)[2] Humphries (Charles[1]) married Isaac T. Gregory prior to 22 November 1830, when Isaac T. Gregory sold one hundred thirty-seven acres to D. A. Mitchell, the dower being relinquished by Mrs. Martha Gregory on 30 November 1830. The deed was witnessed by Thomas Humphries.[12] No descendants have been identified.

18. Aggatha (or Agnes)[2] Humphries (Charles[1]) was born in 1796 in Union County, South Carolina, and died in 1854 in Monroe County, Mississippi.[13] She married George Young, who was born in 1797, Union County, and died 12 October 1856 in Monroe County.[14] The names of their children are found in the estates papers. The birth years of Agnes, George, and their children were computed from the ages on the 1850 census.[15] The children:

49   i.   Charles C.[3] Young, b. 1827, in SC, living in Chickasaw Co., MS, in 1859.[16]
50   ii.   Thomas J.[3] Young, b. 1829, in SC, living in Chickasaw Co., MS, in 1859.
51   iii. Pauline Elizabeth H.[3] Young, b. 1832 in TN, m. John T. McCandless 26 Sept 1848.[17]
52   iv.   Paul F.[3] Young, b. 1834 in AL.
53   v.   Mary J.[3] Young, b. 1839 in AL, m. James Cockburn.

19. Thomas[2] Humphries (Charles[1]) was born 11 April 1799 in Union County, South Carolina, and died 31 January 1859, Union District, South Carolina. He married, second, Lettie N. Huggins, who was born 18 September 1806 and died 2 March 1844. Both are buried at the Humphries Cemetery, Sardis Community in Union County. The name of the first wife of Thomas Humphries is not known. The tombstone of Lettie Humphries states the she was the "second wife of Thomas Humphries." Thomas Humphries wrote a will on 8 March 1856, in which he bequeathed slaves to several of his children. He mentioned a pre-deceased daughter "who was the wife of Thomas H. D. Johnson and her child is now dead." Thomas Humphries appears on the 1850 Census in Union District, as a planter, with real estate valued at $6700. His sons Thomas, Absalom, and John

were still in the household. The children of Thomas Humphries:

    54   i.   (dau.) m. Thomas H. D. Johnson.
+   55   ii. Elizabeth Jane[3] Humphries, b. 1820.
+   56   iii. Charles G. W.[3] Humphries, b. 25 Dec 1827.
+   57   iv. Thomas Henry Durant[3] Humphries, b. 5 Sept 1834.
+   58   v.   Hester Charlotte[3] Humphries, b. 1836.
+   59   vi. Absalom C. C.[3] Humphries, b. 4 Sept 1839.
    60   vii. John William Montgomery[3] Humphries, b. 1843.

20. Charlotte (Lottie)[2] Humphries (Charles[1]) was born 11 July 1806 in Union District, South Carolina, died there on 6 May 1892. She is buried at Salem Baptist Church, Santuc (Union County). She married, first, Charner[2] Humphries (John[1]), #10, her first cousin, who was born 11 November 1795, and died 6 April 1838.[18] She married, second, Isaac Franklin Gregory, born 1811 in Union District, and died 9 September 1868; he is buried at Gilliam Methodist Chapel in Santuc. In 1850, the two daughters of Charlotte by her first husband Charner Humphries, as well as the Gregory children, who had been born up to that point, were living with Isaac and Charlotte Gregory.[19] In 1860, Isaac, Charlotte, and their Gregory children were all in the household, and Thomas Peake, aged 37, a doctor, was living with them as well.[20] The will of Isaac Gregory, dated 15 August 1868, and proved 21 September 1868, names his wife Charlotte, and their children: Charlotte Frances, wife of Thomas Bowker Peake; Sarah Ellen Medora, wife of William F. Smith; Martha Ann Henrietta; and John Wesley.[21] The two children of Charlotte[2] Humphries by Charner[2] Humphries and five children by Isaac Franklin Gregory:[22]

+   61   i.   Elizabeth Jane[3] Humphries, b. 6 Jun 1829.
+   62   ii. Mary Ann[3] Humphries, b. 19 Jan 1831.
+   63   iii. Charlotte Frances[3] Gregory, b. 27 Oct 1843(twin).
    64   iv. Isaac Franklin[3] Gregory, Jr., b. 27 Oct 1843(twin),
              d. 6 May 1864, killed in the Battle of the Wilderness,
              VA. His photograph is reproduced on the following page.
+   65   v.   Sarah Ellen Medora[3] Gregory, b. 8 Oct 1844.
+   66   vi. Martha Ann Henrietta[3] Gregory, b. 26 Mar 1847.
+   67   vii. John Wesley[3] Gregory, b. 24 Nov 1851.

Isaac Franklin Gregory, Jr.

1843-1864

NOTES AND REFERENCES

1. Union Co., SC, Real Estate Book, 1835-1868, p. 91, original at Union Court House.

2. Union Co., SC, Probate Records, Box 29, Package 24.

3. Union Co, SC, Deed Book W, pp. 470-471.

4. Union Co., SC, Probate Records, Box 26, Package 14.

5. The dates are from a Bible record, the original of which is not now extant. However, a photograph of the record was made in the 1940s, a copy of which is in possession of the writer. Dates agree with the tombstones.

6. "Confederate Service Record for John B. Young," Compiled Service Records of Confederate Soldiers, Microcopy Number 267, Roll 303.

7. Union Co., SC, Probate Records, Box 44, Package 18, original at Union Court House.

8. "Confederate Service Record for C. C. Young," Compiled Service Records of Confederate Soldiers, Microcopy Number 267, Roll 303.

9. Union County, SC, Probate Records, Box 47, Package 7.

10. 1850 U. S. Census, Union Dist, SC, p. 32, #484/484.

11. Union County, SC, Probate Records, Box 64, Package 9, originals at Union Court House.

12. Union Co., SC, Deed Book T, pp. 497-8.

13. Monroe Co., MS, Probate Court, Cause #690.

14. Ibid., Cause #805.

15. 1850 U. S. Census of Monroe Co., MS, Eastern Division, #122/129 and #80/85.

16. Deed from C. C. Young and Thomas J. Young to John F. Young, dated 15 June 1859, Monroe Co., MS, Deeds, Book 21, pp. 137-8.

17. Monroe Co., MS, Marriages, Book 1834-50, p. 814.

18. Estate of Charner Humphries, Union Co., SC, Probate Records, Box 24, Package 22, original at Union Court House.

19. 1850 U. S. Census, Union Dist., SC, p. 94, #72/72.

20. 1860 U. S. Census, Union Dist., SC, p. 200, #265/271.

21. Union Co., SC, Probate Records, Box 51, Package 3.

22. The data on the descendants of Charlotte[2] Humphries Gregory have been supplied by T. H. Peake, Jr., of Trinity, NC.

THIRD GENERATION

28. John[3] Humphries (Charles[2], John[1]) was born 1 March 1817, died 18 August 1860, and married Margaret R. _____, who was born 8 January 1823, and died 9 August 1884. Both are buried at the "Polly Young" Graveyard. They had five children,[1] (their years of birth computed from the census):[2]

68   i. George[4] Humphries, b. 1842.
69   ii. Lettie A.[4] Humphries, b. 27 Aug 1847, m. her second cousin once removed, Christopher C.[3] Young, Jr. (see above, #40).
70   iii. John[4] Humphries, b. b. 7 Dec 1853, d. 13 Apr 1872, bur. at the "Polly Young" Graveyard.
71   iv. Louisa[4] Humphries, b. 1857.
72   v. Sallie M.[4] Humphries, b. 10 Oct 1860, d. 20 Aug 1906, m. 1st James S.[4] Sanders (Katherine[3],William[2], Charles[1]) (see #145 below), 2nd Samuel S. Lankford. She and both husbands bur. Sardis United Methodist Church.

31. Dr. Christopher[3] Young (Sarah[2], Charles[1]) was born 23 October 1806, and died 4 July 1850 in Union District, South Carolina. He married Margaret (Peggy) Beaty, who was born in 1804, and died after 1850. Christopher Young was a medical doctor, as is shown on the census of 1850, where his estate was valued at $18,000.[3] He was instrumental in organizing and building Mt. Vernon Presbyterian Church, near Union, South Carolina, where he is buried.[4] He wrote his will on 25 March 1850, in which he named his wife and three children: Sarah A., Robert, and Martha Elizabeth Young. The will was recorded on 13 July 1850. Mary Phillips was a witness to this will.[5]

The children of Dr. Christopher[3] Young and wife Margaret Beaty were as follows:

+ 73.   i. Sarah A.[4] Young, b. 2 Aug 1832.
74.   ii. Robert[4] Young, b. 1834, d. unm.
+ 75.   iii. Martha Elizabeth[4] Young, b. 31 May 1837.

32. Mary[3] Young (Sarah[2], Charles[1]) was born in 1811 in Union District, South Carolina, and married Henry Dunn, according to the will of her father Jared Young. Henry Dunn, aged 42, a hotel keeper, born in North Carolina; Mary

Dunn, aged 39, born in South Carolina; with Elizabeth, aged 15; Nancy, aged 13; Mary, aged 11; and Silas, aged 9; are found in the 1850 census of Union District, South Carolina. She may be the Mary Phillips who witnessed the will of Dr. Christopher Young (see #40 above), and who wrote a will dated 8 October 1868, in which she bequeathed to Robert Young one-third of the estate; to Martha E. Hix, wife of Dr. James E. Hix, one-third of the estate; and to the children of George W. Hill, one-third of the estate. Witnesses to this will were J. W. E. Young, J. D. Smith, and T. C. Hart.[6] If she were this Mary Young who had married Henry Dunn, it is difficult to explain why none of her estate were left to her children, or any of the children of the other children of Jared Young. If she is, indeed, that Mary Dunn, then the children listed in the census with her and Henry Dunn must have been her step-children, or else they had all died leaving no heirs. However, since she is not mentioned as a legatee in the will of Dr. Christopher Young, it is assumed that she is not his daughter.

33. The Rev. Thomas[3] Young (Sarah[2], Charles[1]) was born in 1812 and died 2 June 1853, in Union District, South Carolina. He married Elizabeth A. (Betsy) Skelton, who was born 18 November 1812 and died 16(?) June 1853, Union District, South Carolina. Both are buried in the Humphries Cemetery, Sardis Community, near Union, South Carolina, although there are no headstones to mark their graves. The Rev. Thomas Young was an early pastor of Sardis United Methodist Church, where many of his descendants and other Humphries descendants are buried. His lengthy obituary notice appears in The Southern Christian Advocate, the Methodist newspaper of South Carolina and Georgia, which states that he joined the church in 1841 and that he had been a preacher of the Gospel for more than eight years.[7] A painting of Elizabeth Skelton Young survives in the family, a copy of which is reproduced on the following page. The Rev. Thomas Young died intestate, leaving an estate worth less than $100.[8]

The children of the Rev. Thomas[3] Young and wife Elizabeth A. Skelton:

+ 76 i. Jared W. E.[4] Young, b. 1833.
  77 ii. John C. N.[4] Young, b. 1835.
  78 iii. Sarah Louisa Jane[4] Young, b. 23 Jul 1838, d. 27 Jun 1856,

Elizabeth (Skelton) Young

ca. 1830

bur. Mt. Vernon Pres. Ch.
+ 79   iv.   Martha Ellen W.[4] Young, b. 24 Jan 1841.
  80   v.   Mary E. C.[4] Young, b. 1847.

34. Charles[3] Young (Sarah[2], Charles[1]) was born in 1814, and died ca. 1882. He married Emiline Perry Gregory, who was born in 1818. He was a planter, and in 1860 his real estate was valued at $2,000 and his personal estate at $2,000. His children, according to the 1860 census:[9]

  81   i.   J. Simpson[4] Young, b. 1842, d. in hospital in Frederick
            City, MD., 1 Oct 1862, from a wound received 14 Sept. He was
            a private in Co. A, 13th Regt. SCV.[10]
  82   ii. Nancy[4] Young, b. 1846, m. Jared W. E.[4] Young
            (See #76 for descendants).
+ 83   iii. J. Christopher[4] Young, b. 19 Oct 1851.
  84   iv. Benjamin[4] Young, b. 1856.

35. Thomas[3] Young (Mary[2], Charles[1]) was born in 1807, Union District, South Carolina, and married Elizabeth Saunders, who was born in 1814, Union District, daughter of John Saunders, Jr. and wife Permelia (Milly).[11] They moved to Monroe County, Mississippi, and are found on the 1870 census there.[12] They were living in Union District, at the taking of the 1850 census.[13] Their children, according to these census reports:

  85   i.   Mary[4] Young, b. 1833.
  86   ii.   Elizabeth[4] Young, b. 1838.
  87   iii. John[4] Young, b. 1841.
  88   iv.   Rachel[4] Young. b. 1842.
  89   v.   Thomas[4] Young, b. 1847.
  90   vi.   Milly Ann[4] Young, b. 1850.
  91   vii. James[3] Young, b. 1852.

36. George McCrary[3] Young (Mary[2], Charles[1]) was born 14 September 1815 in Union District, South Carolina, and died there on 27 June 1887. He married, on 25 December 1834, his second cousin Lettice Gregory[3] Humphries, #27 (Charles[2], John[1]), who was born 27 July 1814, and died 28 December 1850. They are both buried at the Young Cemetery, now in the Sumter National Forest in Union County, off Forest Road #239. He married, second, on 30 June 1857, Julia Victoria Myers,[14] daughter of Mathias and Sabry (Turner) Myers. Julia V. Myers

was born 4 July 1837, and died 1 December 1910; she is buried at Rosemont Cemetery, Union, South Carolina. A photograph of her, as well as her obituary notice from The Progress, dated 2 December 1910, is reproduced herein.

George Young was a planter of some means, his real estate being valued in the 1850 census at $4370.[15] However, like many people after the Confederate War, he went "land poor," and his estate was deemed virtually worthless at the time of his death.[16] A daguerreotype of George Young, probably from the 1850s, is reproduced on the following page. A later photograph of him survives, which is also reproduced herein. He had seven children by each wife.

The children of George McCrary[3] Young and wife Lettie Humphries:

```
92   i. Charles H.[4] Young, b. 6 Nov 1835, d. 13 Mar 1848, bur.
        at the Young Cemetery, said to have been a cripple.
93  ii. Christopher[4] Young, b. 27 May 1837, d. Jun 1906.
94 iii. John Henry[4] Young, b. 16 Sep 1839, d. 7 Jun 1887.
+ 95  iv. Thomas Jefferson[4] Young, b. 29 Mar 1842.
+ 96   v. Mary Jane[4] Young, b. Nov 1844.
97  vi. Francis Marion[4] Young, b. 10 Mar 1846, d. 1864.
98 vii. George W.[4] Young, bur. Young Cem. [stone broken].
```

The children of George McCrary[3] Young and wife Julia V. Myers: a photograph of this family group made in December 1910, on the day of the burial of Julia V. Young, is reproduced herein.

```
+  99   i. James B.[4] Young, b. 8 Aug 1858.
+ 100  ii. Katherine[4] Young, b. 18 Mar 1860.
+ 101 iii. Rachel Ann[4] Young, b. 19 Mar 1862.
  102  iv. William P. Young, b. 7 Oct 1865, m. Hattie Greer.
+ 103   v. Conquest McCrary[4] Young, b. 7 Oct 1866.
+ 104  vi. Jackson Eldrich[4] Young, b. 30 Nov 1869.
+ 105 vii. Robert Lee[4] Young, b. 27 Nov 1875.
```

38. Sarah (Sallie)[3] Young (Mary[2], Charles[1]) was born 10 April 1821(?) and died 7 July ____ (before 1870). The years of birth and death are broken from her tombstone at the "Polly Young" Graveyard. She married John W. Sartor. The estates papers of her mother Mary Young list Julia Jeter, wife of Thomas R. Jeter and C. C. Sartor, as children of a pre-deceased daughter. The 1850 census

Death of a Good Woman.

Mrs. Julia V. Young, widow of the late George M Young, died Thursday morning at 8 o'clock at the home of her son, Mr. Robert L Young, on R F D. No. 2. Mrs Young had been in a very critical condition since August and her death was expected by her large family of children and her many friends. She was seventy-three years of age and was a devoted mother and an earnest and consecrated christian woman and was a member of the First Presbyterian church of Union. The funeral services were conducted yesterday at the city cemetery at three o'clock by Rev. L L Wagnon

Mrs. Young is survived by seven children, namely, J. B. Young, Mrs. T J Alverson, W P Young, Mrs. J P Holcomb, C M Young, J E Young and Robert L Young, thirty-six grand children, four great grand children and one sister, Mrs. T J Young of this county. The family of Mrs Young have the sincere sympathy of the entire community in their sorrow.

Julia Victoria (Myers) Young

1837-1910

28

George McCrary Young

ca. 1855

George McCrary Young

ca. 1885

The children of George McCrary and Julia (Myers) Young

Katherine Y. Alverson, Rachel Ann Y. Holcombe, James B.
Young, Robert L. Young, Jackson E. Young, Conquest M. Young,
William P. Young

31

lists another child, Thomas, with this family.[17] The children of Sarah[3] Young and her husband John W. Sartor:

106   i. Thomas[4] Sartor, b. 1839, said to have been killed
        in Confederate service, unm.
+ 107 ii. Christopher C. (Kit)[4] Sartor, b. 24 Dec 1841.
  108 iii. Julia[4] Sartor, b. 1845, m. Thomas R. Jeter.

39. Catherine Brandon[3] Young (Mary[2], Charles[1]) was born 12 October 1825, died 12 July 1875, married on 30 January 1840 William Henry Sartor, who was born 22 August 1814, and died 12 November 1873. The estates papers of Catharine B. Sartor name the heirs:[18]

109   i. John Young[4] Sartor, b. 19 May 1841, d. __ Mar 1906,
        m. Elizabeth Catherine Gross.
+ 110 ii. Mary J.[4] Sartor, b. 20 Dec 1842.
  111 iii. Ann J.[4] Sartor, b. 1845, m. Dr. Thomas B. Bates.
+ 112 iv. James Christopher[4] Sartor, b. 25 Apr 1847.
  113 v. William Henry[4] Sartor, b. 17 Jan 1859, d. 21 Mar 1919,
        m. Effie Moore, bur. Grace Methodist Church.
+ 114 vi. Caroline Virginia[4] Sartor, b. 10 Feb 1861.
+ 115 vii. Emma Frances[4] Sartor, b. 24 Jan 1868.

41. John Thomas[3] Humphries (William[2], Charles[1]) was born 20 January 1821, died 3 October 1869, and married Louisa Pressley, who was born 13 January 1818, died 1 December 1899. Both are buried at Sardis United Methodist Church in Union County, South Carolina. John Thomas Humphries was known as "John Cob," because he smoked a corncob pipe. Their children:

+ 116   i. Adelade[4] Humphries, b. 10 Nov 1841.
+ 117   ii. Mary Ann[4] Humphries, b. 24 Apr 1843.
+ 118 iii. Sarah (Sallie)[4] Humphries, b. 4 Mar 1845.
  119   iv. Victoria (Vic)[4] Humphries, b. 16 Nov 1846 (twin).
        (see #59 for further information.)
+ 120   v. Medora (Dora)[4] Humphries, b. 16 Nov 1846 (twin).
+ 121   vi. Lena[4] Humphries, b. 3 Mar 1848.
+ 122 vii. Josephine[4] Humphries, b. 26 May 1849.
+ 123 viii. Christopher Young[4] Humphries, b. 15 Jul 1852.
+ 124   ix. John Wylie[4] Humphries, b. 28 Sept 1853.
+ 125.   x. J. Calhoun[4] Humphries, b. Sept 1860.

42. Absalom B.[3] Humphries (William[2], Charles[1]) was born 22 October 1824, and died 20 March 1892 in Union County, South Carolina. He married ca. 1872 Caroline (Carrie) Burgess (over thirty years his junior), who was born 15 March 1857, died 30 May 1932. Both are buried at Sardis United Methodist Church in Union County.

Absalom B. Humphries was known as "Big Ab" or "Cherry Ab" to distinguish him from his first cousin, known as "Little Ab." Absalom was a corporal in Co. H, 15th S. C. Infantry, and was wounded on 28 August 1862. He served in the Confederate army from 1861-1864.[19] A letter from J. Clarence Gregory (b. 1876) to the author undated (ca. 1966), says: "he married late in life a young woman name[d] Caroline Burgess. He died sudden, lef[t] a large family mostly small children and a big debt on his place. The widow turned the place over to the creditors and moved the family to Pacolet Mills." Most of the family eventually moved to Greenville, South Carolina. The children of Absalom B.[3] Humphries and wife Caroline Burgess:

126   i. Mary[4] Humphries, b. 25 May 1873, d. 30 May 1932, m.
       John W. Willard, bur. Sardis United Methodist Church.
+ 127   ii. Annie[4] Humphries, b. 16 May 1877.
128   iii. Maude[4] Humphries, b. 16 Nov 1879, d. 20 Dec 1939, m.
       John Ward, bur. Springwood Cemetery.
+ 129   iv. W. Bartow[4] Humphries, b. 19 Jan 1882.
130   v. Jonathan Edwards (John)[4] Humphries, b. 4 Feb 1884, d.
       7 June 1968, unm.
+ 131   vi. Charles Hilliard[4] Humphries, b. 26 Jul 1886.
132   vii. Sallie[4] Humphries, m. Adam F. Hunt (lived Marion, NC).
+ 133   viii. Cleora[4] Humphries.

43. Mary E.[3] Humphries (William[2], Charles[1]) was born 2 March 1826, died 7 September 1891, and married, first, on 18 December 1844, Isaac E. Peek, who was born 9 March 1818, and died 10 January 1861. [Isaac E. Peek had first married Abigail Howard, and had other issue.][20] There is a monument to Isaac Peek in Rosemont Cemetery in Union, South Carolina. Mary E. Humphries Peek married, second, in July 1864, Jonathan Bennett Edwards, who was born in 1809, and died 16 April 1884. Mary E. Humphries Peek Edwards is buried at the Edwards Family Cemetery in Union County.

The children of Mary E.[3] Humphries and her first husband, Isaac Peek:

+ 134   i. Frances Catherine[4] Peek, b. 8 Feb 1847.
  135 ii. Florence Rebecca[4] Peek, b. 1849, d. 14 Mar 1860.
+ 136 iii. Martha Louise[4] Peek, b. 3 Feb 1852.

The children of Mary E.[3] Humphries and her second husband, Jonathan Bennett Edwards:

  137   i. Eugene Lee Davis[4] Edwards, b. 30 Dec 1865, d. 30 Aug 1866,
          bur. Tinker Creek Baptist Church Cemetery, Union Co., SC.
+ 138 ii. Inez[4] Edwards, b. 25 Aug 1867.

44. Charles H.[3] Humphries (William[2], Charles[1]) was born in 1828 in Union District, South Carolina, and was killed by a train near Santuc, South Carolina, in 1869. He married a widow, Nancy (Jones) Hodge, who was born in 1823 in South Carolina. After this death, the family removed to Upshur County, Texas. He and his family appear on the 1860 census in Union District.[21] The children of Charles H.[3] and his wife Nancy Jones Hodge:

+ 139   i. John[4] Humphries, b. 1849.
+ 140 ii. Cornelia[4] Humphries, b. 1852.
  141 iii. Nathaniel G.[4] Humphries, b. 1854.
  142 iv. Laura[4] Humphries, b. 1856.
  143   v. Mary[4] Humphries, b. 1858.

46. Katherine[3] Humphries (William[2], Charles[1]) was born in 1832, died in 1897, and married William Sanders (born 1824, died prior to 1864, son of John Saunders and his wife Permelia). William Sanders was a brother of Elizabeth Sanders who married Thomas[3] Young, #35, (Mary[2], Charles[1]). Katherine H. Sanders is buried at Sardis United Methodist Church in Union County, South Carolina. Their children:

+ 144   i. Frances[4] Sanders, b. 23 Nov 1855.
  145 ii. James S.[4] Sanders, b. 15 Nov 1856, d. 22 May 1882,
          m. 25 Dec 1879[22] to Sallie M.[4] Humphries, #72,
          b. 10 Oct 1860, d. 20 Aug 1906, who m. 2nd Samuel
          S. Lankford. All are bur. at Sardis United Methodist Church.
+ 146 iii. Susan Fair[4] Sanders, b. 25 Dec 1862.
+ 147 iv. Janie[4] Sanders, b. 25 Sept 1865.
  148   v. Cora Mae[4] Sanders, b. 7 May 1869. (See descendants of #103).

149   vi. Wallace[4] Sanders m. Sidney Jackson; they had one son Manly
      Sanders who d. unm.

48. Frances Anne[3] Humphries (William[2], Charles[1]) was born in 1835, and died
prior to 1876. She married _____ Gowing. Two children are reported for this
marriage:

150 Lula[4] Gowing, m. Dr. Smith.
151 Edward[4] Gowing.

55. Elizabeth Jane[3] Humphries (Thomas[2], Charles[1]) was born in 1820, died after
1870, and married George Washington Becknell, who was born 12 August 1812,
and died 4 November 1873. Both are buried at Old Union Cemetery, Monarch,
South Carolina (near Union). Their children:[23]

152   i. Louisa[4] Becknell, b. 14 Sept 1849, d. 16 Sept 1869, bur. at
         Old Union Cem.
153   ii. Cornelia L. C.[4] Becknell, b. 18 July 1851, d. 7 Feb 1873, bur.
         at Old Union Cem.
154   iii. Christopher[4] Becknell, b. 1853.
155   iv. Charles[4] Becknell, b. 1855.
156   v. Elizabeth[4] Becknell, b. 1858.
157   vi. Hester[4] Becknell, b. 1862.
158   vii. Aurelia[4] Becknell, b. 1868.

56. Charles G. W.[3] Humphries (Thomas[2], Charles[1]) was born 25 December 1827,
Union District, South Carolina, and died 10 March 1908 in Darlington County,
South Carolina. He married ca. 1847 Meras Marcena Jeffords, who was born 27
August 1828, and died 4 September 1891, Darlington County. Charles G. W.
Humphries moved to Darlington County (then District) from Union District with
his brother Thomas Henry Durant Humphries and sister Hester Charlotte
Humphries before 1860, as he (Charles) is found on the Darlington District census
in that year.[24] He married, second, in 1896, Mrs. Annie Kilgore.[25] The children
of Charles G. W.[3] Humphries and wife Meras Marcena Jeffords:

159   i. Lettie[4] Humphries, b. 2 Nov 1848, d. 17 Mar 1918, m. 1st
         _____ Sexton, 2nd Walter F. White. She is bur. Pisgah
         Methodist Church, Florence Co., SC.
160   ii. Susannah[4] Humphries, b. 14 June 1850, d. 18 Mar 1917, m.
         Charles A. Melton. She is bur. Grove Hill Cem, Darlington.

161   iii. Samuel King[4] Humphries, b. 17 Oct 1854, d. 14 June 1915, m. 1st Amanda Colvin, 2nd _____. He is bur. Pisgah Methodist Church.

+ 162   iv. Elizabeth Levenia[4] Humphries, b. 7 Jun 1856.

163   v. Margaret M.[4] Humphries, b. 2 May 1858, d. 7 Nov 1825, m. William J. Windham. She is bur. Newman Swamp Methodist Church, Darlington Co.

164   vi. Charles G. W.[4] Humphries, b. 6 Apr 1863, d. 11 May 1930, bur. Grace Methodist Church, Union, SC.

165   vii. William Eliphas Gary[4] Humphries, b. 11 Dec 1864. (See #138 for descendants.)

166 viii. Ella[4] Humphries, b. 6 Dec 1866, d. 17 Feb 1946, m. Joseph F. Saverance, She is bur. Fair Hope Presbyterian Church, Darlington Co.

167   ix. J. Walter A.[4] Humphries, m. 13 Sept 1891, Fannie Elwood Reynolds.

168   x. Edward David[4] Humphries, b. 19 Jan 1872, d. 23 Jan 1943, m. Margaret Doyle. He is bur. Grove Hill Cem., Darlington.

57. Thomas Henry Durant[3] Humphries (Thomas[2], Charles[1]) was born 5 September 1834 in Union District, South Carolina, died 16 May 1892, Darlington County, South Carolina. He married ca. 1852, Maria Jeffords, who was born 18 July 1833, and died 10 November 1917 in Darlington County. Their children:

+ 169   i. Charles G. W.[4] Humphries, b. 24 Oct 1853.

+ 170   ii. Samuel King[4] Humphries b. 17 Oct 1855.

171   iii. Meras Marcena[4] Humphries, b. 17 Jan 1857, m. 1st Heyward McCall, 2nd, 2 Oct 1884, Caleb Boone.

172   iv. Thomas Eliphas[4] Humphries, b. 21 Nov 1858, m. Emmie Huggins.

173   v. Lettie Elizabeth Jane[3] Humphries, b. 28 June 1860, d. 1 Aug 1936, m. 29 Oct 1879, John Reynolds Kirven, b. 9 Aug 1859, d. 25 Nov 1920.

174   vi. John William[4] Humphries b. 18 Jun 1862, d. 15 Oct 1862.

175   vii. Alexander Theodore[4] Humphries b. 18 Sept 1863, d. Jun 1948, m. 25 Dec 1890, Mary Hatchell. d. Jun 1948.

176 viii. Lula Mariah[4] Humphries, b. 29 Jul 1866, d. 3 Sept 1866.

177   ix. Jesse Waterman[4] Humphries, b. 28 Jan 1868, d. 7 Jun 1940, m. 25 Dec 1890, Maude Gee.

178   x. Henry Arthur[4] Humphries. b. 27 Nov 1869, d. 16 Jun 1947, m. Fannie Huggins.

179   xi. Robert Wells[4] Humphries, b. 23 Jul 1871, d. 20 Nov 1937, m. 1st Bertha Kirven, 2nd Mary[5] Odom, his first cousin once removed (see below as #480).

180   xii. (infant), b. 11 Jan 1873.

181 xiii. Hettie Sarah[4] Humphries, b. 12 Dec 1873, d. 2 Nov 1925, m. Joseph Allen Jones.

182   xiv.   Carrie Piggie[4] Humphries, b. ___ Feb 1876, d. 5 Jun 1876.
183   xv.   Hampton Kirkland[4] Humphries, b. 2 Jul 1878, d. 29 Jun 1958,
        m. 31 Oct 1901, Nelle Lide.

58. Hester Charlotte[3] Humphries (Thomas[2], Charles[1]) was born in 1836 in Union District, South Carolina, died 5 May 1911, was married five times, but had only one son (below) by her first husband. She married, first, ca. 1855, Samuel J. Odom, who died 12 June 1862, in hospital, a corporal in Confederate service, at Richmond, Va. She married, second, on 16 April 1863, William (Billy) Pierce. After his death, she married, third, on 10 April 1879, J. Alexander James.[26] She married, fourth, on 8 February 1888, William J. Stuckey. This marriage notice bears quoting in full, from The Darlington News, issue of 16 February 1888:

"On the 8th inst., at the residence of Mr. S. K. Jeffords, Mr. W.
J. Stuckey, of this section, led to the altar Mrs. Hester James,
of the Centre; this being his third bride, and when the Rev. J.
W. Murray had concluded the ceremony, she was holding the arm of
her fourth husband. Mr. Stuckey then took his bride to his home,
where a supper suitable to the occasion had been prepared; after
which they enjoyed a serenade tendered them by some of their friends.
Next day they set out on their bridal tour by private conveyance,
visiting their relatives throughout Darlington and Sumter counties.
We congratulate them on their latest venture and once more wish them
much joy, as they go forth in the evening of their lives happy in
each other's love."

She survived Mr. Stuckey, and married, fifth, ca. 1897, Thomas Calhoun Jeffords, who was born 7 March 1836, and died 10 March 1911. Her death is recorded in the Pisgah Methodist Church records, Timmonsville Circuit, Florence County, South Carolina. The child of Hester Charlotte[3] Humphries and her first husband, Samuel J. Odom:

+ 184   1.   Charles Lafayette[4] Odom, b. 9 Nov 1855.

59. Absalom C. C.[3] Humphries (Thomas[2], Charles[1]) was born 4 September 1839 and died 28 February 1918 in Union County, South Carolina. He married his first cousin once removed, Victoria[4] (Vic) Humphries (John Thomas[3], William[2], Charles[1]), #119, who was born 16 November 1846 and died 21 December 1917, Union County. A photograph of Victoria with her twin sister Medora is

reproduced later in this volume. Absalom C. C. Humphries was known as "Little Ab" Humphries. Both are buried at Sardis United Methodist Church in Union County. Their children:

185   i. (dau.) 1870-1873, bur. Sardis Methodist Church.
186   ii. John T.^{4} Humphries, b. 11 Jan 1872, d. 10 Oct 1874,
        bur. Sardis Methodist Church.
+ 187   iii. Thomas Smith^4 Humphries, b. 8 Jan 1876.
+ 188   iv. Henry B.^{4} Humphries, b. 1878.
+ 189   v. Lettie^4 Humphries, b. 12 June 1883.

61. Elizabeth Jane^3 Humphries (Charlotte^2, Charles^1) [and Charner^2, John^1] was born 6 June 1829 in Union District, South Carolina and died 6 April 1858, Union District; she is buried at the Presbyterian Cemetery in Union. She married Edwin Richter, a painter, who was born in 1822. There was apparently only one child. By 1860, Edwin Richter had remarried, and the second wife was Martha$_{.}^{27}$

190   i. Elizabeth^4 Richter, b. 1857, m. _____ Wilson.

62. Mary Ann^3 Humphries (Charlotte^2, Charles^1) [and Charner^2, John^1] was born 19 January 1831 in Union District, South Carolina, and died 26 March 1880 in Union County, South Carolina. She married Henry Ruskin Johnson, who was born 19 December 1817, and died 31 July 1872, Union County. Their nine children:

191   i. W. H.^{4} Johnson, b. 15 Dec 1851, d. 15 May 1854.
192   ii. Susan Lola^4 Johnson, b. 5 Dec 1853, d. 9 May 1910.
193   iii. Worthy Howell^4 Johnson, b. 26 Mar 1856.
194   iv. Henry Newton^4 Johnson, b. 30 Apr 1858.
195   v. Sarah Ann^4 Johnson, b. 23 Oct 1861, d. 16 Oct 1929.
196   vi. John Franklin^4 Johnson, b. 2 Aug 1863, d. 3 Oct 1939.
197   vii. E. Clarence^4 Johnson, b. 15 Feb 1866(twin), d. 8 Feb 1876.
198   viii. E. Laurens^4 Johnson, b. 15 Feb 1866(twin), d. 11 June 1929.
199   ix. Zachariah Greenbury^4 Johnson, b. 5 Apr 1869, d. 13 Feb 1944.

63. Charlotte Frances^3 (Fannie) Gregory (Charlotte^2, Charles^1) was born 27 October 1843 in Union District, South Carolina, and died 15 September 1928 at Glenn Springs, South Carolina. She married Dr. Thomas Bowker Peake, who was born 23 July 1829 in Union District, and died 3 May 1893 at Glenn Springs.

Both are buried at Bogansville Methodist Church, Union County. They had ten children:

+ 200   i. Isaac Frank[4] Peake, b. 8 Jul 1864.
  201   ii. Victoria Anna[4] Peake m. Capt. _____ Townsend, d. Tallahassee, FL. d. s. p.
  202   iii. Thomas Bowker[4] Peake, Jr., d. young, bur. in unmarked grave beside his parents.
+ 203   iv. Glenn David[4] Peake, b. 15 Mar 1875.
  204   v. Frances Gregory[4] Peake, b. 8 Jul 1879, d. 12 Jan 1940, unm., bur. beside her parents.
+ 205   vi. George Washington[4] Peake, b. 25 Nov 1881.
  206   vii. Mary Jones[4] Peake, b. 26 Mar 1883, d. 3 Oct 1952, unm., bur. beside her parents.
+ 207   viii. John Lamartine[4] Peake, b. 27 Jul 1885.
  208   ix. Hopkins[4] Peake, d. at age one year, bur. in Peake-Hamm Cemetery, Glenn Springs, Spartanburg Co., SC.

65. Sarah Ellen Medora (Sallie)[3] Gregory (Charlotte[2], Charles[1]) was born 8 October 1844 in Union District, South Carolina, and died 23 June 1925 in Chester County, South Carolina. She married William Franklin Smith of Rodman in Chester County. Both are buried at Calvary Baptist Church in the Baton Rouge section of Chester County. They had five children:

  209   i. Charlotte (Lottie)[4] Smith.
+ 210   ii. Jennie Mae[4] Smith, b. 20 Apr 1882.
+ 211   iii. Annie Lou[4] Smith.
  212   iv. William Frank[4] Smith, m. Mary _____, no issue.
  213   v. Oscar[4] Smith, unm.
  214   vi. Fannie[4] Smith, m. _____ Mobley, lived Dalzell, SC.

66. Mary Ann Henrietta[3] Gregory (Charlotte[2], Charles[1]) was born 26 March 1847 in Santuc, Union District, South Carolina, and died 5 September 1935 in Landrum, Spartanburg County, South Carolina. She married James Henry Randolph, who was born 25 May 1852, and died 11 August 1918 in Landrum, South Carolina. Both are buried in the Landrum City Cemetery. They had six children:

+ 215   i. Charlotte Cornelia[4] Randolph, b. 27 Nov 1877.
  216   ii. Annie Tekoah[4] Randolph, b. 1879, d. 1966, Greenville, SC, bur. Landrum City Cem.
+ 217   iii. Elizabeth[4] Randolph, b. 1881.
  218   iv. Fannie Belle[4] Randolph, b. 1883, Santuc, SC, d. 1933,

Saluda, NC, m. the Rev. Ralph H. Morgan, Baptist minister.
Bur. Landrum City Cem. No issue.

+ 219   v. William Isaac[4] Randolph, b. 6 June 1885.
   220   vi. James Henry[4] Randolph, Jr., b. 1887, d. 1889, bur.
       at Salem Baptist Church, Santuc, SC.

67. John Wesley[3] Gregory (Charlotte[2], Charles[1]) was born 24 November 1851 at Santuc, Union District, South Carolina, and died there 8 March 1925. He married Emma Adyl Chapin, who was born 11 September 1855, and died 28 December 1932, the daughter of Martin and Laura Benjamin Chapin of Chapin, South Carolina. J. W. Gregory served as Deputy Clerk of Court for Union County, South Carolina, for twenty-five years and was also a farmer. A photograph of him is reproduced on the following page. Both are buried in Rosemont Cemetery in Union, South Carolina. They had ten children:

+ 221   i. Claude Chapin[4] Gregory, b. 3 Sept 1878.
   222   ii. Charlotte[4] Gregory, b. 15 Jun 1880, d. 6 Dec 1971,
       Santuc, SC, unm.; bur. Rosemont Cem, Union, SC.
+ 223   iii. Annie Laura[4] Gregory, b. 10 May 1882.
   224   iv. Benjamin Wyse[4] Gregory, b. 28 Nov 1883, Santuc, SC, d.
       2 July 1960, Santuc, m. Danie E. Merritt Coleman. No
       issue; bur. Rosemont Cem, Union, SC.
   225   v. Mary Virginia[4] Gregory, b. 5 July 1886, Santuc, SC, d.
       17 May 1935, unm.; bur. Rosemont Cem, Union, SC.
+ 226   vi. Sarah Eleanor[4] Gregory, b. 11 Jan 1889.
   227   vii. John Wesley[4] Gregory, b. 6 May 1891, d. 1947, Jacksonville, FL,
       m. Frances Thuber, no issue.
   228   viii. Martha Eloise[4] Gregory, b. 22 Nov 1893, d. 27 Nov 1979, unm.;
       bur. Rosemont Cem, Union, SC.
+ 229   ix. Frederick Paige[4] Gregory, b. 26 Jan 1896.
   230   x. Curtis Humphries[4] Gregory, b. 4 Apr 1898, Santuc, SC, d.
       27 Feb 1982, Santuc, m. Harriet Holmes, no issue; bur. Rosemont
       Cem, Union, SC.

John Wesley Gregory
1851-1925

NOTES AND REFERENCES

1. Estate of John Humphries, Union Co., SC, Probate Records, Box 43, Package 12.

2. 1860 U. S. Census, Union Dist., SC, p. 212, #478/411; 1870 U. S. Census, Union Co., SC, p. 46-7, #355/376.

3. 1850 U. S. Census, Union Dist., SC, p. 33, #493/493.

4. Frank D. Jones, History of the Presbyterian Church in South Carolina since 1850, p. 747.

5. Union Co., SC, Probate Records, Box 35, Package 13.

6. Union Co., SC, Probate Records, Box 57, Package 11.

7. Brent H. Holcomb, Marriage and Death Notices from the Southern Christian Advocate, Vol. I: 1837-1860, p. 310.

8. Union Co., SC, Probate Records, Box 39, Package 3.

9. 1860 U. S. Census, Union Dist., SC, p. 247, #1021/924

10. Brent H. Holcomb, Marriage and Death Notices from the Southern Christian Advocate, Vol. II: 1860-1867, p. 112.

11. Union Co., SC, Probate Records, Box 48, Package 18.

12. 1870 U. S. Census, Monroe Co., MS, #25/36.

13. 1850 U. S. Census, Union Dist., SC, p. 33, #487/487.

14. Bible record not now extant, photocopy in possession of the author.

15. 1850 U. S. Census, Union Dist., SC, p. 2, #19/19.

16. Union Co., SC, Probate Records, Box 78, Package 17.

17. 1850 U. S. Census, Union Dist., SC, p. 35, #518/518.

18. Union Co., SC, Probate Records, Box 61, Package 11.

19. Compiled Service Records of Confederate Soldiers, Microcopy #267, Roll 280.

20. Bible records and other records quoted in The J. C. Edwards Branch of the Edwards Family Tree, by Myrtle Smith Simmons and Mannie Lee Edwards Mabry.

21. 1860 U. S. Census, Union Dist., SC, p. 245, #1005/905.

22. Marriage notice in The Weekly Union Times, issue of 9 Jan 1880.

23. 1860 U. S. Census, Union Dist., SC, p. 315; 1870 U. S. Census, Union Co., SC, p. 59, # 448/488.

24. 1860 U. S. Census, Darlington Dist., SC, p. 380, #162/157.

25. Information on this and other members of the Humphries family who went to Darlington District is from the Darlington County Historical Commission, courtesy of Mr. Horace F. Rudisill; data also supplied by Mr. Franklin Lambert, Florence, SC, a descendant.

26. Marriage notice in Darlington News, issue of April 1879.

27. 1860 U. S. Census, Union Dist., SC, p. 272, #1421/1310.

FOURTH GENERATION

73. Sarah A.[4] Young (Dr. Christopher[3], Sarah[2], Charles[1]) was born 2 August 1832 in Union District, South Carolina, and died 12 December 1862. On 28 October 1851, she married George Washington Hill,[1] who was born 5 May 1822 at Carlisle, South Carolina, and died there 3 May 1909. Sarah Young attended Salem College, in Salem, North Carolina, entering there 14 November 1847.[2] George Washington Hill was a graduate of South Carolina College (now USC), at Columbia. After the Confederate War, he lived at "Hillside" and farmed until his death in 1909. At his death the home went to his daughter (by a second marriage) Jeannette Hill May, and is now [1984] owned and occupied by her daughter Jeannette May Christopher, who has supplied most of the information on the descendants of Sarah A.[4] Young and George Washington Hill.[3] A copy of a portrait of Sarah A. Young Hill is reproduced on the following page. The three children of George W. Hill and wife Sarah A.[4] Young:

+ 231 i. Margaret[5] Hill, b. 3 Nov 1852.
+ 232 ii. Sarah Glenn[5] Hill, b. 15 Jan 1856.
+ 233 iii. Martha Elizabeth[5] Hill, b. 1858.

75. Martha Elizabeth[4] Young (Dr. Christopher[3], Sarah[2], Charles[1]) was born 31 May 1837 in Union District, South Carolina and died in 1906. She married Dr. James Edward Hix, son of Jesse S. Hix and wife Julia Ann Meng. Martha Elizabeth Young attended Salem College, in Salem, North Carolina, from 10 September 1850-18 September 1851.[4] She is buried at Grace Methodist Church in Union, South Carolina. The four children of Dr. James Edward Hix and wife Martha Elizabeth[4] Young:[5]

234   i. John C.[5] Hix, b. 1 Oct 1855, d. 1887, unmarried; bur.
          Grace Methodist Church, Union, SC.
+ 235 ii. Jesse Robert[5] Hix, b. 28 Oct 1857.
+ 236 iii. Sarah[5] Hix, b. 1866 or 1867.
237 iv. James Wallace[5] Hix, b. 1863, d. 1885, unmarried,
          bur. Grace Methodist Church, Union, SC.

76. Jared W. E.[4] Young (Thomas[3], Sarah[2], Charles[1]) was born in 1833, and died prior to 1880. He married his first cousin Nancy[4] (or Nannie) Young, #82,

Sarah A. (Young) Hill

1832-1862

(Charles[3], Sarah[2], Charles[1]), who was born in 1846, and died after 1880. Jared W. E. Young was a bookkeeper.[6] Jared and Nancy Young are both buried at Bogansville Church, but there are no dates on the tombstones. The children of Jared W. E.[4] Young and wife Nancy[4] Young:

    238   i. Anna[5] (or Ann) Young, b. 1 Sept 1863, m. Levy Edge.
+ 239   ii. Simpson[5] Young, b. 9 Feb 1867.
    240   iii. Thomas J.[5] Young, b. 9 Dec 1868, d. 16 Dec 1928, bur.
              Sardis United Methodist Church.
    241   iv. Sallie[5] Young, b. 1870, m. 1st ____ Smith, 2nd Leland
              Triplet.
    242   v. Jared W. E.[5] Young, b. 16 Mar 1872, d. 15 Mar 1912,
              bur. Sardis United Methodist Church.
    243   vi. Cleora[5] Young, b. 15 Dec 1876, d. 13 Nov 1967, m.
              Gibson Ivey, bur. Rosemont Cemetery, Union, SC. No children.
    244   vii. Bennie[5] Young, a child reported to have died young, but
              no record found.
    245 viii. Clayton[5] Young, also reported to be a child in
              this family.

79. Martha Ellen W.[4] Young (Thomas[3], Sarah[2], Charles[1]) was born 24 January 1841, Union District, South Carolina, and died there 6 May 1918. She married in 1860, Micheal Robert Betenbaugh, Sr., who was born 22 November 1827, and died 19 November 1906. Both are buried at Sardis United Methodist Church.

After the death of her parents, her cousin Robert[4] Young, #74, (Dr. Christopher[3], Sarah[2], Charles[1]) became her guardian. Like her cousins, Martha Ellen W. Young attended Salem College, in Salem, North Carolina, from 6 August 1858 until 1 June 1860.[7] According to family tradition, she "ran away" to get married and did not return to school. A photograph of Martha and her husband Micheal Betenbaugh is reproduced on the following page. They had nine children:[8]

    246   i. Thomas Joseph[5] Betenbaugh, b. 28 Aug 1862.(see #146
              below for descendants.)
+ 247   ii. John Calhoun[5] Betenbaugh, b. 16 Oct 1864.
+ 248   iii. Elizabeth Ann Freelove[5] Betenbaugh, b. 30 Jul 1867.
+ 249   iv. Micheal Robert[5] Betenbaugh, Jr., b. 15 Feb 1870.
    250   v. William David[5] Betenbaugh, b. 11 Nov 1872, d. 10 Feb
              1895, unm., bur. Sardis United Methodist Church.

Micheal Robert and Martha Ellen W. (Young) Betenbaugh

ca. 1900

+ 251   vi. James Claude[5] Betenbaugh, b. 24 Jun 1875.
+ 252   vii. Powell Higgerson[5] Betenbaugh, b. 27 Dec 1877.
+ 253   viii. Sallie E.[5] Betenbaugh, b. 4 Jul 1881.
+ 254   ix. Beaty Harden[5] Betenbaugh, b. 28 Nov 1884.

83. J. Christopher[4] (Kit) Young (Charles[3], Sarah[2], Charles[1]), was born 19 October 1851 in Union District, South Carolina, and died 22 August 1921, Spartanburg County, South Carolina. He married Sarah Jane (Sallie) Edge, who was born 17 October 1858, and died 8 April 1935, the daughter of W. W. and Julia Edge. Both are buried at Graham Chapel Wesleyan Church in Mayo, Spartanburg County, South Carolina. J. Christopher Young was a schoolteacher as early as 1860, when he was living in the household of Sarah Humphries.[9] J. Christopher[4] Young and wife Sallie Edge had four children:

+ 255   i. Bertha[5] Young, b. 18 Nov 1878.
+ 256   ii. Ulalah (Leila)[5] Young, b. 14 Jun 1886.
+ 257   iii. Julia[5] Young, b. 5 Aug 1889.
  258   iv. William McFarland[5] Young, b. 6 Jul 1896, d. 17 May 1929,
        m. Elvia Lindsey. They had only one child who was stillborn.

95. Thomas Jefferson[4] Young (George McCrary[3], Mary[2], Charles[1]) [and Lettie G.[3], Charles[2], John[1]] was born 29 March 1842 in Union District, South Carolina, and died there on 25 May 1923. He married Amanda Myers, who was born 2 October 1844, and died 22 February 1913, daughter of Mathias and Sabry (Turner) Myers, and sister of his step-mother Julia Victoria Myers Young. A photograph of Thomas Jefferson and Amanda Myers Young is reproduced on the following page. Thomas Jefferson Young was known as "Bud Tom" Young to most members of the family. Both are buried at Sardis United Methodist Church.

Any discussion of this family at reunions or get-togethers brings up the fact that father (George) and son (Thomas) married sisters. Thomas Jefferson[4] Young and wife Amanda Myers had only two children:

  259   i. Lettie[5] Young, b. 2 Jun 1877, d. 4 Jun 1964, m. as his
        second wife Samuel S. Lankford, b. 16 Oct 1866, d. 16 Nov 1937.
        They had no children. Samuel S. Lankford m. 1st Sallie M.[4]
        Humphries Sanders, #72.
+ 260   ii. George Ernest[5] Young, b. 17 May 1890.

Thomas Jefferson and Amanda (Myers) Young

96. Mary Jane[4] Young (George McCrary[3], Mary[2], Charles[1]) [and Lettie G.[3], Charles[2], John[1]] was born in November 1844, and died after 1900. She married David Lane, who was born January 1837, and died after 1900. They were living Union County in 1880,[10] but by 1900 had removed to Spartanburg County, South Carolina.[11] They had six children:

```
261   i. G. Robert[5] Lane, b. 1866.
262  ii. Lettie[5] Lane, b. 1869.
263 iii. Fannie[5] Lane, b. 1875.
264  iv. Sallie[5] Lane, b. July 1877.
265   v. Rosalee[5] Lane.
266  vi. David[5] Lane.
```

99. James B.[4] Young (George McCrary[3], Mary[2], Charles[1]) was born 8 August 1858 in Union District, South Carolina, and died 19 January 1949, Union County, South Carolina. He married on 21 November 1889, Josie Bailey,[12] who was born 8 January 1874, and died 14 March 1943, daughter of George Bailey. Both are buried at Sardis United Methodist Church. They had ten children:

```
+ 267   i. Josie[5] Young.
+ 268  ii. Mary[5] Young.
  269 iii. George M.[5] Young, b. 12 Nov 1893, d. 29 Nov 1969, m. Laura
           Barnett Holcombe, b. 24 Mar 1886, d. 28 June 1958,  widow
           of his first cousin William Hazel[5] Holcombe, #287 (see below).
           Both bur. in Rosemont Cem, Union, SC.
+ 270  iv. Leland Cunningham[5] Young, b. 25 Sept 1896.
+ 271   v. Carrie[5] Young.
+ 272  vi. Clark Hamilton[5] Young.
  273 vii. Inez[5] Young, b. ____, d. __ Oct 1984, Granite Falls,
           NC, m. J. W. Blankenship.
+ 274 viii. James Heyward[5] Young, b. 20 Aug 1903.
  275  ix. Marie[5] Young, unm.
  276   x. Benjamin[5] Young, unm.
```

100. Katherine[4] Young (George McCrary[3], Mary[2], Charles[1]) was born 18 March 1860 in Union District, South Carolina, and died there 26 December 1953. She married Thomas J. Alverson, who was born 26 January 1852, and died 9 June 1911. Both are buried at Padgett's Creek Baptist Church in Union County, South Carolina. Available information on their children:

```
277    i. Raymond⁵ Alverson.
+ 278   ii. Effie⁵ Alverson.
+ 279  iii. Sallie⁵ Alverson, b. 14 Jun 1881.
+ 280   iv. G. Rector⁵ Alverson, b. 1887.
+ 281    v. Julia A.⁵ Alverson, b. 22 Mar 1888.
+ 282   vi. Bess⁵ Alverson, b. 24 Dec 1891.
  283  vii. Thomas J.⁵ Alverson, Jr., b. 14 Jul 1895, d. 9 Sept 1967.
+ 284 viii. Mable⁵ Alverson, b. 1901.
+ 285   ix. William Giles⁵ Alverson.
```

101. Rachel Ann[4] Young (George McCrary[3], Mary[2], Charles[1]), was born 19 March 1862 in Union District, South Carolina, and died 22 May 1950, Union County, South Carolina. She married on 9 January 1883,[13] Jesse President "Wheeler" Holcombe, who was born 22 January 1861, Union District, South Carolina, and died 27 August 1931, Union County, South Carolina, son of Jesse and Mary (Lawson) Holcombe.[14] Wheeler Holcombe was a farmer in Union County all of his life. Both are buried at Sardis United Methodist Church. They were the parents of ten children:

```
+ 286    i. Mattie Victoria⁵ Holcombe, b. 17 Nov 1883.
+ 287   ii. William Hazel⁵ Holcombe, b. 7 Oct 1886.
  288  iii. Robert Dobson⁵ Holcombe, b. 1 Nov 1888, d. 17 Feb 1964,
            m. 20 Jan 1916, Belle Bentley, b. 29 Oct 1890, d. 14
            Jan 1950. Both bur. at Sardis United Methodist Church.
            No issue.
+ 289   iv. Pearl Catherine⁵ Holcombe, b. 1 Apr 1891.
+ 290    v. Rufus Thompson⁵ Holcomb, b. 29 Sept 1893.
+ 291   vi. Kennis Clemson⁵ Holcombe, b. 4 May 1896.
+ 292  vii. Thomas Duncan⁵ Holcombe, b. 8 Oct 1898.
  293 viii. (son) b. 7 Nov 1900, d. 10 Jul 1902.
+ 294   ix. May Inez⁵ Holcombe, b. 1 Dec 1902.
+ 295    x. Sidney Maxel⁵ Holcombe, b. 4 Aug 1905.
```

103. Conquest McCrary[4] Young (George McCrary[3], Mary[2], Charles[1]) was born 7 October 1866 in Union District, South Carolina and died 23 June 1919, Union County, South Carolina. He married his second cousin, Cora Mae[4] Sanders, #148 (Katherine[3], William[2], Charles[1]), who was born 7 May 1869, and died 7 January 1935. Three children:

```
  296    i. Charles⁵ Young.
+ 297   ii. Kathleen⁵ Young, b. 1894.
+ 298  iii. Grace⁵ Young.
```

104. Jackson Eldrich[4] Young (George McCrary[3], Mary[2], Charles[1]) was born 30 November 1869 in Union County, South Carolina and died there 4 December 1941. He married Cecilia E. Sims, who was born 6 November 1877, and died 2 May 1953. Both are buried at Sardis United Methodist Church. Their children:

+ 299   i. Mattie Irene[5] Young, b. 27 Nov 1894.
   300 ii. Annie Lou[5] Young, b. 8 Jan 1899. (See #188 for details.)
   301 iii. Reuben[5] Young, d. young.
+ 302 iv. Ellen[5] Young.
+ 303   v. Thomas E.[5] Young, b. 25 Feb 1900.
+ 304 vi. Ernest Arthur[5] Young, b. 10 Feb 1902.

105. Robert Lee[4] Young (George McCrary[3], Mary[2], Charles[1]) was born 27 November 1875 in Union County, South Carolina and died there 23 September 1953. He married in 1898 Alice Davis, who was born 28 December 1880, and died 30 June 1946. He married, second, on 12 November 1947, Sallie Goforth Betenbaugh, widow of James Beauregard[5] Betenbaugh, #335, (Adelade[4], John Thomas[3], William[2], Charles[1]), who was born 28 September 1876 and died 16 January 1967. Five children:

   305   i. Johnnie R.[5] Young, b. 1898, d. 1899.
+ 306 ii. Ethel[5] Young, b. 7 Jan 1900.
+ 307 iii. Pauline[5] Young, b. 13 Jun 1901.
+ 308 iv. Fred[5] Young, b. 26 Jan 1903.
+ 309   v. Helen[5] Young, b. 22 Feb 1912.

107. Christopher Columbus[4] (Kit) Sartor (Sarah[3], Mary[2], Charles[1]) was born 24 December 1841 in Union District, South Carolina and died 5 November 1911 in Columbia, South Carolina. He married, on 21 November 1861, Mary Cornelia Brandenburg, of Orangeburg County, South Carolina, who was born 20 November 1844, and died 21 October 1920. They are buried at Grace Methodist Church, Union, South Carolina. C. C. Sartor held the office of Union County Commissioner. Their children:[15]

− 310   i. Adella Frances[5] Sartor, b. 9 Oct 1864
   311 ii. Clara Eugenia[5] Sartor, b. 16 Mar 1867, Union Co., SC,
           d. 8 Jan 1894, Salt Lake City, UT, m. John W. Dunbar Moodie.
   312 iii. Thomas Edwin[5] Sartor, b. 20 Aug 1869, d. 25 Aug 1897, unm.

313   iv. Theopa Thomason[5] Sartor, b. 5 Nov 1871, d. 29 Mar 1927, m.
          Jason F. Norman.
+ 314   v. Claude Christopher[5] Sartor, b. 30 Mar 1874.
  315   vi. Mary Cornelia[5] (Neelie) Sartor, b. 25 Dec 1876, d. 21 Oct 1965,
          was librarian in Union for many years.
  316   vii. James Perry[5] Sartor, b. 29 Mar 1879, d. ___ Lawton,
          OK, unm.
  317 viii. Effie Pauline[5] Sartor, b. 10 Oct 1881, d. 24 Mar 1969,
          unm., was a schoolteacher in Union for many years.
  318   ix. Eoline Brandenburg[5] Sartor, b. 16 Mar 1885, d. 5 Dec 1969, unm.

110. Mary J.[4] Sartor (Catherine Brandon[3], Mary[2], Charles[1]) was born 20 December 1842 and died 2 October 1872. She married Dr. Thomas B. Bates, who was born 5 February 1830 and died 8 January 1917. Both are buried at Mt. Vernon Presbyterian Church in Union County, South Carolina. (Dr. Thomas B. Bates married, second, his wife's sister Ann J.[4] Sartor.) They had two children:

319 i. William Farr[5] Bates, b. 11 Nov 1866, d. 29 Apr 1955.
320 ii. John S. Bates, b. 3 Jan 1871, d. 1 May 1891.

112. James Christopher[4] Sartor (Catherine Brandon[3], Mary[2], Charles[1]) was born 25 April 1847 in Union District, South Carolina and died there 11 November 1905. He married, on 3 February 1869, Mary Cornelia Hogan, who was born 29 May 1851, and died 16 September 1925.[16] Both are buried at Grace Methodist Church in Union, South Carolina. They were the parents of five children:

321   i. Robert Wallace[5] Sartor, b. 4 Jan 1873, d. 29 Oct 1911, m.
          Irene Fant, b. 18 Nov 1874, d. 1 Nov 1955.
+ 322   ii. Sarah Frances[5] Sartor, b. 8 Aug 1874.
+ 323   iii. William Daniel[5] Sartor, b. 11 Mar 1878.
+ 324   iv. Kate[5] Sartor, b. 17 Nov 1880.
+ 325   v. Mary[5] Sartor, b. 7 Oct 1882.

114. Caroline Virginia[4] (Carrie) Sartor (Catherine Brandon[3], Mary[2], Charles[1]) was born 10 February 1861 and died 24 July 1949. She married, on 4 April 1889, Frank Edward Davis, who was born 28 March 1859 and died 23 March 1939. Both are buried at Mt. Vernon Presbyterian Church in Union County, South Carolina. They had five children:

+ 326 i. Annie Belle[5] Davis, b. 3 Oct 1891.
327 ii. Kathleen[5] Davis, b. 18 Jun 1892, d. 1 May 1893.
328 iii. Jack Hiram[5] Davis, b. 13 Apr 1894, d. 8 Nov 1895.
329 iv. Ethelind Lucille[5] Davis, b. 7 Jun 1896, d. 23 Sep 1941,
   m. William Matthews Butler, b. 23 Feb 1870, d. 8 May 1945.
   Both are bur. at Cane Creek Presbyterian Church, Union Co., SC.
+ 330 v. Carrie Sartor[5] Davis, b. 1 Jul 1903.

115. Emma Frances[4] Sartor (Catherine Brandon[3], Mary[2], Charles[1]) was born 24 January 1868 and died 3 December 1950. She was married, on 30 September 1889,[17] to Dr. Hampton Kennedy Smith, of Asheville, North Carolina, who was born 3 October 1865; and died 19 May 1946. Both are buried at Grace Methodist Church in Union, South Carolina. Dr. H. K. Smith was a dentist in Union for many years. There were three children:

331 i. Harold Calvert[5] Smith.
+ 332 ii. Edith Kennedy[5] Smith.
333 iii. Emma[5] Smith.

116. Adelade[4] Humphries (John Thomas[3], William[2], Charles[1]) was born 10 November 1841 in Union District, South Carolina and died 16 May 1900. She married, first, John J. Betenbaugh, born 1834, died at Pt. Lookout Maryland, in the Confederate service, 1864, son of David and Freelove Betenbaugh, and brother of Micbeal R. Betenbaugh who married Martha Ellen W.[4] Young, #79. Second, she married Carey W. Willard, (1843-1911) of Union County, South Carolina. Both Adelade and Carey W. Willard are buried at Sardis United Methodist Church in Union County.

By her marriage to John J. Betenbaugh, there were two children:

+ 334 i. Sarah Ellen[5] Betenbaugh, b. 16 May 1859.
335 ii. James Beauregard[5] Betenbaugh, b. Apr 1861, d. 1936,
   m. 1st Sarah Ann Greer, b. 4 Apr 1844, d. 1924, dau. of
   Jason M. Greer, Sr. and wife Sarah Sanders. He m. 2nd
   Sallie Goforth, b. 28 Sep 1876, d. 16 Jan 1967. Sallie Goforth
   Betenbaugh m. 2nd Robert Lee[4] Young, #105. All are bur. at
   Sardis United Methodist Church.

By her marriage to Carey W. Willard, there were seven children:

+ 336 i. Caroline Lorena^5 Willard, b. 14 Feb 1869.
+ 337 ii. Arthur$_5$ Willard, b. 1871.
+ 338 iii. Louisa^5 Willard, b. 6 Feb 1873.
+ 339 iv. Josephine^5 Willard, b. 1874.
+ 340 v. Addie^5 Willard, b. 15 May 1877.
+ 341 vi. Jackson Lee^5 Willard, b. 16 Feb 1879.
  342 vii. Duncan^5 Willard, b. Feb 1883, d. young.

117. Mary Ann^4 Humphries (John Thomas^3, William^2, Charles^1) was born 24 April 1843 and died 23 October 1928. She first married William Stokes. She married, second, Charles Bolt, who was born 5 October 1835 and died 28 August 1902. Mary Ann and Charles Bolt are buried at Grace Methodist Church in Union, South Carolina. There were two children by the first marriage, none by the second:

+ 343 i. Mary Lou$_5$ Stokes, b. 16 Jun 1871.
  344 ii. Walter H.^{5} Stokes, b. 18 Jul 1872, d. 19 Jan 1930, m. Antonie
       Hart, bur. Presbyterian Cem, Union, SC.

118. Sarah (Sallie)^4 Humphries (John Thomas^3, William^2, Charles^1) was born 4 March 1845 and died 18 May 1908. She married Jonathan Edwards, who was born 30 September 1834 and died 30 April 1912. Both are buried at Sardis United Methodist Church in Union County, South Carolina. They had two children:

+ 345 i. Belle^5 Edwards, b. 20 Jul 1870.
+ 346 ii. Bernice^5 Edwards, b. 6 May 1872.

120. Medora^4 (Dora) Humphries (John Thomas^3, William^2, Charles^1) was born 16 November 1876 and died 22 October 1922. She married, on 12 July 1865,[18] Lemuel McDaniel Jr., who was born 1 September 1840 and died 16 March 1907. Both are buried at Sardis United Methodist Church in Union County, South Carolina. A photograph of Medora McDaniel with her twin sister Victoria Humphries is reproduced on the following page. Lemuel and Medora McDaniel had nine children:

  347 i. Ida^5 McDaniel, b. 23 June 1866, d. 9 Jan 1843, m. 1st
       ___ Merrill, 2nd ___ Bailey, no children.
+ 348 ii. John Rufus^5 McDaniel, b. 21 Sep 1869.
+ 349 iii. Robert Lee^5 McDaniel, b. 17 Apr 1871.
+ 350 iv. Victoria^5 McDaniel, b. 8 May 1873.
  351 v. Adam Presley^5 McDaniel, b. 4 June 1875, d. 15 June 1877.

The twin daughters of John Thomas Humphries

Victoria (Humphries) Humphries (left) and
Medora (Humphries) McDaniel (right)

+ 352 vi. Lucy Smith[5] McDaniel, b. 14 Sep 1877.
  353 vii. (son), b. and d. 10 Dec 1880.
  354 viii. Kate[5] McDaniel, b. 18 Oct 1883, d. 28 Sep 1905, m.
    John Lemuel Keisler, had one child who d. in infancy.
+ 355 ix. Mary Ann[5] McDaniel, b. 24 Jan 1887.

121. Lena[4] Humphries (John Thomas[3], William[2], Charles[1]), was born 3 March 1848 and died 29 September 1906; she married Greene Bailey. She is buried at Padgett's Creek Baptist Church in Union County, South Carolina. They had six children:

356 i. Norman[5] Bailey, m. Maggie Brock.
357 ii. Forrest[5] Bailey, b. 26 Aug 1881, d. 22 May 1959, m. Thomas
    Cash, bur. Rosemont Cem, Union, SC.
358 iii. Letty[5] Bailey, b. 1884, d. 1966, m. Laurence Petty, bur.
    Rosemont Cem, Union, SC.
359 iv. Pearl[5] Bailey, b. 12 Apr 1886, d. 6 Nov 1959, m. States
    W. Jolly, bur. Rosemont Cem, Union, SC.
360 v. Evie[5] Bailey, b. 5 Aug 1888, d. 20 May 1910, m. N. Boyd
    Petty, bur. Rosemont Cem, Union, SC.
361 vi. Lela[5] Bailey, b. 5 Jun 1890, d. 20 Jan 1947, m. Marion
    Spillers, bur. Rosemont Cem, Union, SC.

122. Josephine[4] Humphries (John Thomas[3], William[2], Charles[1]), was born 16 May 1849 and died 3 November 1896. She married Joseph Sanders, who was born 23 November 1847 and died 17 September 1916. Both are buried at Gilead Baptist Church in Union County, South Carolina. They had eight children:

362 i. Gus B.[5] Sanders, b. 23 Jul 1874, d. 29 Jun 1939, m. Amanda
    Ledbetter, b. 11 Jan 1875, d. 2 Aug 1962, bur. Rosemont Cem,
    Union, SC.
363 ii. Louise[5] Sanders, b. 26 Nov 1875, d. 20 Jul 1911, m. Thomas
    A. Littlejohn, b. 27 Apr 1876, d. 25 Jun 1956, bur. Littlejohn
    Cem, Union Co., SC.
364 iii. Mattie S.[5] Sanders, b. 15 May 1877, d. 16 Jan 1950, m. John
    C. O'Shields, b. 15 Jul 1875, d. 30 Jul 1924, bur. Gilead Baptist
    Church.
365 iv. Scaife[5] Sanders, m. _____ Johnson.
366 v. Wylie[5] Sanders, m. Kelly Ledbetter.
367 vi. Greene[5] Sanders, m. Clarice _____.
368 vii. Addie[5] Sanders, m. Rev. S. P. Hair.
369 viii. Curtis[5] Sanders.

123. Christopher Young[4] (Kit) Humphries (John Thomas[3], William[2], Charles[1]) was born 15 July 1852 in Union District, South Carolina and died 2 February 1931. He married Nannie Austell, who was born 13 July 1862 and died 17 October 1892. Both are buried at Sardis United Methodist Church in Union County, South Carolina. They had six children:

    370   i.   Blanche[5] Humphries, b. 9 Dec 1880, d. 30 Jan 1966, m.
                Arthur Roland Morris, b. 23 Feb 1871, d. 23 Feb 1944, bur.
                Rosemont Cem, Union, SC.
    371   ii. Daisy[5] Humphries, m. Robert George.
    372   iii. Jack[5] Humphries, m. Dracie May.
    373   iv. Hattie[5] Humphries, m. Eugene Gossett.
    374   v.   Lena[5] Humphries, m. Byron Reed.
    375   vi. Fred[5] Humphries, m. Ella Sharpe.

124. John Wylie[4] Humphries (John Thomas[3], William[2], Charles[1]) was born 28 September 1853 and died 15 January 1936. He married, on 5 December 1878, Othela Caroline Ray, who was born 15 October 1859 and died 14 August 1938, daughter of Robert F. And Charlotte (Sparks) Ray. Both are buried at Padgett's Creek Baptist Church in Union County, South Carolina. They had seven children:

      376   i.   Bertha E.[5] Humphries, b. 18 Jan 1880, d. 23 Jul 1905, unmarried.
    + 377   ii. Evelyn Frances[5] Humphries, b. 29 Aug 1882.
    + 378   iii. Olive[5] Humphries, b. 25 Oct 1883.
    + 379   iv. Robert Ray[5] Humphries, b. 4 Sept 1885.
    + 380   v.   Bessie[5] Humphries, b. 14 Aug 1888.
      381   vi. Willie Thompson[5] Humphries, b. 21 Jun 1891, d. 18 Nov 1952,
                  m. 4 Mar 1920, Ruth Pinson. No issue. W. T. Humphries was
                  a veteran of World War I.
    + 382   vii. Lona Mae[5] Humphries, b. 18 Jul 1895.
             viii. Margaret[5] Humphries (adopted), m. Algie Chumley.

125. J. Calhoun[4] Humphries (John Thomas[3], William[2], Charles[1]) was born September 1860, and married Neely McCreight, daughter of William and Mary Ann (Betenbaugh) McCreight.[19] They had five children:

    383   i.   Edward[5] Humphries, b. Nov 1885, m. Florence Holder.
    384   ii. Annie[5] Humphries, b. Aug 1888, m. Herbert Branch.
    385   iii. John[5] Humphries, b. Apr 1890, m. Inez Fowler.
    386   iv. George[5] Humphries, b. Jan 1895.
    387   v.   Eva[5] Humphries, b. Aug 1899, m. Wallace Fowler.

127. Annie[4] Humphries (Absalom B.[3], William[2], Charles[1]) was born 16 May 1877 in Union County, South Carolina, and died 16 December 1943 in Greenville, South Carolina. She married John Nelson Badger, who wasborn 29 July 1870 and died 22 December 1960. Both are buried at Springwood Cemetery in Greenville, South Carolina. Five children:

388 i. James R.[5] Badger, b. 9 Jan 1898, d. 16 Feb 1976.
389 ii. Estelle[5] Badger, m. James Dean Poole, lives Greenville, SC.
390 iii. Sidney Humphries[5] Badger.
391 iv. Ruby[5] Badger.
392 v. Morris[5] Badger.

129. W. Bartow[4] Humphries (Absalom B.[3], William[2], Charles[1]) was born 19 January 1882 in Union County, South Carolina and died 13 December 1924, Greenville, South Carolina. He married Belle Lewis, who was born 17 January 1887. He is buried at Graceland Cemetery, Greenville, South Carolina. They had five children:

393 i. Roy[5] Humphries.
394 ii. Velma[5] Humphries, b. 2 Sept 1912.
395 iii. Frederee[5] Humphries.
396 iv. Norman[5] Humphries, b. 22 May 1914, d. 2 Jun 1977.
397 v. William Earl[5] Humphries, b. 15 Jun 1923.

131. Charles Hilliard[4] Humphries (Absalom B.[3], William[2], Charles[1]) was born 26 July 1886 in Union County, South Carolina and died 25 October 1976 in Walhalla, South Carolina. He married Olive Maxwell, who was born 23 November 1888 and died 7 September 1946. Both are buried at Westview Cemetery in Walhalla. They had five children:

+ 398 i. Charles Hilliard[5] Humphries, Jr., b. 6 Sept 1911.
+ 399 ii. Julian Maxwell[5] Humphries, b. 1 Oct 1913.
+ 400 iii. Norma Keels[5] Humphries, b. 30 May 1920.
+ 401 iv. George Badger[5] Humphries, b. 27 Sept 1922.
+ 402 v. Olive Elaine[5] Humphries, b. 28 Jul 1925.

133. Cleora[4] Humphries (Absalom B.[3], William[2], Charles[1]) married Ben Holmes. They had three children:

403   i. Frank[5] Holmes.
404 ii. Mary[5] Holmes, m. Sam Moyer.
405 iii. Ruby[5] Holmes, m. Arthur Goforth.

134. Frances Catherine[4] Peek (Mary E.[3], William[2], Charles[1]) was born 8 February 1847 in Union District, South Carolina and died 14 October 1917 Union County, South Carolina. She married, first, Capt. John Sanders, Company C, 18th Regiment, South Carolina Volunteers, who was born in 1819 and died 23 August 1867. He is buried at the Sanders Family Cemetery, Union County, South Carolina. She married, second, John Caldwell Calhoun (J. C.) Edwards, her step-brother, who was born 1 March 1851 and died 31 October 1924. J. C. Edwards and wife Frances Catherine are buried at Rosemont Cemetery in Union, South Carolina. The one child of John Sanders and wife Frances Catherine[4] Peek:

+ 406   Johnnie (Jean)[5] Sanders, b. 20 Dec 1867.

J. C. Edwards and wife Frances Catherine[4] Peek Sanders had five children:

+ 407   i. Coline[5] Edwards, b. 25 Sept 1875.
  408 ii. Mary Elizabeth[5] Edwards, b. 26 Jan 1878, d. 26 Oct 1953,
            Columbia, SC, unmarried, bur. Rosemont Cemetery, Union, SC.
+ 409 iii. Joseph Eugene[5] Edwards, b. 14 Oct 1880.
+ 410 iv. George Douglas[5] Edwards, b. 19 Jul 1883.
+ 411   v. Leila Viola[5] Edwards, b. 1 Aug 1887.

136. Martha Louise[4] (Pet) Peek (Mary E.[3], William[2], Charles[1]) was born 3 February 1852 in Union District, South Carolina and died 23 February 1923 in Union County, South Carolina. She married, in 1871, Joseph Butler Skelton, who was born 12 September 1846 and died 22 July 1925. Both are buried at Hebron Baptist Church in Union County. They had three children:

+ 412   i. William Peek[5] Skelton, b. 30 Apr 1872.
  413 ii. Florence Cornelia[5] Skelton, b. 19 Mar 1874, d. 1900, unmarried.
+ 414 iii. Mary[5] Skelton, b. 11 Feb 1888.

138. Inez[4] Edwards (Mary E.[3], William[2], Charles[1]) was born 25 August 1867 in Union District, South Carolina and died 1 November 1937. She married on 23 April 1891, the Rev. William Eliphas Gary[4] Humphries, #165 (Charles G. W.[3],

Thomas[2], Charles[1]), who was born 11 December 1864 in Darlington District, South Carolina and died 29 August 1948. They had six children:

415   i. Vera[5] Humphries, m. Rev. B. W. Orrick.
416   ii. Christine[5] Humphries, m. C. B. Thomas.
417 iii. Mabel Pauline[5] Humphries, m. A. Fred Cope.
418 iv. Will Lola[5] Humphries, m. C. L. McFarland.
419   v. Estelle[5] Humphries, m. Merrill Evenson.
420 vi. Grace[5] Humphries, m. Floyd Fulton.

139. John[4] Humphries (Charles H.[3], William[2], Charles[1]) was born in 1849 in Union District, South Carolina, resided in Upshur County, Texas, and was a farmer. He married Nancy Hodge, probably in South Carolina; she died in 1880, in Upshur County. They had four children:[20]

421   i. Charles[5] Humphries, b. 1870.
+ 422 ii. John S.[5] Humphries, b. 25 Sept 1873.
423 iii. William[5] Humphries, b. 1876.
424 iv. Walter[5] Humphries, b. 1880.

140. Cornelia[4] Humphries (Charles H.[3], William[2], Charles[1]) was born in 1852 and died prior to 26 August 1895.[21] She married John M. Lyles, who died in Texas. They had only one child:

425 Lettie E.[5] Lyles, m. W. J. Fowler, prior to 26 Aug 1895.

144. Frances[4] Sanders (Katherine[3], William[2], Charles[1]) was born 23 November 1855 and died 20 January 1911.[22] She married Newton Burgess, who was born 15 May 1850, and died 2 June 1906. Both are buried at Sardis United Methodist Church in Union County, South Carolina. There were five sons and three daughters:

+ 426   i. Lawrence[5] Burgess, b. 3 Oct 1875.
+ 427   ii. Minnie[5] Burgess, b. 7 Jun 1877.
428 iii. Albert[5] Burgess, m. Sue _____.
+ 429 iv. Joseph Lilton[5] Burgess.
430   v. Bessie[5] Burgess, b. 12 Dec 1882. (See #341 for descendants.)
+ 431 vi. William[5] Burgess.
+ 432 vii. Frank[5] H. Burgess, b. 17 Aug 1893.
+ 433 viii. Nannie[5] Burgess.

146. Susan Fair[4] Sanders (Katherine[3], William[2], Charles[1]) was born 25 December 1862 in Union District, South Carolina and died 23 June 1934 in Union County, South Carolina. She married, on 15 January 1880,[23] Thomas Joseph[5] Betenbaugh, #246 (Martha Ellen W.[4], Thomas[3], Sarah[2], Charles[1]), who was born 28 August 1862 and died 16 October 1915. Thomas J. Betenbaugh was elected Union County Auditor, to take office 28 April 1911.[24] He retained this office until his death. Upon his death, his son James Sanders Betenbaugh was appointed to fill out the unexpired term, and was thereafter elected to that office. Thomas Joseph Betenbaugh and wife Susan Fair Sanders had fourteen children:

+ 434   i. Della Young[5] Betenbaugh, b. 14 Oct 1880.
+ 435   ii. James Sanders[5] Betenbaugh, b. 22 Aug 1882.
  436   iii. Madge[5] Betenbaugh, b. 21 Jan 1884. (See #426 for descendants.)
  437   iv. William Glover[5] Betenbaugh, b. 2 Feb 1886, d. 18 Apr 1905,
          bur. Sardis United Methodist Church.
  438   v. Michael Grover[5] Betenbaugh, b. 2 Feb 1886, d. 11 Jul 1886.
  439   vi. Thomas Boyd[5] Betenbaugh, b. 1888, d. 1941, m.
          Bertha Ann Bentley, b. 1888, d. 1968, no children.
+ 440   vii. Pearl[5] Betenbaugh, b. 30 May 1890.
  441   viii. Annie Lou[5] Betenbaugh, b. 27 Sept 1892. (See #260 for
          descendants.)
+ 442   ix. Morris Douglas[5] Betenbaugh, b. 23 Mar 1895.
  443   x. John Roper[5] Betenbaugh, b. 2 Aug 1897, d. 27 Aug 1919.
+ 444   xi. Walter Russell[5] Betenbaugh, b. 13 Sept 1899.
+ 445 xii. Charlie Norman[5] Betenbaugh, b. 27 Apr 1902.
  446 xiii. Sudie Ruby[5] Betenbaugh, b. 10 Jul 1904, m. Perry
          Smith, and lives at Walker Heights, Union, SC.
+ 447 xiv. Nina Coline[5] Betenbaugh, b. 8 Dec 1906.

147. Janie[4] Sanders (Katherine[3], William[2], Charles[1]) was born 25 September 1865, Union District, South Carolina, and died 10 January 1901, Union County, South Carolina. She married in 1883, David Jefferson Willard, who was born 18 February 1863 and died 5 October 1834, son of John and Elizabeth (Betenbaugh) Willard. They had six children:

+ 448   i. Humphries Henry[5] Willard, b. 15 Feb 1884.
  449   ii. Glover E.[5] Willard, b. 15 Jan 1886, d. 17 Jul 1947, unm.
+ 450   iii. Kate[5] Willard, b. 11 Aug 1888.
+ 451   iv. Mattie Louise[5] Willard, b. 23 Jul 1892.
  452   v. Bessie[5] Willard, b. 20 Sept 1895, m. 18 Jan 1930,
          Sam Sherbert. They had an infant son b. 31 Jan and

d. 1 Feb 1922.

453   vi. Janie S.[5] Willard, b. 5 Jan 1901, d. 29 Jan 1901.

162. Elizabeth Levenia[4] Humphries (Charles G. W.[3], Thomas[2], Charles[1]) was born 7 June 1856 in Darlington District, South Carolina and died 3 March 1944, Darlington County, South Carolina. She married on 26 September 1872, Benjamin Franklin Lambert, who was born 3 October 1843, Marion District, South Carolina and died 12 July 1917 in Darlington County, South Carolina. They had twelve children:

   454   i. (son) b. and d. 16 Sept 1873.
+ 455   ii. Letitia Mary Jane[5] Lambert, b. 7 Apr 1875.
   456   iii. Meres Marcena[5] Lambert, b. 7 June 1877, d. 22 Nov 1971,
            m. 12 Jan 1902, Charles Franklin Howell.
   457   iv. John Wesley[5] Lambert, b. 29 Sept 1879, d. 19 May 1939,
            m. Feb 1901, Hattie Gardner.
   458   v. Bertha Nancy[5] Lambert, b. 13 Nov 1881, d. 1 Nov 1960,
            m. 14 Apr 1902, Hartwell R. Kirby.
+ 459   vi. Lue Ella[5] Lambert, b. 16 Mar 1884.
   460   vii. Henrietta Richmond[5] Lambert, b. 3 July 1887, d. 6 May 1935,
            m. Belton A. Weaver.
   461   viii. James H. Johnson[5] Lambert, b. 28 Jan 1891, d. 5 Oct 1942,
            m. 20 Jan 1919, Bessie Giles.
   462   ix. Mariah Elizabeth[5] Lambert, b. 14 Aug 1893, d. 2 Mar 1894.
+ 463   x. Charles Franklin[5] Lambert, b. 28 Feb 1895.
   464   xi. Lola Juanita[5] Lambert, b. 4 Jun 1897, d. 1 Mar 1981,
            m. 13 May 1916, James Henry Boan.
   465   xii. Robert Leonard[5] Lambert, b. 23 Dec 1899, d. 26 Sept 1900.

169. Charles G. W.[4] Humphries (Thomas Henry Durant[3], Thomas[2], Charles[1]) was born 24 October 1853, Darlington District, South Carolina. He married Sallie Ann Privett. They had six children:

+ 466   i. James Henry[5] Humphries, b. 14 Feb 1875.
   467   ii. Thomas Durant[5] Humphries, b. 21 Jun 1876, d. 19 Oct 1956, m. Ella Howell.
+ 468   iii. John Duncan[5] Humphries, b. 16 Mar 1878, d. 18 Nov 1953,
            m. 1st Meddie Oakley, 2nd Alice McMillan.
   469   iv. Albert Carlisle[5] Humphries, b. 22 Jan 1882, d. 1 Oct 1955,
            m. 1st Emily Katherine Howell, 2nd Fannie Windham Howell.
   470   v. Joseph Liston[5] Humphries, b. 10 Apr 1884, d. 23 Jan 1949, m. Corrine Oakley.
   471   vi. Edith[5] Humphries, b. ____, m. 1st, 7 Oct 1906, T. B. Anderson;
            2nd, 18 Jul 1942, James A. Foust; 3rd, 30 Sept 1951, A. L. Spence.

170. Samuel King[4] Humphries (Thomas Henry Durant[3], Thomas[2], Charles[1]) was born 17 October 1855. He married Sallie E. Melton, who was born in November 1857. They had at least three children:[25]

   472 i. Boyd R.[5] Humphries, b. Sept 1877.
   473 ii. King Jill[5] Humphries, b. 29 Dec 1878. (See #377 for descendants.)
   474 iii. Lilla N.[5] Humphries, b. May 1882.

184. Charles Lafayette[4] Odom (Hester Charlotte[3], Thomas[2], Charles[1] was born 9 November 1855 and died 22 June 1902. He married, ca. 1877, Leila Jesna Rollins, who was born 10 November 1860 and died 10 March 1936. She married, second, John Carter. Charles L. and Leila J. Odom are buried at High Hill Baptist Church in Darlington County, South Carolina. The estate of Charles Lafayette Odom was partitioned in the Court of Common Pleas.[26] The children of Charles Lafayette and Leila Jesna Rollins Odom (not necessarily in order of birth):

   475   i. Jesna[5] Odom
   476   ii. Pearl Odom[5], b. 13 Mar 1881. (See #466 for descendants.)
   477   iii. Albertus Jennings[5] Odom, b. 1883, d. 1954, m. Flonnie High.
   478   iv. Samuel Richard[5] Odom, b. 13 Mar 1884, d. Dec 1968, m. Edna
              Chandler. He served in the S. C. House of Representatives from
              Darlington County, 1937-38, 1941-2, 1943-4.
   479   v. Eloise[5] Odom, b. 1889, d. Aug 1967, m. M. Patrick McDonald.
   480   vi. Mary[5] Odom, b. 1890, m. Robert Wells[4] Humphries, #179,
              her first cousin once removed.
   481   vii. Otho[5] Odom.
   482 viii. Harry[5] Odom.
   483   ix. Hettie[5] Odom, b. 1895, m. Snow Weaver.
   484   x. Agnes Juanita[5] Odom, b. 1897, d. 7 Jan 1924, m. Mertz C. Broach.
   485   xi. Leon[5] Odom.

187. Thomas Smith[4] Humphries (Absalom C. C.[3], Thomas[2], Charles[1]) [and Victoria[4], John Thomas[3], William[2], Charles[1])] was born 8 January 1876 and died 22 June 1953, Newberry, South Carolina. He married Annie Pauline Lee, who was born 24 August 1886 and died 6 November 1966. Both are buried at Rosemont Cemetery in Newberry, South Carolina. They had eight children:

+ 486   i. Lena Beaufort[5] Humphries.
   487   ii. Lillian[5] Humphries, m. George Rodelsperger.
   488   iii. Mary Eva[5] Humphries, m. William Marshall Cox.

+ 489   iv. Catherine[5] Humphries.
+ 490   v. Thomas Smith[5] Humphries, Jr.
+ 491   vi. Wilbur Absalom[5] Humphries.
  492   vii. Horace L.[5] Humphries, b. 30 May 1911.
  493 viii. Henry[5] Humphries, d. 1909.

188. Henry B.[4] Humphries (Absalom C. C.[3], Thomas[2], Charles[1]) [and Victoria[4], John Thomas[3], William[2], Charles[1]] was born in 1878 and died 14 January 1935. He married, on 26 December 1912, Annie Lou[5] Young, #300, who was born 9 January 1899 and died 4 April 1977. Annie Lou Young Humphries married, second, on 12 April 1960, James Blaine Edwards, who was born 1 September 1889 and died 19 March 1974. She married, third, _____ Weaver. Henry B.[4] Humphries and wife Annie Lou[5] Young had three children:

  494   i. James Beaty[5] Humphries, b. 15 Mar 1914, d. 1 Apr
          1976, m. Ann Robinson.
+ 495 ii. Lucille[5] Humphries, b. 8 Jan 1918.
+ 496 iii. Woodrow Wilson[5] Humphries.

189. Lettie[4] Humphries (Absalom C. C.[3], Thomas[2], Charles[1]) [and Victoria[4], John Thomas[3], William[2], Charles[1]] was born 12 June 1883 in Union County, South Carolina, and died 7 June 1971 in Union, South Carolina. She married Charles Watson Lawson, who was born 12 October 1880 and died 11 February 1945. They are both buried at Rosemont Cemetery in Union, South Carolina. They had five children:

+ 497   i. Louise[5] Lawson.
+ 498   ii. John Minter[5] Lawson.
+ 499 iii. Guy[5] Lawson.
+ 500   iv. Lena Victoria[5] Lawson.
+ 501   v. Charles Richard[5] Lawson.

200. Isaac Frank[4] Peake (Charlotte Frances[3], Charlotte[2], Charles[1]) was born 8 July 1864 in Union District, South Carolina, and died 13 July 1933 at Glenn Springs, South Carolina. He married, on 28 June 1897, in Union, South Carolina, Mae Anna Cockrell, who was born 27 August 1870 at Harper's Ferry, West Virginia, and died 29 April 1962 in Union, daughter of Adam and Elisabeth (Merritt) Cockrell. Isaac Frank Peake served as Clerk of Court for Union

County. Both are buried at Bogansville Methodist Church in Union County. They had five children:

+ 502   i. Frank Ernell[5] Peake, b. 10 Apr 1898.
+ 503   ii. Keith Cockrell[5] Peake, b. 23 Sept 1900.
+ 504   iii. Thomas Hopkins[5] Peake, b. 20 Jun 1903.
+ 505   iv. Frances Elisabeth[5] Peake, b. 13 Oct 1905.
+ 506   v. Isaac Frank[5] Peake, Jr., b. 11 Sept 1908.

203. Glenn David[4] Peake (Charlotte Frances[3], Charlotte[2], Charles[1]) was born 15 March 1875 at Glenn Springs, South Carolina, and died 16 March 1940 in Spartanburg, South Carolina. He married in 1901 Elizabeth Etta Baines, who was born 1 July 1880 and died November 1937, daughter of Elisha and Mary Bogan Baines. Glenn David and Elizabeth Baines Peake are buried at Oak Grove Baptist Church in Spartanburg, South Carolina. They had two children:

+ 507   i. Lucia Glennie[5] Peake, b. 22 Sept 1904.
+ 508   ii. Patricia Myra[5] Peake, b. 11 Apr 1907.

205. George Washington[5] Peake (Charlotte Frances[3], Charlotte[2], Charles[1]) was born 25 November 1881 at Glenn Springs, South Carolina, and died 31 August 1960, Union County, South Carolina. He was married on 24 May 1911 to Loula Pearl Smith, who was born 12 October 1886 and died 18 December 1970. Both are buried at Bogansville Methodist Church in Union County, South Carolina. They had one child:

509   i. Fanny Lucille[5] Peake, b. 23 Aug 1912, Union Co, SC,
        m. 1 Mar 1930, in Spartanburg, SC, Frank Owen Pruitt, b. 1
        Feb 1909, d. 28 March 1975. She m. 2nd, Boyce Lawson, and
        currently lives at Route 1, Buffalo, SC.

207. John Lamartine[4] Peake (Charlotte Frances[3], Charlotte[2], Charles[1]) was born 27 July 1885 at Glenn Springs, South Carolina, and died 3 August 1968 at Glenn Springs. He married, on 2 June 1917, in Spartanburg, South Carolina, Hattie Ennon West, who was born 19 September 1898, daughter of Joe M. and Ellen Cannon West. They had three children:

+ 510   i. Hattie Elizabeth[5] Peake, b. 5 Jun 1920.
  511 ii. Mary Lamartine[5] Peake, b. 14 Sept 1924, m. Donald
       Browning, and lives currently at Glenn Springs, SC.
       No children.
+ 512 iii. John Lamartine[5] Peake, Jr., b. 14 Dec 1928.

210. Jennie Mae[4] Smith (Sarah Ellen Medora[3], Charlotte[2], Charles[1]) was born 20 April 1882 in the Baton Rouge section of Chester County, South Carolina, and died 8 December 1978, in the Rodman section of Chester County. She married Chalmers Edgar Waters, who was born 4 May 1876 and died 20 September 1949, son of James Alexander and Sarah Elizabeth (Waters) Waters. Jennie Mae and Chalmers Waters are buried at Union Associate Reformed Presbyterian Church at Richburg, South Carolina. They had no children.

211. Annie Lou[4] Smith (Sarah Ellen Medora[3], Charlotte[2], Charles[1]) married John Oliver Barwick of Paxville and Sumter, South Carolina. She was educated at Limestone College (Gaffney, South Carolina) and was teaching school in Paxville, South Carolina, when she married John Oliver Barwick, who was a bookkeeper. Five known children:

+ 513   i. John Oliver[5] Barwick Jr., b. 1905.
  514 ii. Leon[5] Barwick.
  515 iii. Gregory[5] Barwick.
  516 iv. Raymond[5] Barwick.
  517   v. Eleanor[5] Barwick, m. William B. Gibson.

215. Charlotte Cornelia[4] Randolph (Mary Ann Henrietta[3], Charlotte[2], Charles[1]) was born 27 November 1877 in Santuc, South Carolina, and died in 1963 in Greenville, South Carolina. She is buried at Landrum City Cemetery in Landrum, South Carolina. She married Leland Shumpert. They had one child:

  518 i. Randolph[5] Shumpert, m. Miriam_____, and had one daughter Randolph[6] Shumpert.

217. Elizabeth[4] Randolph (Mary Ann Henrietta[3], Charlotte[2], Charles[1]) was born in 1881 in Santuc, South Carolina, and died in 1925 in Landrum, South Carolina. She married A. Clea Carpenter of Landrum. Both are buried at Landrum City Cemetery. They had two children:

⊦ 519 i. Elizabeth[5] Carpenter, b. 29 Jul 1914.
   520 ii. Dorothy[5] Carpenter, b. 10 Sept 1916, Landrum, SC, m.
       8 Aug 1941 in Atlantic City, NJ, Joseph Tozzie, b. 16 Feb
       1918, Pleasantville, NJ. They were living in Greenville, SC, in 1982.

219. William Isaac[4] Randolph (Mary Ann Henrietta[3], Charlotte[2], Charles[1]) was born 6 June 1885 in Santuc, South Carolina, and died 27 September 1979 in Taylors, South Carolina. He married Evelyn Grogan, who was born 2 October 1880 at Pauline, South Carolina, and died 24 November 1968 in Spartanburg, South Carolina, daughter of Thomas and Martha Ann Smith Grogan. They had one child:

+ 521 i. Mary Evelyn[5] Randolph, b. 27 Nov 1922.

221. Claude Chapin[4] Gregory (John Wesley[3], Charlotte[2], Charles[1]), was born 3 September 1879 in Santuc, South Carolina, and died 1 December 1939 in Jacksonville, Florida. He married Emma Elizabeth Fulmer, who was born 6 September 1873, at Peak, South Carolina, and died 30 April 1949. Both are buried at Rosemont Cemetery in Union, South Carolina. They had one child:

+ 522 i. Paige Chapin[5] Gregory, b. 27 Nov 1900.

223. Annie Laura[4] Gregory (John Wesley[3], Charlotte[2], Charles[1]), was born 10 May 1882 in Santuc, South Carolina, and died 2 July 1983, Eastover, South Carolina. She was educated at Clifford Seminary, Union, South Carolina, and taught music in Williston, Santuc, and Eastover, South Carolina. She was married, on 3 July 1912, in Cane Creek Presbyterian Church, Santuc, to Sultan Westmoreland McKenzie, Jr., who was born 31 October 1875 and died 13 September 1919 at Eastover, South Carolina. They had two children:

+ 523 i. Martin Chapin[5] McKenzie, b. 10 May 1914.
   524 ii. Eppie Elizabeth[5] McKenzie, b. 29 Jul 1918, unmarried, lives Eastover, SC.

226. Sarah Eleanor[4] (Sadie) Gregory (John Wesley[3], Charlotte[2], Charles[1]) was born 11 January 1889 in Santuc, South Carolina, and died 29 June 1983 in Columbia, South Carolina. She married on 13 September 1911, in Columbia,

Llewellyn Fletcher Pearce, who was born 11 June 1886 in Prattville, Alabama, and died 24 December 1972 in Columbia, South Carolina, son of William Wallace and Mary Augusta Spigener Pearce. Llewellyn Pearce was employed by the South Carolina Electric and Gas Company for almost fifty years, and was assistant secretary and treasurer at the time of his retirement in 1957. Sadie and Llewellyn were charter members of Shandon Presbyterian Church in Columbia, South Carolina. They had three children:

+ 525 i. Llewellyn Gregory[5] Pearce, b. 31 Mar 1914.
   526 ii. Edmund Spigener[5] Pearce, b. 22 Jun 1915, Columbia, SC., d. 28 Oct 1963, Hanover, NH, m. Rose Marie Lanigan, in Tacoma, WA, in 1936.
+ 527 iii. Mary Emily[5] Pearce, b. 17 Jul 1916.

229. Frederick Paige[4] Gregory (John Wesley[3], Charlotte[2], Charles[1]) was born 26 January 1896 in Santuc, South Carolina. He was married on 7 March 1936 in Gaffney, South Carolina, to Ida Christine Jeter, who was born 23 December 1906 in Santuc, daughter of Little Berry Jeter and Mary Adeline Crosby Jeter, of Santuc, South Carolina. In 1982, they were living in Santuc, South Carolina. They had two children:

  528 i. Paige Christine[5] Gregory, b. 22 June 1946, Union, S. C., a graduate of Erskine College, m. Samuel Grant Kelly, b. 14 Jan 1924, Hampton Roads, VA. In 1982, they were living in Charleston, SC.
  529 ii. Malcolm Chapin[5] Gregory, b. 12 Dec 1942, Union, SC, a graduate of Erskine College, unm., lives Santuc, SC.

NOTES AND REFERENCES

1. Marriage notice in The Unionville Journal, issue of 28 Oct 1851.

2. Records of Salem College Alumnae Association, Book 3, p. 259.

3. See Glenn and Kin, ed. by Lucile Miller and Jeannette Christopher, 1975.

4. Records of Salem College Alumnae Association, Book IV, p. 275.

5. Data on these people and descendants has been supplied by Mrs. Frances H. Price, Black Mountain, NC.

6. 1870 U. S. Census, Union Co., SC, Union Township, p. 6.

7. Records of Salem College Alumnae Association, Book IV, p. 342.

8. Bible record of Micheal Betenbaugh, photocopy in possession of the author.

9. 1860 U. S. Census, Union Dist., SC, p. 54, #466/399.

10. 1880 U. S. Census, Union Co., SC, Union Twp, p. 49, #495/305.

11. 1900 U. S. Census, Spartanburg Co., SC, Campobello Twp, p. 49, #453/453.

12. Marriage notice in The Weekly Union Times, issue of 29 November 1889.

13. Marriage date from day book of Young S. Bobo who performed the ceremony. This book was in possession of his granddaughter Mrs. Vera Smith Spears.

14. Bible record of Jesse Holcombe, Bible in possession of the author.

15. Information on this family and descendants supplied by Mrs. Malcolm G. Gray, Starkville, MS, a descendant.

16. Data from family Bibles supplied by Rachel Sartor Gilliam Williams (Mrs. Robert C.), Union, SC.

17. Marriage notice in The Weekly Union Times, issue of 4 Oct 1889.

18. Marriage date and list of children from undated letter to Mrs. Ruth Humphries from Ida Bailey, oldest child of Medora and Lemuel McDaniel, copy in possession of the author.

19. See The Bedenbaugh-Betenbaugh Family of South Carolina, by Brent H. Holcomb.

20. Information supplied by L. C. Honeycutt, Kansas City, Mo., a descendant.

21. Estate papers of William Humphries, Union Co., SC, Probate Records, Box 64, Package 9.

22. An obituary notice appears in The Progress, issue of 24 Jan 1911.

23. Marriage date from obituary of T. J. Betenbaugh, The Progress, issue of 19 Oct 1915.

24. News item in The Progress, issue of 24 Jan 1911.

25. 1900 U. S. Census, Darlington County, High Hill Twp, Sheet 19.

26. Leila J. Carter, formerly Leila J. Odom against Pearl Humphries, et al., Darlington County Records of the Court of Common Pleas, copy supplied to the author by Darlington Historical Commission.

FIFTH GENERATION

231. Margaret[5] Hill (Sarah A.[4], Dr. Christopher[3], Sarah[2], Charles[1]) was born 3 November 1852 in Union District, South Carolina, and died 27 May 1921. She married William Kelly Thomas, who was born 18 October 1847 and died 23 June 1909. Both are buried at Fishdam Cemetery in Union County, South Carolina. They had five children:

530   i. Glenn Hill[6] Thomas, b. 7 Apr 1879, d. 2 Jan 1918, unm.; bur. Fishdam Cem.
531   ii. Will H.[6] Thomas, d. unm.
532   iii. Sarah[6] Thomas, d. unm.
+ 533   iv. George W.[6] Thomas, b. 15 Oct 1889.
534   v. Mary Ruth[6] Thomas, b. 29 May 1894, d. 15 Apr 1980, m. D. C. Heustess, lived Clinton, SC., no issue.

232. Sarah Glenn[5] Hill (Sarah A.[4], Dr. Christopher[3], Sarah[2], Charles[1]) was born 15 January 1856 at "Hillside," Carlisle, South Carolina, and died at Union, South Carolina, 8 May 1910. She is buried at Cane Creek Presbyterian Church at Santuc, South Carolina. She married, on 20 January 1872, James Fleming Willard, who was born 15 March 1853, died 6 January 1935 in Union. They had four children who died in infancy, and are not shown in the list of descendants and six other children:

535   i. Laura[6] Willard, died at age three.
+ 536   ii. Annie[6] Willard.
+ 537   iii. Bernice Gertrude[6] Willard, b. 17 Apr 1885.
+ 538   iv. Mary[6] (Mamie) Willard.
539   v. Sarah[6] (Sadie) Willard, b. 29 Sept 1892, d. 3 Aug 1976, m. Hubert H. Beason, b. 30 Oct 1900, d. 31 Oct 1970. Sarah W. Beason is listed in Who's Who in the Arts. They lived in Pageland, SC.
+ 540   vi. Thomas Hancock[6] Willard, b. 29 Oct 1896.

233. Martha Elizabeth[5] (Mattie) Hill (Sarah A.[4], Dr. Christopher[3], Sarah[2], Charles[1]) was born in 1858 and died in 1906. She married Reuben Sims Thomas, who was born in 1865 and died in 1906. They lived at Carlisle, South Carolina, and are buried are Fishdam Cemetery there. They had two children:

+ 541 i. James Guy[6] Thomas, b. 28 Dec 1891.
+ 542 ii. Rowland Farr[6] Thomas, b. 8 Apr 1897.

235. Jesse Robert[5] Hix (Martha Elizabeth[4], Dr. Christopher[3], Sarah[2], Charles[1]) was born 28 October 1857 and died 6 May 1921; he married in 1875 Rebecca Williamson, who was born 3 February 1856 and died 28 June 1924, daughter of Walter Blount and Angeronia (Cook) Williamson, of Fairfield County, South Carolina. Both are buried at the Presbyterian Cemetery in Union, South Carolina. They had eleven children:

543 i. James Preston[6] Hix, m. _____ and had one son Robert Hix. James Preston Hix was a veteran of the Spanish-American War.
+ 544 ii. Roberta[6] Hix, b. 1879.
+ 545 iii. Jessie[6] Hix, b. 1881.
546 iv. Sarah[6] Hix, b. _____ d. 1963, m. Hurl W. Edgar, no children.
547 v. Martha[6] Hix, m. _____ Shaw, no children.
548 vi. Louise[6] Hix, b. 5 Mar 1891, m. Robert Ray[5] Humphries (see #379).
549 vii. Daniel Townsend[6] Hix, b. 1893, d. 1966, m. Lucy McBride, no issue.
+ 550 viii. Walter[6] Hix.
+ 551 ix. Kathleen[6] Hix.
+ 552 x. Ruth[6] Hix.
+ 553 xi. Joseph Alston[6] Hix, b. 1900.

236. Sarah[5] Hix (Martha Elizabeth[4], Dr. Christopher[3], Sarah[2], Charles[1]) was born in 1866 or 1867 in Union District, South Carolina. She married Roy Townsend. They lived in Union, South Carolina, until 1919 when they moved to Maxton, North Carolina. They had five children:

554 i. Edward[6] Townsend, m. Marguerite _____.
555 ii. Sarah Marguerite[6] Townsend, was a school teacher, d. unm.
556 iii. Lois[6] Townsend, was a school teacher, and d. unm.
557 iv. Agnes[6] Townsend, m. Victor Burrell.
558 v. James[6] Townsend.

239. Simpson[5] Young (Jared W. E.[4], Thomas[3], Sarah[2], Charles[1]) was born 9 February 1867 in Union District, South Carolina, and died 9 September 1912 in Union County, South Carolina. He married Docia Julia Spears (1871-1955). She married, second, _____ Willard. Simpson Young and Docia Spears Young

Willard are buried at Sardis United Methodist Church in Union County. They had seven children:

559   i. Doris[6] Young, b. 23 Nov 1892, d. 8 Sept 1948, m.
        1st Tillman Parks, 2nd Buell Rippey.
560   ii. Ida[6] Young, b. 1896, d. 1907.
561   iii. Kate[6] Young, b. 23 Nov 1897, d. 12 Apr 1928, m. Willie
        Sumner.
562   iv. Willie[6] Young, b. 20 Dec 1899, d. 1903.
563   v. Julia[6] Young, b. 24 Feb 1902, m. 1st Oliver Austin,
        2nd Charlie Trammell, lives Union, SC.
+ 564   vi. Paul H.[6] Young, b. 11 Aug 1906.
565   vii. Simpson[6] Young, b. 23 Jun 1911, d. 12 Feb 1977, m.
        Ada Mae Grady.

247. John Calhoun[5] Betenbaugh (Martha Ellen W.[4], Thomas[3], Sarah[2], Charles[1] was born 16 October 1864 in Union District, South Carolina, and died 23 August 1911 at Glendale, South Carolina.[1] He married, on 21 February 1889,[2] Aurelia Adell Greer, born 27 February 1868 in Union County, South Carolina, died 3 December 1931 in High Point, North Carolina, daughter of Charner Sanders Greer and wife Mary Ann Malone. John Calhoun Betenbaugh and wife Aurelia are buried at Sardis United Methodist Church in Union County, South Carolina. A photograph of them and their children is reproduced on the following page. They had six children:

+ 566   i. Martha Ann[6] (Mattie) Betenbaugh, b. 18 Nov 1889.
+ 567   ii. William David[6] (Will) Betenbaugh, b. 16 May 1894.
568   iii. Mary Morris[6] Betenbaugh, b. 29 Jan 1897. (See #290 for details.)
569   iv. Margaret Aurelia[6] (Maggie) Betenbaugh, b. 22 Jan 1900,
        d. 20 Jan 1969, m. Clyde Everhart, no issue.
570   v. Gordan[6] Betenbaugh, b. 21 Jan 1904, d. 13 Mar 1913.
+ 571   vi. Charner Michael[6] Betenbaugh, b. 14 Aug 1907.

248. Elizabeth Ann Freelove[5] (Annie Elizabeth) Betenbaugh (Martha Ellen W.[4], Thomas[3], Sarah[2], Charles[1]), was born 30 July 1867 in Union District, South Carolina, and died 30 October 1946 in Union, South Carolina. She was married on 25 Dec 1884 to Thomas Calhoun (Cal) Jolly, who was born 8 June 1863 and died 10 October 1938. Both are buried at Sardis United Methodist Church. They had six children:

The family of John Calhoun and Aurelia (Greer) Betenbaugh

(top row) William David and Martha Ann, (second row) John
Calhoun, Charner Michael, Aurelia, Mary (standing) Margaret
Aurelia (seated) and Gordan (on bottom step)

+ 572   i. Alvin S.^{6} Jolly, b. 12 Apr 1886.
  573 ii. Bertran^6 (Bert) Jolly, b. 21 Jan 1889, d. 7 Apr 1976, unm.
+ 574 iii. Thomas Claude^6 Jolly, b. 11 Nov 1892.
+ 575 iv. Herbert M.^{6} Jolly, b. 17 Dec 1896.
  576   v. Floretta^6 Jolly, b. 6 Jun 1899, d. 18 Jul 1902.
+ 577 vi. Leila Pearl^6 Jolly, b. 17 Aug 1903.

249. Michael Robert^5 Betenbaugh, Jr. (Martha Ellen W.^{4}, Thomas^3, Sarah^2, Charles^1) was born 15 February 1870 and died 10 November 1895. He married Nannie Barnett, who married, second, David Johnson. Michael Robert Betenbaugh, Jr., is buried at Sardis United Methodist Church. Two children:

  578   i. Blanche^6 Betenbaugh, m. _____ Shirley.
  579 ii. Willie^6 Betenbaugh.

251. James Claude^5 Betenbaugh (Martha Ellen W.^{4}, Thomas^3, Sarah^2, Charles^1) was born 24 June 1875 in Union County, South Carolina, and died 10 October 1964 in Decatur, Georgia. He married Dovie Fuller, who was born 11 September 1891 and died 16 December 1967. They had seven children:

  580   i. Dovie Marie^6 Betenbaugh, m. Willis Andrew Bailey.
  581 ii. James Raymond^6 Betenbaugh.
  582 iii. William Hubert^6 (Bill) Betenbaugh.
  583 iv. Thomas Alvin^6 Betenbaugh.
  584   v. Cecil Robert^6 Betenbaugh.
  585 vi. George Carlton^6 Betenbaugh.
  586 vii. Annie Cornelia^6 Betenbaugh.

252. Powell Higgerson^5 Betenbaugh (Martha Ellen W.^{4}, Thomas^3, Sarah^2, Charles^1) was born 27 December 1877 and died 25 July 1961. He married on 26 December 1901 Corrie Letha Hodge, who was born 19 January 1879 and died 25 December 1961. Both were born and died in Union County, South Carolina, and are buried at Sardis United Methodist Church. They had five children:

  587   i. Alma^6 Betenbaugh, b. 11 Jan 1903, ret. schoolteacher, lives Union, SC.
  588 ii. Myrtle^6 Betenbaugh, b. 19 Jan 1905, ret. schoolteacher, lives Union, SC.
  589 iii. Lunette^6 Betenbaugh, b. 11 May 1911, ret. schoolteacher, lives Union, SC.
+ 590 iv. Margaret^6 Betenbaugh, b. 15 Jan 1916.
  591   v. Ruth^6 Betenbaugh, b. 24 Nov 1919, d. 16 Apr 1976.

253. Sallie E.^{5} Betenbaugh (Martha Ellen W.^{4}, Thomas^3, Sarah^2, Charles^1) was born 4 July 1881 and died 27 November 1909. She married, first, Sam O'Shields, who was born 22 December 1876, and died 8 February 1906; she married, second, John Sanders. Sallie E. Sanders is buried at Sardis United Methodist Church. She had four children:

592   i. James Wesley^6 O'Shields.
593 ii. Eunice Mae^6 O'Shields.
594 iii. Lewis Willis^6 O'Shields.
595 iv. Sarah Elizabeth^6 Sanders, b. 8 Nov 1909, d. 17 Dec 1910.

254. Beaty Harden^5 Betenbaugh (Martha Ellen W.^{4}, Thomas^3, Sarah^2, Charles^1) was born 28 November 1884 and died 14 August 1957. He married Maude Cunningham, who was born 8 May 1896 and died 23 December 1977, while on a visit in California. Both are buried at Rosemont Cemetery in Union, South Carolina. They had three children:

+ 596   i. Cyril Charles^6 (Mike) Betenbaugh, b. 24 Sept 1915.
+ 597 ii. Neal Harden^6 Betenbaugh.
+ 598 iii. Hubert Stanley^6 Betenbaugh.

255. Bertha^5 Young (J. Christopher^4, Charles^3, Sarah^2, Charles^1) was born 18 November 1878, died 18 January 1957. She was married, on 12 December 1895, to John Clarence^6 Gregory, #760, (Sarah Ellen^5, Adelade^4, John Thomas^3, William^2, Charles^1) (see below), who was born 4 September 1976 and died 24 February 1974. Both are buried at Hebron Baptist Church in Union, South Carolina. They had five children:

599   i. Lola Lawson^6 Gregory, b. 27 Oct 1897. (See #442 for details.)
600 ii. Ernest Talmadge^6 Gregory, b. 1902.
601 iii. Clyde Carlisle^6 Gregory, b. 1905.
602 iv. Ralph Gilliam^6 Gregory, b. 1907.
603   v. John Clarence^6 Gregory, Jr., b. 1918.

256. Ulalah (Leila)^5 Young (J. Christopher^4, Charles^3, Sarah^2, Charles^1) was born 14 June 1886 and died 21 June 1961. She was married, on 1 March 1903 to Edgar Allen Robbins, who was born 23 January 1976 and died 1 August 1949.^{3}

They are buried at Mt. Olive Baptist Church, near Cowpens, South Carolina. They had five children:

604 i. Theodore Monroe[6] Robbins, b. 13 Jun 1904, d. 22 Apr 1970,
m. 12 Jan 1925, Gladys Pettit.
605 ii. Lydia Ophelia[6] Robbins, b. 25 Feb 1907, m. 16 Dec 1934,
Troy Elbert Dalton.
606 iii. Clara Pauline[6] Robbins, b. 21 Apr 1909, m. 24 Dec 1931,
James Ralph Clary.
607 iv. Sarah Esma Maudie[6] Robbins, b. 5 Aug 1912, m. 4 Dec 1932,
William McCraw.
608 v. Hellen Antapha[6] Robbins, b. 15 Dec 1914, m. 21 Nov 1931,
Oscar Wright Gardner.

257. Julia[5] Young (J. Christopher[4], Charles[3], Sarah[2], Charles[1]) was born 5 August 1889 and died 8 November 1979. She married William Forrest Sellars, who was born 8 October 1881 and died 16 July 1973. Both are buried at Graham Chapel Wesleyan Church at Mayo, South Carolina. They had twelve children: *

    i. inf. dau., b. & d. 18 Oct 1906
    ii. Roy Robert[6] Sellars, b. 11 Jan 1908, d. 11 Jul 1909.
609 iii. Guy Calvin[6] Sellars, b. 9 Apr 1910, d. 10 Apr 1984.
610 iv. Robert Elonzo[6] Sellars, b. 23 Sept 1912.
611 v. James Nelson[6] Sellars, b. 25 Apr 1915, d. Aug 1979.
    vi. Tallulah[6] Sellars, b. 1 June 1918, d. 15 Apr 1958.
612 vii. Lela Bertha[6] Sellars, b. 24 Mar 1921.
613 viii. Albert Perry[6] Sellars, b. 18 Sept 1923.
614 ix. Maenette[6] Sellars, b. 22 Feb 1926.
615 x. Mildred Virginia[6] Sellars, b. 9 Nov 1928.
616 xi. William Forrest[6] Sellars, Jr., b. 6 Apr 1931.
    xii. Theron Eugene[6] Sellars, b. 8 Oct 1933, d. Apr 1959.

260. George Ernest[5] Young (Thomas Jefferson[4], George McCrary[3], Mary[2], Charles[1]) [and Thomas Jefferson[4], Lettie G.[3], Charles[2], John[1]] was born 17 May 1890 in Union County, South Carolina, and died there 12 October 1962. He married Annie Lou[5] Betenbaugh, #441, (Susan Fair[4], Katherine[3], William[2], Charles[1]) [and Thomas Joseph[5], Martha Ellen W.[4], Thomas[3], Sarah[2], Charles[1]], who was born 27 September 1892 and died 21 July 1984. They had two children:

+ 617 i. Leila Mae[6] Young, b. 17 Mar 1920.
618 ii. Frances Thomas[6] Young, b. 14 Feb 1926, m. Isaac
Smith Vaughan, b. 10 May 1918, d. 4 Apr 1975.

* *Some do not have numbers, as a portion of the information was received
after numbers had been assigned.*

267. Josie[5] Young (James B.[4], George McCrary[3], Mary[2], Charles[1]) married Marion Gallman. They lived in Ft. Myers, Florida, and had four children:

+ 619 i. Jimmy[6] Gallman.
+ 620 ii. George Heyward[6] Gallman.
  621 iii. Allen[6] Gallman.
  622 iv. Billy[6] Gallman.

268. Mary[5] Young (James B.[4], George McCrary[3], Mary[2], Charles[1]) was born 29 September 1891 and died 3 January 1978; she married Henry Brewington, who was born 4 May 1875 and died 6 August 1962. Both are buried at Sardis United Methodist Church in Union County, South Carolina. They had one child:

  623 Louico[6] Brewington.

270. Leland Cunningham[5] Young (James B.[4], George McCrary[3], Mary[2], Charles[1]) was born 25 September 1896 and died 29 September 1969; he married, first, Ida[6] Gregory, #770, (Sarah Ellen[5], Adelade[4], John Thomas[3], William[2], Charles[1]), who was born 10 April 1902 and died 2 January 1945 (see below). He married, second, Inez Garner. There were four children, all by Ida Gregory.

  624 i. (infant).
  625 ii. Connie[6] Young.
+ 626 iii. Ellen Jo[6] Young.
+ 627 iv. Morris[6] Young.

271. Carrie[5] Young (James B.[4], George McCrary[3], Mary[2], Charles[1]) married, first, William Reid; second, Albert P. Kirby of Granite Falls, North Carolina. There was one child:

  628 Margaret Carolyn[6] Reid m. 21 Jun 1959, Willie Dean Bumgarner.

272. Clark Hamilton[5] Young (James B.[4], George McCrary[3], Mary[2], Charles[1]) married Anne Tinker. They had two children:

  629 i. Joe[6] Young.
  630 ii. Clark[6] Young.

274. James Heyward^5 Young (James B.^{4}, George McCrary^3, Mary^2, Charles^1) was born 20 August 1903 and died 5 April 1969. He was married on 1 May 1926 to Annie Greer, who was born 24 July 1904, daughter of Charner Lester Greer and his wife Martha Vaughan. They had one child:

+ 631 i. Annie Laurie^6 Young.

278. Effie^5 Alverson (Katherine^4, George McCrary^3, Mary^2, Charles^1) married Jesse Whitmire. They had two children:

632 i. William^6 Whitmire.
633 ii. Sara Evelyn^6 Whitmire.

279. Sallie^5 Alverson (Katherine^4, George McCrary^3, Mary^2, Charles^1) was born 14 June 1881 and married Frank Caldwell. They had two children:

+ 634 i. Margaret^6 Caldwell.
635 ii. Sara^6 Caldwell.

280. G. Rector^5 (Rex) Alverson (Katherine^4, George McCrary^3, Mary^2, Charles^1) was born in 1887 and married Carrie Estes. They had three children:

636 i. Catherine^6 Alverson, m. _____ Waal.
637 ii. Francis L.^{6} Alverson, b. _____ d. 3 Jul 1978, m. Billie Jean Sprouse.
638 iii. George^6 Alverson, m. Annie Belle Maybin.

281. Julia A.^{5} Alverson (Katherine^4, George McCrary^3, Mary^2, Charles^1) was born 22 March 1888 and died 19 December 1967, married Eugene E. Sanders. They had two children:

+ 639 i. Jean^6 Sanders.
+ 640 ii. Catherine^6 Sanders.

282. Bess^5 Alverson (Katherine^4, George McCrary^3, Mary^2, Charles^1) was born 24 December 1891 and died 29 June 1959, married Orin B. Hollis, who was born 8 February 1884 and died 14 July 1953. They had six children:

641   i. Betty[6] Hollis, m. 1st Walter C. Smith, 2nd J. D. Lewis.
642 ii. Orin B.[6] Hollis, Jr.
643 iii. J. Thomas[6] Hollis.
644 iv. Truett[6] Hollis.
645   v. Charles Myers[6] Hollis.
646 vi. Richard[6] Hollis, m. Janet Melter Caldwell.

284. Mable[5] Alverson (Katherine[4], George McCrary[3], Mary[2], Charles[1]) was born in 1901 and died 26 November 1962; she married Arthur Russell Collins. They had one child:

+ 647 i. Arthur Russell[6] Collins, Jr.

285. William Giles[5] (Bill) Alverson (Katherine[4], George McCrary[3], Mary[2], Charles[1]) married Coleen Elizabeth Bishop. They had two children:

  648 i. William Giles[6] Alverson, Jr.
+ 649 ii. Walter Bishop[6] Alverson.

286. Mattie Victoria[5] Holcombe (Rachel Ann[4], George McCrary[3], Mary[2], Charles[1]) was born 17 November 1883 (tombstone has 1882) and died 13 March 1952. She was married on 24 December 1901 to William Wesley (Will) Greer, who was born 30 May 1871 and died 1 December 1946, son of Charner Sanders Greer and his wife Mary Ann Malone. Both are buried at Sardis United Methodist Church in Union County, South Carolina. They had ten children:

  650   i. Nettie Marie[6] Greer, b. 13 Sept 1903, d. 8 Jan 1980,
              m. 22 Dec 1933 to Eugene Hawkins, d. 16 Mar 1973. No issue.
              Both are buried at Rosemont Cem, Union, SC.
+ 651   ii. Claudia Sue[6] Greer, b. 18 Sept 1904.
+ 652 iii. Charner Jason[6] (Buddy) Greer, b. 1 May 1907.
+ 653   iv. Della Amanda[6] Greer, b. 19 Aug 1911.
+ 654   v. Mason Louise[6] Greer, b. 4 Apr 1914.
+ 655   vi. George Wesley[6] (Ned) Greer, b. 1 Jul 1917.
+ 656 vii. Lillian Virginia[6] Greer b. 31 Mar 1920.
+ 657 viii. Lydia Loretta[6] Greer, b. 14 Dec 1922.
+ 658   ix. Mattie Hazel[6] Greer, b. 7 Dec 1926.
  659   x. Mary[6] Greer, d. in childhood.

287. William Hazel[5] Holcombe (Rachel Ann[4], George McCrary[3], Mary[2], Charles[1]) was born 7 October 1886 in Union County, South Carolina, and died 27 October

1918 at Camp Lewis, Washington, while in military service. He is buried at Rosemont Cemetery in Union, South Carolina. On 3 May 1908 he married Laura Barnett, and they had one daughter:

660 i. Laura Everette[6] Holcombe, b. 28 June 1909, unm., lives in Union, SC.

289. Pearl Catherine[5] Holcombe (Rachel Ann[4], George McCrary[3], Mary[2], Charles[1]) was born 1 April 1891 in Union County, South Carolina, and died there 3 May 1913. In August 1907 she married James Bert May. They had two children:

+ 661 i. Cornelia[6] May, b. 18 Mar 1909.
+ 662 ii. Pearl Frances[6] May, b. 25 Oct 1911.

290. Rufus Thompson[5] Holcomb (Rachel Ann[4], George McCrary[3], Mary[2], Charles[1]) was born 29 September 1893 in Union County, South Carolina and died 11 January 1952 at Cross Anchor, Spartanburg County, South Carolina. He was married on 24 December 1915 to Mary Morris[6] Betenbaugh, #568, (John Calhoun[5], Martha Ellen W.[4], Thomas[3], Sarah[2], Charles[1]) born 29 January 1897, at White Stone, Spartanburg County. This family moved about 1926 to High Point, North Carolina, but in 1932 moved back to South Carolina, and lived near Cross Anchor. Rufus Thompson Holcomb dropped the "e" from his surname, while other members of the family retained it. He is buried at Sardis United Methodist Church in Union County, South Carolina. Mary Betenbaugh Holcomb currently [1984] resides with her daughter Jessie H. Wolfe, 557 Leonora Drive, Memphis, Tennessee. Rufus Thompson[5] Holcomb and wife Mary Morris Betenbaugh had five children:

+ 663 i. Gary Hope[6] Holcomb, b. 30 Nov 1916.
  664 ii. Mary Ruth[6] Holcombe, b. 6 May 1919, unmarried, currently lives in Columbia, SC.
+ 665 iii. Rufus T.[6] Holcomb, Jr., b. 31 Jan 1924.
+ 666 iv. Jessie Marie[6] Holcomb, b. 10 Jul 1932.
  667 v. Nancy Janet[6] Holcomb, b. 17 Apr 1937, d. 23 May 1961, in Virginia Beach, VA., m. 8 Mar 1958 to Ben Nix, Jr. No issue. Nancy is bur. at Sardis United Methodist Church.

Rufus T. and Mary (Betenbaugh) Holcomb

ca. 1915

291. Kennis Clemson[5] Holcombe (Rachel Ann[4], George McCrary[3], Mary[2], Charles[1]) was born 4 May 1896, Union County, South Carolina, and died 10 December 1969 in Loudon, Tennessee. He married, 31 July 1915, Janie Grady, and they had four children. In 1924, Kennis Clemson Holcombe removed to Tennessee and changed his name to Casey Hawkins. After the death of his first wife, he married Fannie Lou Pickle, and had seven children by her. After her death, he married Bessie (Murr) Carden, but there were no children by that marriage. The children of Kennis Clemson Holcombe were as follows:

+ 668 i. Sidney Earl[6] Holcombe, b. 25 Apr 1918.
+ 669 ii. Sara Frances[6] Holcombe, b. 11 Apr 1920.
+ 670 iii. Annie[6] Holcombe.
+ 671 iv. Virginia[6] (Jenny) Holcombe.

The children of Casey Hawkins in Tennessee:

+ 672 i. Jesse Rufus[6] Hawkins.
+ 673 ii. Casey Conrad[6] Hawkins.
+ 674 iii. Wanda June[6] Hawkins.
+ 675 iv. Billie Sue[6] Hawkins.
+ 676 v. Sarah Lou[6] Hawkins, b. 12 Dec 1931.
+ 677 vi. Paul David[6] Hawkins.
+ 678 vii. Don Gary[6] Hawkins.

292. Thomas Duncan[5] Holcombe (Rachel Ann[4], George McCrary[3], Mary[2], Charles[1]) was born 8 October 1898 in Union County, South Carolina, and died 24 February 1964 in Union. He was married on 12 October 1918 to Eileen[6] Vaughan, #842, (Lucy Smith[5], Medora[4], John Thomas[3], William[2], Charles[1]), who was born 16 August 1900 and died 15 June 1965. They are buried at Sardis United Methodist Church in Union County, South Carolina. Thomas Duncan[5] Holcombe was a sergeant in World War I and was about to enter Officer's Candidate School when he lost a leg at Chateau-Thierry and was sent home. Thomas Duncan[5] Holcombe and wife Eileen Vaughan had three children:

  679 i. Thomas Duncan[6] Holcombe, Jr., b. Aug 1920, d. 8 Jan 1922.
+ 680 ii. Helen[6] Holcombe, b. 29 Jan 1922.
  681 iii. Ray[6] Holcombe, b. 4 Jul 1924, unm., lives Union, SC.

294. May Inez[5] Holcombe (Rachel Ann[4], George McCrary[3], Mary[2], Charles[1]) was born 1 December 1902 in Union County, South Carolina, and died there 13 March 1982. On 4 December 1920, she married Thomas Frank Vaughn, who was born 1 July 1882 and died 21 May 1935. He is buried at Rosemont Cemetery in Union. They had no children. Mary Inez married, second, on 2 July 1937, Willie Edward[7] (Ed) Greer #1401, (Sallie[6], Bernice[5], Sarah[4], John Thomas[3], William[2], Charles[1]), who was born 19 February 1912 and died 23 May 1965. May Inez and Willie Edward Greer are buried at Sardis United Methodist Church in Union County. They had one child:

+ 682 i. Willie Edward[6] Greer, Jr., b. 6 Mar 1939.

295. Sidney Maxel[5] Holcombe (Rachel Ann[4], George McCrary[3], Mary[2], Charles[1]) was born on 4 August 1905. He married Alma Henderson, who was born 8 September 1898 and died 8 April 1952, and by whom he had six children, listed below. He married, second, Amy Henson Mease (div.). Sidney Maxel[5] Holcombe lives in Union County, near his daughter Catherine.

+ 683 i. Catherine[6] Holcombe.
  684 ii. Sidney A.[6] Holcombe, d. 1925.
  685 iii. William J.[6] Holcombe, d. 1927.
  686 iv. Thomas Franklin[6] Holcombe, m. Glenda _____, lives CA.
+ 687 v. Martha Juanita[6] (Shirley) Holcombe.
+ 688 vi. Curtis[6] Holcombe.

297. Kathleen[5] Young (Conquest[4], George McCrary[3], Mary[2], Charles[1]) was born in 1894 and died in 1949; she married William Hughes Sinclair (1888-1930). They had four children:

  689 i. Hazel[6] Sinclair, b. 1923, d. 1930.
+ 690 ii. Ione[6] Sinclair.
  691 iii. Ruby[6] Sinclair, m. Raymond[6] Jolly, #701.
  692 iv. William[6] (Bill) Sinclair m. Ruby Lawson.

298. Grace[5] Young (Conquest[4], George McCrary[3], Mary[2], Charles[1]) married Walter Wilson Jolly. Grace Young Jolly currently [1984] lives in Union, South Carolina. There were three children:

Thomas D. Holcombe, Sidney M. Holcombe, Inez H. Greer,
and R. Dobson Holcombe

ca. 1955

693 i. Stanley[6] Jolly, m. Ethel Cohen.
694 ii. Tessie[6] Jolly.
+ 695 iii. J. C.[6] Jolly.

299. Mattie Irene[5] Young (Jackson[4], George McCrary[3], Mary[2], Charles[1]) was born 27 November 1894 and died 18 August 1947; she married Milton Jolly, who was born 25 November 1883 and died 28 January 1961. Both are buried at Hebron Baptist Church in Union County, South Carolina. They had fourteen children:

696 i. Beulah Irene[6] Jolly, b. 1911, d. 1912.
697 ii. Mattie Pearl[6] Jolly, b. 1913, d. 1914.
+ 698 iii. Reubin[6] Jolly.
+ 699 iv. Ben[6] Jolly.
+ 700 v. Lois[6] Jolly.
701 vi. Raymond[6] Jolly, m. Ruby[6] Sinclair, #691.
702 vii. Lillian[6] Jolly, m. William Bentley.
703 viii. Milton[6] Jolly, Jr., b. 17 Dec 1919, d. Dec 1944.
+ 704 ix. Ralph[6] Jolly.
+ 705 x. Roy[6] Jolly.
+ 706 xi. Margaret[6] Jolly.
+ 707 xii. Mary Nell[6] Jolly.
708 xiii. Johnnie C.[6] Jolly, d. 12 May 1947, aged 15.
+ 709 xiv. Charlie B.[6] Jolly.

302. Ellen[5] Young (Jackson[4], George McCrary[3], Mary[2], Charles[1]) married Steven Burnett Cogdell. They had three children:

710 i. Herman B.[6] Cogdell, m. Helen C. Griffie.
711 ii. Ernest A.[6] Cogdell, m. Connie Cogdell.
712 iii. Steve B.[6] Cogdell, m. Janette C. Quinn.

303. Thomas E.[5] Young (Jackson[4], George McCrary[3], Mary[2], Charles[1]) born 25 February 1900 and died 14 August 1979; he married Mary James. They had three children:

+ 713 i. Hazel[6] Young.
714 ii. Douglas James[6] Young.
715 iii. Donald Ray[6] Young.

304. Ernest Arthur[5] Young (Jackson[4], George McCrary[3], Mary[2], Charles[1]) was born 10 February 1902 and died 21 March 1976, married Marie Gregory. They had three children:

+ 716 i. Peggy[6] Young.
+ 717 ii. Reeda[6] Young.
+ 718 iii. Ernest Arthur[6] (Sonny) Young, Jr.

306. Ethel[5] Young (Robert[4], George McCrary[3], Mary[2], Charles[1]) was born 7 January 1900 and died 29 September 1982; she married George B. Bailey, who was born 20 March 1895 and died 21 April 1966. They had seven children:

+ 719 i. James[6] Bailey.
+ 720 ii. Fred Richard[6] Bailey.
+ 721 iii. Dolly[6] Bailey.
+ 722 iv. Louise[6] Bailey.
+ 723 v. Mabel Alice[6] Bailey.
+ 724 vi. Frances[6] Bailey.
+ 725 vii. Ann[6] Bailey.

307. Pauline[5] (Polly) Young (Robert[4], George McCrary[3], Mary[2], Charles[1]) was born 13 June 1901 and died 19 February 1969, married Boyd (Bud) Keisler. They had three children:

  726 i. Adeline[6] Keisler, d. in infancy.
+ 727 ii. Betty[6] Keisler, b. 15 May 1925.
  728 iii. Hazel[6] Keisler, d. in infancy.

308. Fred[5] Young (Robert[4], George McCrary[3], Mary[2], Charles[1]) was born 26 January 1903 and died 13 February 1965. On 3 April 1926, he married Jettie Pearl Greer, who was born 16 December 1902 and died 17 May 1982, daughter of Charner Lester Greer and his wife Mattie Vaughan. Fred and Jettie are buried at Sardis United Methodist Church in Union County, South Carolina. They had two children:

729 i. Fred[6] Young, Jr., b. 11 Jan 1931, m. 9 Apr 1950, Carol Ann Brooks.
730 ii. Robert Leslie[6] Young, b. 7 Sept 1937, m. 1 Jul 1960, Tommie Rebecca Nickles.

309. Helen[5] Young (Robert[4], George McCrary[3], Mary[2], Charles[1]) was born 22 February 1912. On 30 December 1937, she married Brooks Bailey, Jr., who was born 30 December 1902, and died 15 July 1978, son of Brooks Bailey, Sr., and his

wife Elizabeth Bolt. Helen Young Bailey lives at Route 2, Union, South Carolina. There were two children:

731 i. George Russell[6] Bailey, b. 29 May 1942, d. 12 Nov 1943.
+ 732 ii. Roger Dale[6] Bailey, b. 4 May 1947.

310. Adelia Frances[5] Sartor (Christopher C.[4], Sarah[3], Mary[2], Charles[1]) was born 9 October 1864 in Union, South Carolina and died in July 1945 in Charleston, South Carolina. She married in 1891, Melvin Bookman Kelly, who was born 21 March 1865 and died 29 February 1912 at Spartanburg, South Carolina. He is buried at Oakwood Cemetery in Spartanburg. They had five children:

+ 733 i. Frances[6] (Polly) Kelly, b. 6 Dec 1891.
+ 734 ii. John Granberry[6] Kelly, b. 7 Mar 1893.
+ 735 iii. William Houston[6] Kelly.
+ 736 iv. Samuel Sartor[6] Kelly.
+ 737 v. Thomas Edwin[6] Kelly, b. 13 Aug 1900.

314. Claude Christopher[5] Sartor (Christopher C.[4], Sarah[3], Mary[2], Charles[1]) was born 30 March 1874 in Union, South Carolina and died 19 January 1964 in Union, South Carolina. He married Pearl Irene Humphries, (1879-1917), daughter of Milton McSwain Humphries and wife Mary Gee (apparently not related to this Humphries family). Both are buried at Grace Methodist Church in Union, South Carolina. They had four children:

+ 738 i. Claude Christopher[6] Sartor, Jr., b. 19 Oct 1902.
+ 739 ii. Milton Humphries[6] Sartor, b. 20 Jun 1908.
  740 iii. Thomas Bradenburg[6] Sartor, b. 9 Oct 1910, d. 17 Feb 1977, m. Katherine Yazvac of Brookfield, OH. No issue.
+ 741 iv. Mary Cornelia[6] (Mamie) Sartor, b. 21 Jul 1914.

322. Sarah Frances[5] Sartor (James Christopher[4], Catherine Brandon[3], Mary[2], Charles[1]) was born 8 August 1874 and died 7 July 1964. On 17 October 1897, she married David Fant Gilliam, Sr., who was born 14 August 1870 and died 4 June 1926. They had six children:

+ 742 i. James Louis[6] Gilliam.
  743 ii. Mary Frances[6] Gilliam, schoolteacher in Union, SC.
+ 744 iii. Lillian Zeng[6] Gilliam.
+ 745 iv. David Fant[6] Gilliam, Jr.

+ 746   v. Rachel Sartor[6] Gilliam, b. 26 Jun 1910.
+ 747 vi. Ruth Cornelia[6] Gilliam, b. 6 May 1913.

323. William Daniel[5] Sartor (James Christopher[4], Catherine Brandon[3], Mary[2], Charles[1]) was born 11 March 1878 and died 14 December 1962. On 29 March 1908, he married Mary E. Thomas, who was born 17 October 1886 and died 31 May 1939. They had three children:

748   i. Elizabeth[6] Sartor.
749 ii. Frances Agnes[6] Sartor.
750 iii. Robert W.[6] Sartor.

324. Kate[5] Sartor (James Christopher[4], Catherine Brandon[3], Mary[2], Charles[1]) was born 17 November 1880 and died 23 May 1937. On 27 February 1907, she married William Wallace Nix, who was born 3 October 1882 and died 23 September 1937. They had one child:

751 i. Kathryn[6] Nix.

325. Mary[5] Sartor (James Christopher[4], Catherine Brandon[3], Mary[2], Charles[1]) was born 7 October 1882 and died 30 May 1973. She married, first, on 4 November 1914, Clanton Gould Estes of Mississippi, who was born 15 September 1889 and died 3 January 1921. She married, second, on 16 January 1931, F. G. McHugh, who was born 21 September 1874 and died 17 June 1948. Mary Sartor and her first husband Clanton Gould Estes had one child:

752 i. Mary Electa[6] Estes.

326. Annie Belle[5] Davis (Caroline[4], Catherine Brandon[3], Mary[2], Charles[1]) was born 3 October 1891, Union County, South Carolina. She married on 5 April 1911,[4] William Thaddeus Holcomb, who was born 9 July 1874 and died 24 February 1932. He is buried at New Hope Methodist Church, near Jonesville, South Carolina. Annie Belle married, second, on 10 November 1936, Jefferson Bennette Stone, who was born 27 January 1885, died 20 June 1973. He is buried at Union Memorial Gardens. Annie Belle Stone, at age ninety-three, in 1984 lives in Union, South Carolina.

330. Carrie Sartor^5 Davis (Caroline^4, Catherine Brandon^3, Mary^2, Charles^1) was born 1 July 1903 and married 20 September 1936, Robert Marcus White, who was born 27 August 1900. They adopted two children:

+ 753 i. Edward Marcus^6 White, b. 2 Apr 1941.
  754 ii. Charles Glenn^6 White, b. 26 Aug 1943, m. Zendra Tollison.

332. Edith Kennedy^5 Smith (Emma^4, Catherine Brandon^3, Mary^2, Charles^1) was married on 7 September 1918 to Philip Dunn Flynn, Sr. She currently [1984] lives in Union, South Carolina. They had five children:

+ 755 i. Edith^6 Flynn.
+ 756 ii. Frances^6 Flynn.
+ 757 iii. Philip Dunn^6 Flynn, Jr.
+ 758 iv. Edward Dunn^6 Flynn.
+ 759 v. John Sartor^6 Flynn.

334. Sarah Ellen^5 Betenbaugh (Adelade^4, John Thomas^3, William^2, Charles^1) was born 16 May 1859 and died 20 February 1934. In 1875 she married Ralph Gilliam Gregory, who was born 1 January 1854 and died 20 January 1926. Both are buried at Hebron Baptist Church in Union County, South Carolina. They had eleven children:

  760 i. John Clarence^6 Gregory, b. 4 Sept 1876, m. Bertha^5 Young, #255 (see above for descendants).
  761 ii. Mamie^6 Gregory, b. 25 Jan 1878, d. 3 Jan 1964, m. Rev. Jesse C. Lawson.
  762 iii. Theodore Monroe^6 Gregory, b. 12 Dec 1879, d. 12 Nov 1954, bur. Hebron Baptist Church, m. Della Foster.
  763 iv. Leila Pearl^6 Gregory, b. 12 Dec 1879, d. 25 Dec 1883.
+ 764 v. Grover Cleveland^6 Gregory, b. 13 Nov 1884.
  765 vi. Nelle^6 Gregory, b. 20 Jan 1887, d. 15 Oct 1977, m. Hunter Finney.
  766 vii. Eugene^6 Gregory, b. 2 May 1889 (twin).
  767 viii. Colene^6 Gregory, b. 2 May 1889(twin), m. Luke Scott.
  768 ix. Sarah Louise^6 Gregory, b. 23 Jun 1892, d. 1971, m. Fletcher Clark.
  769 x. Gilliam Maurice^6 Gregory, b. 25 Oct 1896, d. 16 May 1946, m. Helen Sweeney.
  770 xi. Ida^6 Gregory, b. 20 Apr 1902, m. Leland Cunningham^5 Young, #270 (see above for descendants).

336. Caroline Lorena[5] Willard (Adelade[4], John Thomas[3], William[2], Charles[1]) was born 14 February 1869 and died 17 September 1908; she married W. J. (Jess) Jolly. They had ten children:

```
    771   i.  Nora[6] Jolly.
    772  ii.  Rosa[6] Jolly.
    773 iii.  Sue[6] Jolly.
    774  iv.  Addie[6] Jolly.
    775   v.  Mamie[6] Jolly.
    776  vi.  Clara[6] Jolly.
    777 vii.  Jessie[6] Jolly.
    778 viii. Janice[6] Jolly.
+   779  ix.  Paul[6] Jolly, b. 1904.
    780   x.  Richard[6] Jolly.
```

337. Arthur[5] Willard (Adelade[4], John Thomas[3], William[2], Charles[1]) was born in 1871 and died in 1912. He married Fannie J. Williams, who was born 7 July 1870 and died 23 September 1903. Both are buried at Putman Baptist Church in Union County, South Carolina. They had five children:

```
    781   i.  Monroe[6] Willard.
    782  ii.  Laura[6] Willard.
    783 iii.  Ann[6] Willard.
    784  iv.  Vickie[6] Willard.
    785   v.  Frances[6] Willard.
```

338. Louisa[5] Willard (Adelade[4], John Thomas[3], William[2], Charles[1]) was born 6 February 1873 and died 1 October 1901. On 9 January 1889, she married John R. Greer.[5] She married, second, John Thomas Bishop. Louisa and John R. Greer had five children:

```
+   786   i.  Robert Christopher[6] Greer, b. 6 Mar 1891.
+   787  ii.  Clarence Eugene[6] Greer, b. 1893.
    788 iii.  Glover[6] Greer.
    789  iv.  John[6] Greer, m. Leara _____.
+   790   v.  Sue[6] Greer.
```

Louisa and John Thomas Bishop had two children:

```
    791   i.  Herman[6] Bishop.
    792  ii.  Louise[6] Bishop.
```

339. Josephine[5] Willard (Adelade[4], John Thomas[3], William[2], Charles[1]) was born in 1874 and died 26 May 1911, at Pacolet, South Carolina.[6] She married Eular Eison. They had two children:

    793 i. Irene[6] Eison.
    794 ii. Daisy[6] Eison.

340. Addie[5] Willard (Adelade[4], John Thomas[3], William[2], Charles[1]) was born 15 May 1877 and died in May 1973, in Easley, South Carolina. In 1901, she married Jason Claudius Greer, who was born 16 May 1876 and died 27 April 1937, son of Charner Sanders Greer and wife Mary Ann Malone. They had six children:

    795   i. Ernest[6] Greer, m. Callie Scott.
    796 ii. Lewis[6] Greer, m. Mattie Brown.
    797 iii. Leonard[6] Greer, m. Cora Harris.
    798 iv. Vera[6] Greer, m. Alonzo Meeks.
    799   v. Forrest[6] Greer.
    800 vi. J. C.[6] Greer, Jr.

341. Jackson Lee[5] Willard (Adelade[4], John Thomas[3], William[2], Charles[1]) was born 16 February 1879 and died 16 November 1955 in Clinton, South Carolina. He married his second cousin Bessie[5] Burgess, #430, (Frances[4], Katherine[3], William[2], Charles[1]), who was born 12 December 1882 and died 17 August 1955 in Clinton. Both are buried at Rosemont Cemetery in Clinton. They had six children:

    801   i. Clemson[6] Willard, b. 1900, d. 1978, m. Gladys Bobo.
  + 802 ii. Adelaide[6] Willard, b. 1902.
    803 iii. Cleora[6] Willard.
  + 804 iv. John[6] Willard, b. 1906.
    805   v. Thomas[6] Willard, b. 1918, d. 1976.
  + 806 vi. Sara Lee[6] Willard, b. 1920.

343. Mary Lou[5] Stokes (Mary Ann[4], John Thomas[3], William[2], Charles[1]) was born 16 June 1871 and died 11 February 1937. She married Perry C. Whisenant, who was born 5 January 1863 and died 4 December 1942. They are buried at Rosemont Cemetery in Union, South Carolina. (Perry C. Whisenant was married first to Belle[5] Edwards, #345 (see below). They had three children:

+ 807 i. Lillian[6] Whisenant.
  808 ii. Carolina A.[6] Whisenant.
  809 iii. Louise[6] Whisenant.

345. Belle[5] Edwards (Sarah[4], John Thomas[3], William[2], Charles[1]) was born 20 July 1870 and died 29 July 1896. She married Perry C. Whisenant, who married, second, Mary Lou[5] Stokes, #343, (see above). Belle Edwards Whisenant is buried at the Whisenant-Rogers Cemetery in Union County, South Carolina. Belle and Perry C. Whisenant had five children:

  810 i. Robert Theodore[6] (Bob) Whisenant, b. 2 Apr 1888,
    d. 14 Dec 1972.
+ 811 ii. Ed[6] Whisenant.
  812 iii. Lampley[6] Whisenant, b. 10 Oct 1891, d. 3 Jun 1981, m.
    Lillie Chapman.
  813 iv. Hoyt[6] Whisenant, b. 1893, d. 1974.
  814 v. Nell Ossie[6] Whisenant, b. 7 Sept 1895, d. 8 Mar 1970,
    m. Harry Allison.

346. Bernice[5] Edwards (Sarah[4], John Thomas[3], William[2], Charles[1]) was born 6 May 1872 and died 15 May 1922. She married William Thomas Edwards, who was born 19 December 1862 and died 10 February 1908. Both are buried at Sardis United Methodist Church in Union County, South Carolina. They had nine children:

+ 815 i. Sallie[6] Edwards, b. 18 Nov 1893.
  816 ii. Clarence Earl[6] Edwards, b. 9 May 1895, d. 7 Jul 1980,
    m. Margaret Lowrey.
  817 iii. Love Berry[6] Edwards, b. 31 Dec 1896, d. 9 Jul 1964, unm.
  818 iv. John William[6] Edwards, b. 20 Dec 1898, d. 5 Nov 1939,
    m. Lula Keisler.
  819 v. Joseph Hamilton[6] Edwards, b. 1 May 1900, d. 2 Jun 1936,
    m. Sara Lee Finney.
  820 vi. Bessie[6] Edwards, b. 30 Apr 1903 (twin), d. 13 Jun 1975, m.
    Frank Smith.
  821 vii. Bell[6] Edwards, b. 30 Apr 1903(twin), d. 23 Nov 1903.
  822 viii. Thomas Clyde[6] Edwards, b. 9 Sept 1904, m. Corine Estes,
    lives Union, SC.
+ 823 ix. Lewis Crawford[6] Edwards, b. 16 Nov 1906.

348. John Rufus[5] McDaniel (Medora[4], John Thomas[3], William[2], Charles[1]) was born 21 September 1869 in Union County, South Carolina, and died 5 June 1931;

he is buried at Rosemont Cemetery, Union, South Carolina. He married Blanche
Barnett, by whom he had seven children:

824   i. Antonia[6] McDaniel, b. 1890, m. J. L. Doggett, b. 1875, d. 1930.
825   ii. Louis[6] McDaniel, m. Katie Saltonstall.
826   iii. Leila[6] McDaniel, m. S. W. Hopper.
827   iv. Nannie[6] McDaniel, m. F. M. Willard.
828   v. Louise[6] McDaniel, m. Coy Smith.
829   vi. Jane[6] McDaniel.
830   vii. John[6] McDaniel, m. Nena Gladden.

349. Robert Lee[5] McDaniel (Medora[4], John Thomas[3], William[2], Charles[1]) was
born 17 April 1871 in Union County, South Carolina, and died 8 May 1943. He
married Annie Belle Barnett, who was born 15 November 1881 and died 9 July
1969. Both are buried at Rosemont Cemetery in Union. They had three children:

831   i. Annie Belle[6] McDaniel, unm.
832 ii. Marion[6] McDaniel, b. 6 Apr 1905, d. 4 Apr 1975, unm.
+ 833 iii. Robert Monroe[6] McDaniel.

350. Victoria[5] McDaniel (Medora[4], John Thomas[3], William[2], Charles[1]) was born 8
May 1873 and married Carrie Barnett. They had six children:

834   i. Myrtice[6] Barnett.
835   ii. Douglas[6] Barnett.
836   iii. Robert[6] Barnett.
837   iv. Rufus[6] Barnett.
838   v. Beaty[6] Barnett.
839   vi. Lunette[6] Barnett.

352. Lucy Smith[5] McDaniel (Medora[4], John Thomas[3], William[2], Charles[1]) was
born 14 September 1877 in Union County, South Carolina and died 19 August
1961. On 9 September 1896, she married Wallace Hamilton Vaughan, who was
born 27 November 1877 in Union County, and died 24 January 1950, son of
James Thomas Byrd Vaughan and his wife Ann Vaughan. Both Lucy Smith
McDaniel and her husband, Wallace Hamilton Vaughan, are buried at Rosemont
Cemetery in Union. They had six children:

+ 840   i. Ida Florence[6] Vaughan, b. 24 Dec 1897.
+ 841 ii. Annie Estelle[6] Vaughan, b. 1 Mar 1899.
842 iii. Eileen[6] Vaughan, b. 16 Aug 1900, m. Thomas Duncan[5]

Holcombe (see #292 for descendants).
843 iv. James Thomas Byrd[6] Vaughan, b. 26 Apr 1902, d. 2 May 1932,
m. Catherine Grice, no issue.
+ 844 v. Lindsey[6] Vaughan, b. 6 Nov 1903.
+ 845 vi. Katie Louise[6] Vaughan, b. 7 Apr 1908.

355. Mary Ann[5] (Mame) McDaniel (Medora[4], John Thomas[3], William[2], Charles[1])
was born 24 January 1887, and died 24 June 1958. She married John Lewis Jolly,
who was born 21 February 1882 and died 29 March 1939. Both are buried at
Grace Methodist Church in Union, South Carolina. They had four children:

846 i. Martha[6] Jolly, b. 23 Dec 1908, Union Co., SC, d. 1980, San
Diego, CA, m. John Sannes, no issue.
847 ii. Mary Victoria[6] Jolly, b. 13 Jan 1913, d. 15 May 1914.
+ 848 iii. Helen Ruth[6] Jolly, b. 11 May 1919.
849 iv. John Lewis[6] Jolly, Jr., b. 24 Aug 1925, d. 5 Feb 1963, unm.

377. Evelyn Frances[5] Humphries (John Wylie[4], John Thomas[3], William[2], Charles[1]),
was born 29 August 1882 and died 9 September 1962. On 24 December 1903, she
married King Jill[5] Humphries, #473, (Samuel King[4], Thomas Henry Durant[3],
Thomas[2], Charles[1]), who was born 29 December 1878 in Darlington County, South
Carolina, and died 8 March 1942. They had two children:

850 i. Sarah Othella[6] Humphries, b. 22 Jul 1915, d. 5 Nov 1916.
+ 851 ii. Jack Wylie[6] Humphries, b. 14 Nov 1911.

378. Olive[5] Humphries (John Wylie[4], John Thomas[3], William[2], Charles[1]) was born
25 October 1883 and died 22 February 1982. On 19 July 1903, she married
Clarence W. Kirven, who was born 18 December 1881 and died 14 October 1955.
They had four children:

+ 852 i. Roy Humphries[6] Kirven, b. 20 May 1904.
+ 853 ii. Bertha E.[6] Kirven, b. 8 Dec 1905.
854 iii. Raymond Bernard[6] Kirven, b. 24 Jul 1908, d. 22 Oct 1909.
+ 855 iv. Edith Mae[6] Kirven, b. 26 Oct 1911.

379. Robert Ray[5] Humphries (John Wylie[4], John Thomas[3], William[2], Charles[1])
was born 4 September 1885 and died 25 September 1973. He married on 1 June
1910, Lillie Mae Bussey, who was born 14 May 1890 and died 18 May 1912. He
married, second, on 26 November 1913, Louise[6] Hix, #548, (Jesse Robert[5],

Martha Elizabeth[4], Dr. Christopher[3], Sarah[2], Charles[1]) who was born 5 March 1891 and died 19 May 1969. They had two children:

+ 856   i. Frances Williamson[6] Humphries, b. 9 Dec 1919.
   857 ii. Beverly Ray[6] Humphries, b. 9 May 1926, d. 11 Apr 1980, unm.

380. Bessie[5] Humphries (John Wylie[4], John Thomas[3], William[2], Charles[1]) was born 14 August 1888 and died 10 October 1984 in Union, South Carolina.   On 14 June 1906, she married Albert Jefferson Taylor, who was born 2 January 1875 and died 27 November 1961. They had seven children:

+ 858   i. Elizabeth[6] Taylor, b. 3 Mar 1910.
+ 859 ii. Harry Ray[6] Taylor, b. 8 Aug 1912.
+ 860 iii. William Marion[6] Taylor, b. 23 Aug 1914.
+ 861 iv. Frances Alberta[6] Taylor, b. 20 June 1916.
+ 862 v. Martha Victoria[6] Taylor, b. 30 Apr 1918 (twin).
+ 863 vi. Mary Lenora[6] Taylor, b. 30 Apr 1918 (twin).
+ 864 vii. Doris Ruth[6] Taylor, b. 19 Oct 1931.

382. Lona Mae[5] Humphries (John Wylie[4], John Thomas[3], William[2], Charles[1]) was born 18 July 1895. On 6 October 1915, she married William Clough Rice, Sr. Eight children:

+ 865   i. Mary Alice[6] Rice, b. 28 Jul 1917.
+ 866 ii. Helen[6] Rice, b. 19 Feb 1919.
+ 867 iii. William[6] Rice, b. 8 Aug 1920.
+ 868 iv. Louise[6] Rice, b. 18 Oct 1922.
+ 869 v. Donald[6] Rice, b. 5 May 1924.
+ 870 vi. Harriett Lucille[6] Rice, b. 11 Jan 1926.
+ 871 vii. Cornelia Othela[6] Rice, b. 19 May 1928.
+ 872 viii. James McDowell[6] Rice, b. 18 Oct 1933.

398. Charles Hilliard[5] Humphries, Jr. (Charles Hilliard[4], Absalom B.[3], William[2], Charles[1]) was born 6 September 1911 and married Lucille Caldwell.   Three children:

+ 873   i. Charles Hilliard[6] Humphries, III, b. 29 May 1945.
   874 ii. Thomas Caldwell[6] Humphries, b. 11 Nov 1948.
   875 iii. Nancy Maxwell[6] Humphries, b. 6 Dec 1955.

399. Julian Maxwell[5] Humphries (Charles Hilliard[4], Absalom B.[3], William[2], Charles[1]) was born 1 October 1913 and married Claire Joyner. They live in Jacksonville, Florida. Three children:

876 i. Julian Maxwell[6] Humphries, Jr., b. 1 May 1949, m. Nancy Collier.
+ 877 ii. Ralph Joyner[5] Humphries, b. 24 Jan 1952.
+ 878 iii. Susan Claire[6] Humphries, b. 5 Jul 1954.

400. Norma Keels[5] Humphries (Charles Hilliard[4], Absalom B.[3], William[2], Charles[1]) was born 30 May 1920 and married Robert Emmett Love, Jr. They live in Walhalla, South Carolina. Three children:

+ 879 i. Robert Maxwell[6] Love, b. 3 Aug 1947.
+ 880 ii. Julia Elizabeth[6] Love, b. 8 Apr 1950.
881 iii. Sue Kendrick[6] Love, b. 9 Oct 1956, m. Patman Sherer Eberhart.

401. George Badger[5] Humphries (Charles Hilliard[4], Absalom B.[3], William[2], Charles[1]) was born 27 September 1922 and married Elaine Clark. They live at Johnston, South Carolina. Two children:

+ 882 i. George Badger[6] Humphries, Jr., b. 24 Mar 1947.
+ 883 ii. Claude Maxwell[6] Humphries, b. 16 Dec 1953.

402. Olive Elaine[5] Humphries (Charles Hilliard[4], Absalom B.[3], William[2], Charles[1]) was born 28 July 1925 and married John Lester Paschal. They live in Dallas, Texas. Two children:

+ 884 i. Elizabeth Ann[6] Paschal, b. 24 Aug 1954.
885 ii. John Lester Paschal, Jr., b. 30 Aug 1960.

406. Johnnie (Jean)[5] Sanders (Frances Catherine[4], Mary E.[3], William[2], Charles[1]) was born 20 December 1867 in Union County, South Carolina, and died 18 April 1926, at Nashville, Tennessee. On 6 February 1904, she married the Rev. Albert Crosland Bowen, who was born 4 October 1865, Lawrenceville, Alabama, and died 10 January 1951, Shanghai, China, son of Dr. O. B. Bowen and his wife Amanda Whitehurst. Both were missionaries. They had two children:

886 i. Frances Jean[6] Bowen, b. 21 Nov 1905, Soochow, China,
       d. 16 Apr 1977, Nashville, TN, was educated at Vanderbilt
       University, m. June 1961, Thomas Edmund Durrett Jr., died in
       1961, bur. Mt. Calvary Cemetery, Nashville, TN, no issue.
887 ii. Albert Lander[6] Bowen, b. 18 Apr 1908, Shanghai, China,
       m. 1 May 1943 Olive Graves, b. 19 Mar 1907, Atlanta, GA.
       Albert Lander Bowen lives in Nashville. No issue.

407. Coline[5] Edwards (Frances Catherine[4], Mary E.[3], William[2], Charles[1]) was
born 25 September 1875 in Union County, South Carolina, and died 18 May 1957,
at Monroe, North Carolina. She was educated at Clifford Seminary in Union,
South Carolina. On 6 September 1897, she married Charles Richardson Smith,
who was born 17 November 1870, Union County, South Carolina, and died 31
December 1927 in Union, son of William Smith and his wife Eliza Jane Long.
Both Coline Edwards and her husband are buried at Rosemont Cemetery in
Union. They had two children:

+ 888 i. Myrtle Coline[6] Smith, b. 7 June 1899.
  889 ii. William Calhoun[6] Smith, b. 28 Sept 1915, Union, SC,
         m. 15 June 1946, Harriet Evelyn Wallace, div. 1965, no issue.

409. Joseph Eugene[5] Edwards (Frances Catherine[4], Mary E.[3], William[2], Charles[1])
was born 14 October 1880, Union County, South Carolina and died 7 June 1959 in
Union. He married, first, in 1905, Sue Thomas, who was born 4 August 1882 and
died 13 July 1942 (they were divorced). He married, second, 15 August 1918,
Mattie Belle Lake, who was born 3 June 1884, and died 22 August 1966, in
Union, daughter of Middleton Columbus Lake and his wife Laura Olive Smith.
Joseph Eugene Edwards was a postal clerk in Union, and a veteran of the
Spanish-American War. He and his wife Mattie Belle Lake had three children:

+ 890 i. Frances Lake[6] Edwards, b. 29 May 1919.
+ 891 ii. Joseph Eugene[6] Edwards, Jr., b. 23 Oct 1920.
+ 892 iii. Martha Louise[6] (Marty) Edwards, b. 29 May 1923.

410. George Douglas[5] Edwards (Frances Catherine[4], Mary E.[3], William[2], Charles[1])
was born 19 July 1883 in Union County, South Carolina, and died 21 December
1965 in Union County. On 11 June 1911, he married Lillie Blanche Adams, who
was born 13 December 1885 and died 9 November 1967, daughter of Josiah

Franklin Adams and his wife Mary Ida Smith. George Douglas Edwards was a farmer, and his wife Lillie was a public school teacher, educated at Winthrop College in Rock Hill, South Carolina. Both are buried at Rosemont Cemetery in Union. They had two children:

+ 893 i. Mannie Lee[6] Edwards, b. 13 Mar 1912.
+ 894 ii. Johnathan Franklin[6] Edwards, b. 21 Nov 1925.

411. Leila Viola[5] Edwards (Frances Catherine[4], Mary E.[3], William[2], Charles[1]) was born 1 August 1887 in Union County, South Carolina, and died 19 December 1978 in Clinton, South Carolina. On 8 October 1919, she married William Hugh Simpson, who was born 23 January 1884, Laurens County, South Carolina and died 17 February 1950, Clinton, South Carolina, son of James Lewis Simpson and his wife Martha Ann Wright. Leila Edwards Simpson was a public school teacher, a graduate of Littleton College, near Raleigh, North Carolina. William Hugh Simpson was a business man, and well-known citizen of Clinton, South Carolina. Both are buried at Rosemont Cemetery in Clinton. They had one child:

+ 895 Frances[6] Simpson, b. 15 June 1921.

412. William Peek[5] Skelton (Martha Louise[4], Mary E.[3], William[2], Charles[1]) was born 30 April 1872 in Union County, South Carolina, and died 29 November 1932 in Union County. On 12 December 1897, he married Bessie Smith Black, born 22 November 1878 and died 15 October 1962 in Spartanburg County, South Carolina. William Peek (or Peake) Skelton was a policeman in Union. They are both buried at Upper Fairforest Baptist Church in Union County, South Carolina. They had four children:

896 i. Victor[6] Skelton, b. 15 Oct 1901, d. 15 Feb 1903.
897 ii. William Paul[6] Skelton, b. 16 Jul 1899, m. Ruby Powell.
898 iii. Hazel Compton[6] Skelton, b. 4 May 1908, d. 26 Feb 1980, m. Lucy Sims, no children.
899 iv. Ned Woodrow[6] Skelton, b. 15 Jan 1912, m. 6 Aug 1943, Nina Lee[6] Willard, #964, (Humphries Henry[5], Janie[4], Katherine[3], William[2], Charles[1]), b. 29 Apr 1916.

414. Mary[5] Skelton (Martha Louise[4], Mary E.[3], William[2], Charles[1]) was born 11 February 1888, and married Kay Hawkins. They had nine children:

900   i. Boyce[6] Hawkins.
901 ii. Ethel[6] Hawkins.
902 iii. Coline[6] Hawkins.
903 iv. Louise[6] Hawkins.
904   v. Ned[6] Hawkins.
905 vi. Fred[6] Hawkins (twin).
906 vii. Frances[6] Hawkins (twin).
907 viii. Inez[6] Hawkins.
908 ix. Leonard[6] Hawkins.

422. John S.[5] Humphries (John[4], Charles H.[3], William[2], Charles[1]) was born 25 September 1873, in Louisiana and died 4 September 1931 in Gilmer, Upshur County, Texas. On 10 November 1892, in Gilmer, Texas, he married Elizabeth Welborn, who was born 20 September 1876 in Pritchett, Upshur County, Texas, and died there 17 October 1918. Both are buried at Pleasant Hills Cemetery in Pritchett, Texas. They had six children:

909   i. Charles William[6] Humphries, b. 14 Sept 1895, Pritchett,
        TX, m. 1919, Bertha _____, d. 7 June 1957, Pritchett,
        bur. Pleasant Hills Cem.
910 ii. Willie[6] Humphries, b. 3 Jan 1897, m. 16 Apr 1916,
        Henry Chapman.
911 iii. Zoula May[6] Humphries, b. 22 May 1901, Pritchett, TX,
        d. 11 Nov 1959, Gladewater, Gregg Co., TX, m. 20 Jul 1918,
        at Gilmer, TX, Evel Timothy Marsh, bur. Pleasant Hills Cem.
912 iv. Myrtle Mary[6] Humphries, b. 8 Aug 1903, Pritchett, TX,
        m. 1st, 7 Oct 1922, John Honeycutt, m. 2nd, 12 Nov 1943,
        Austin W. Folles.
+ 913 v. Joy Elizabeth[6] Humphries, b. 25 Dec 1905.
914 vi. William Clifford[6] Humphries, b. 29 Mar 1912, Pritchett,
        TX, d. 9 Sept 1922, Pritchett, TX, bur. Pleasant Hills Cem.

426. Lawrence[5] Burgess (Frances[4], Katherine[3], William[2], Charles[1]) was born 3 October 1875 and died 26 May 1913. He married his first cousin, Madge Cloria[5] Betenbaugh, #436, (Susan Fair[4], Katherine[3], William[2], Charles[1]), who was born 21 June 1884 and died 25 June 1938. Both are buried at Sardis United Methodist Church in Union County, South Carolina. They had two children:

915 i. Lewis Manley^6 Burgess.
+ 916 ii. Paul Heyward^6 Burgess.

427. Minnie^5 Burgess (Frances^4, Katherine^3, William^2, Charles^1) was born 7 June 1877 and died 9 March 1936. She is buried at Sardis United Methodist Church, Union County, South Carolina. She married a Lee, and had three children:

917 i. Nellie^6 Lee.
918 ii. Blanche^6 Lee.
919 iii. "Buster"^{6} Lee.

429. Joseph Lilton^5 Burgess (Frances^4, Katherine^3, William^2, Charles^1) married Nellie Parks. They had five children:

+ 920 i. Cleo^6 Burgess.
921 ii. Violet^6 Burgess.
+ 922 iii. LaVerne^6 Burgess.
+ 923 iv. Roy^6 Burgess.
924 v. Louis^6 Burgess.

431. William^5 Burgess (Frances^4, Katherine^3, William^2, Charles^1) married Claudia _____, and had five children:

925 i. Marie^6 Burgess.
926 ii. Blanche^6 Burgess.
927 iii. Colleen^6 Burgess.
928 iv. Janie^6 Burgess.
929 v. Louise^6 Burgess.

432. Frank H.^{5} Burgess (Frances^4, Katherine^3, William^2, Charles^1) was born 17 August 1893 and married Josephine Fowler, who was born 22 November 1890 and died 22 May 1962. They had four children:

930 i. Frances^6 Burgess.
931 ii. Lena^6 Burgess.
932 iii. Paul^6 Burgess.
933 iv. Arthur^6 Burgess.

433. Nannie^5 Burgess (Frances^4, Katherine^3, William^2, Charles^1) married Jesse Thompson, and had four children:

448. Humphries Henry[5] Willard (Janie[4], Katherine[3], William[2], Charles[1]) was born 15 February 1884 in Union County, South Carolina and died there 9 September 1960. He married, on 28 February 1906, Carrie Burgess, who was born 29 May 1891, Union County, South Carolina, and died there 30 July 1977. Both are buried at Forest Lawn Cemetery in Union. They had six children:

+ 962 i. Ezell Manly[6] Willard, b. 10 Nov 1910.
  963 ii. Mary Louise[6] Willard, b. 2 Oct 1913, d. 8 Jan 1942, unm.
  964 iii. Nina Lee[6] Willard, b. 29 Apr 1916, m. Ned Woodrow[6] Skelton, #899 (see above).
+ 965 iv. Helen Ruth[6] Willard, b. 9 Oct 1918.
  966 v. Humphries Henry[6] Willard, Jr., b. 3 Nov 1920, m. 8 Jan 1942, Kathryn Howell.
  967 vi. Dorothy Sanders[6] Willard, b. 26 Feb 1923, m. 17 Apr 1946, William Preston Mabry.

450. Kate[5] Willard (Janie[4], Katherine[3], William[2], Charles[1]) was born 11 August 1888 and died 20 March 1932. She married, on 8 December 1912, Robert Jenkins, who was born 16 November 1884 and died 23 April 1954. Both are buried at Beulah Baptist Church in Union County, South Carolina. They had five children:

  968 i. David Willard[6] Jenkins, b. 15 Oct 1913.
  969 ii. Margaret Louise[6] Jenkins, b. 16 Sept 1916.
  970 iii. Thomas Douglas[6] Jenkins, b. 21 Dec 1918.
  971 iv. Robert[6] Jenkins, Jr., b. 16 Sept 1921.
  972 v. Janie Sue[6] Jenkins, b. 16 Feb 1932.

451. Mattie Louise[5] Willard (Janie[4], Katherine[3], William[2], Charles[1]) was born 23 July 1892 and died 1 August 1974. She married, on 12 December 1915, Charles Preston Bailey, who was born 18 January 1892 and died 18 March 1960. Both are buried at Sardis United Methodist Church in Union County, South Carolina. They had five children:

  973 i. Charles[6] Bailey, Jr., b. 21 Jun 1919.
  974 ii. Paul[6] Bailey, b. 15 Feb 1922.
  975 iii. Morris Sanders[6] Bailey, b. 11 Apr 1926, d. 18 Jan 1978, unm.
  976 iv. Marion Eugene[6] Bailey, b. 19 Sept 1930.
  977 v. Sue Catherine[6] Bailey, b. 5 Jan 1933.

455. Letitia Mary Jane[5] (Lettie) Lambert (Elizabeth Levenia[4], Charles G. W.[3], Thomas[2], Charles[1]) was born 7 April 1875 in Darlington, South Carolina, and died there 2 March 1919. She married, on 24 September 1893, James Edward Wilson, who was born 6 May 1872 and died 28 November 1929 in Florence, South Carolina. Both are buried at Grove Hill Cemetery in Darlington. They had ten children:

+ 978   i. Herbert Earl[6] Wilson, b. 3 Jan 1895.
+ 979   ii. Mary Elizabeth[6] Wilson, b. 23 Oct 1897.
+ 980   iii. James Bertram[6] Wilson, b. 25 Jul 1899.
+ 981   iv. Virgil William[6] Wilson, b. 2 Sept 1901.
+ 982   v. Robert Stevenson[6] Wilson, b. 1 Sept 1903.
+ 983   vi. Oscar LaFaye[6] Wilson, b. 10 Dec 1905.
+ 984   vii. Myrtle Leona[6] Wilson, b. 1 Oct 1909.
   985   viii. Bertha Juanita[6] Wilson, b. 6 Oct 1911, d. 21 Jul
          1925, at Columbia, SC, bur. Grove Hill Cem, Darlington, SC.
+ 986   ix. Woodrow Frank[6] Wilson, b. 1 Dec 1915.
+ 987   x. Emerson Edward[6] Wilson, b. 11 Oct 1917.

459. Lue Ella[5] Lambert (Elizabeth Levenia[4], Charles G. W.[3], Thomas[2], Charles[1]) was born 16 March 1884 in Darlington County, South Carolina and died there 12 April 1960. She married, on 17 November 1901, David Melvin Hatchell, who was born 6 October 1877 and died 17 January 1919. Both are buried at Magnolia Cemetery in Darlington. They had five children:

+ 988   i. Ella Louise[6] Hatchell, b. 6 Apr 1906.
   989   ii. Earnest[6] Hatchell, d. in infancy.
   990   iii. Jason[6] Hatchell, d. in infancy.
   991   iv. Pearly Elizabeth[6] Hatchell, b. 23 Mar 1915, d. 5 Apr
          1968, m. 1st Guy Gibbs, 2nd Theo Clark.
+ 992   v. Meres Evelyn[6] Hatchell, b. 31 Mar 1918.

463. Charles Franklin[5] Lambert (Elizabeth Levenia[4], Charles G. W.[3], Thomas[2], Charles[1]) was born 28 February 1895 in Darlington, County, South Carolina, and died there 31 May 1935. He married, on 12 April 1917, in Darlington, Kathleen Smith, who was born 6 August 1897 in Chesterfield County, South Carolina, and died 19 April 1975, in Darlington. Both are buried at Grove Hill Cemetery in Darlington. They had four children:

993 i. Franklin Julius[6] Lambert, b. 10 May 1918, d. 26 Jan 1940.
+ 994 ii. Cecil Edgar[6] Lambert, b. 15 Jun 1920.
+ 995 iii. Monroe Terry[6] Lambert, b. 25 Jan 1922.
+ 996 iv. Gena Ray[6] Lambert, b. 14 Dec 1925.

466. James Henry[5] Humphries (Charles G. W.[4], Thomas Henry Durant[3], Thomas[2], Charles[1]) was born 14 February 1875 in Darlington County, South Carolina and died 3 May 1944. He is buried at High Hill Baptist Church in Darlington County. He married his second cousin, Pearl[5] Odom, #476 (Charles Lafayette[4], Hester Charlotte[3], Thomas[2], Charles[1]) who was born 13 March 1881 and died in July 1966. They had nine children (not necessarily in order of birth):

997 i. James Wallace[6] Humphries, b. 1901, d. ___ Aug 1960,
        m. 23 Sept 1924, Ruby Hill, bur. at High Hill
        Baptist Church, Darlington Co., SC.
998 ii. Raymond L.[6] Humphries, b. 1902, d. 19 Dec 1982.
999 iii. Earl Albert[6] Humphries, m. _____ Snipes, d. Oct 1967.
1000 iv. Nell[6] Humphries, m. Gus Hoffmeyer.
1001 v. Alice[6] Humphries, m. Burris Tedder.
1002 vi. Maude A.[6] Humphries, m.1st ___ Caves, 2nd ____ Brown.
1003 vii. Rosa[6] Humphries, b. 1912, d. 23 Jul 1979, m. 1st ___ Walker,
        2nd Ira Lowman.
1004 viii. James Henry[6] Humphries, Jr., b. 23 Nov 1922.
1005 ix. George B.[6] Humphries, b. 23 Nov 1922.

468. John Duncan[5] Humphries (Charles G. W.[4], Thomas Henry Durant[3], Thomas[2], Charles[1]) was born 16 March 1878 and died 18 November 1953. He is buried at Wesley Chapel in Lydia, South Carolina. He married Meddie M. Oakley, who was born 16 September 1877 and died 13 October 1918. She is buried at Mt. Elon Church in Hyman, South Carolina. John Duncan[5] Humphries, married, second Alice McMillan. John Duncan[5] Humphries and wife Meddie M. Oakley had nine children:

1006 i. James Henry[6] Humphries, b. 12 Dec 1903.(See #988
        for descendants.)
1007 ii. Bysie Sims[6] Humphries, b. 25 Jul 1905, d. 19 May
        1982, m. 1st Della Feagin, 2nd Grace Barnhill.
1008 iii. Maggie[6] Humphries, b. 9 Oct 1906, d. 23 Apr 1933,
        m. Robert Langston.
1009 iv. Sallie[6] Humphries, b. 6 Aug 1908, m. John Hood
        Bass, Sr.
1010 v. Charles G. W.[6] Humphries, b. 20 Oct 1909, d. 1

Jun. 1981.
1011 vi. Ella[6] Humphries, b. 17 Oct 1911 (twin), m. 21 May 1930, Harlee Stewart.
1012 vii. Newell Benjamin[6] Humphries, b. 17 Oct 1911 (twin), d. 1 May 1948, unm.
1013 viii. Edith[6] Humphries, b. 5 Jan 1915, m. 1st Benton Blackwell, 2nd Joel Ellis.
1014 ix. Jake Duncan[6] Humphries, b. 17 Sept 1918, d. 18 Nov 1918.

486. Lena Beaufort[5] Humphries (Thomas Smith[4], Absalom C. C.[3], Thomas[2], Charles[1]) married Ralph Edward Cooper, and they reside [1984] in Columbia, South Carolina. They had two children:

1015 i. Ralph Edward[6] Cooper, Jr.
1016 ii. Thomas Glenn[6] Cooper.

489. Catherine[5] Humphries (Thomas Smith[4], Absalom C. C.[3], Thomas[2], Charles[1]) married Charles W. Gordon. They had two children:

1017 i. Charlotte[6] Gordon.
1018 ii. Dorothy Pamela[6] Gordon.

490. Thomas Smith[5] Humphries, Jr. (Thomas Smith[4], Absalom C. C.[3], Thomas[2], Charles[1]) married Frances Prelloman. They had two children:

1019 i. John Marshall[6] Humphries.
1020 ii. Jayne[6] Humphries.

491. Wilbur Absalom[5] Humphries (Thomas Smith[4], Absalom C. C.[3], Thomas[2], Charles[1]) married Helen Force. They have one child:

1021 Steven[6] Humphries.

495. Lucille[5] Humphries (Henry B.[4], Absalom C. C.[3], Thomas[2], Charles[1]) was born 8 January 1918, married Eugene Bishop. They had one child:

+ 1022 Marion Eugene[6] Bishop.

496. Woodrow Wilson[5] Humphries (Henry B.[4], Absalom C. C.[3], Thomas[2], Charles[1]) married Sara Riggs. They had two children:

+ 1023 i. Terry Wilson[6] Humphries.
  1024 ii. Vickie Dianne[6] Humphries, m. 2 Sept 1978, E. Perry Haney.

497. Louise[5] Lawson (Lettie[4], Absalom C. C.[3], Thomas[2], Charles[1]) married C. Garvin Hughes. They had two children:

+ 1025 i. Carroll G.[6] Hughes.
+ 1026 ii. Phillip L.[6] Hughes.

498. John Minter[5] Lawson (Lettie[4], Absalom C. C.[3], Thomas[2], Charles[1]) married Grace Rodgers. They had two children:

+ 1027 i. June Mavis[6] Lawson.
+ 1028 ii. Ann[6] Lawson.

499. Guy H.[5] Lawson (Lettie[4], Absalom C. C.[3], Thomas[2], Charles[1]) married Lillian Donnan. Guy H. Lawson is a Baptist minister. They live at Route 3, Inman, South Carolina, and had four children:

  1029 i. Guy H.[6] Lawson, Jr. m. Sandra _____.
+ 1030 ii. K. Donnan[6] Lawson.
  1031 iii. Mary Lillian[6] Lawson.
+ 1032 iv. Glenda Jo[6] Lawson.

500. Lena Victoria[5] Lawson (Lettie[4], Absalom C. C.[3], Thomas[2], Charles[1]) married John LeRoy Allen. They reside [1984] at Arcadia, South Carolina, and had two children:

+ 1033 i. John LeRoy[6] Allen, Jr.
+ 1034 ii. William Conrad[6] Allen.

501. Charles Richard[5] Lawson (Lettie[4], Absalom C. C.[3], Thomas[2], Charles[1]) married Orgla Powell. Charles Richard Lawson is a Baptist minister, and resides at Walterboro, South Carolina. They had two children:

  1035 i. Jane Margaret[6] Lawson.
  1036 ii. Carla Louise[6] Lawson.

502. Frank Ernell[5] Peake (Isaac Frank[4], Charlotte Frances[3], Charlotte[2], Charles[1]) was born 10 April 1898 in Union, South Carolina, and died 20 September 1981 at

St. Petersburg Beach, Florida. He married, on 18 March 1923, in Conway, South Carolina, Inez Stalvey, who was born 10 November 1900, daughter of Albert Derrick and Ellen Victoria (Sanders) Stalvey, of Georgetown, South Carolina. Frank Ernell Peake served in the 42nd Rainbow Division, World War I. Inez Stalvey Peake still resides at St. Petersburg Beach. They had three children:

+ 1037 i. Frank Ernell[6] Peake, Jr., b. 12 Feb 1924.
+ 1038 ii. Robert Sanders[6] Peake, b. 20 Oct 1926.
+ 1039 iii. William Derrick[6] Peake, b. 11 June 1929.

503. Keith Cockrell[5] Peake (Isaac Frank[4], Charlotte Frances[3], Charlotte[2], Charles[1]) was born 23 September 1900 at Harper's Ferry, West Virginia, and died 12 October 1963, Washington, D. C., and is buried at Rock Creek Cemetery, Washington, D. C. He married first, in August 1925, Brownlee Elizabeth Neely, who was born 12 April 1910, Rock Hill, South Carolina, and died in October 1948, in Washington, D. C. She is buried Laurelwood Cemetery in Rock Hill, South Carolina, daughter of Eugene Moore and Eunice (Cameron) Neely. Keith Cockrell Peake and wife Elizabeth Neely had two children. He married, second, Emma Manolia Garlington Warren, who was born 14 July 1918 in Columbia, South Carolina. They had one child. The children of Keith Cockrell[5] Peake:

+ 1040 i. Jean Neely[6] Peake, b. 7 May 1926.
  1041 ii. Eunice Elizabeth[6] Peake, b. 9 May 1927, Chester, SC,
         d. 12 Dec 1952, Washington, DC, bur. Arlington National
         Cemetery, m. Luther Monroe Eastep, in 1949, no issue.
  1042 iii. Marcia[6] Peake, b. 28 Mar 1955, Washington, DC, after
         the death of her father was adopted by an aunt and uncle,
         and her name was legally changed to Marcia Peake Sorrell.

504. Thomas Hopkins[5] (Hop) Peake (Isaac Frank[4], Charlotte Frances[3], Charlotte[2], Charles[1]) was born 20 June 1903 in Union, South Carolina, died there 4 January 1969, and is buried at Rosemont Cemetery in Union. He was married, 6 August 1925, at the Associate Reformed Presbyterian Church at Abbeville, South Carolina, to Mary Elizabeth McMurray, who was born 25 February 1902 at Clinton, South Carolina, daughter of Otis Miller and Bessie Selina (Garvin) McMurray. Mary Elizabeth (Betty) McMurray was a graduate of Queen's College, Charlotte, North Carolina. Thomas Hopkins[5] Peake was an automobile salesman

in Union for approximately thirty years. They had two children:

+ 1043 i. Thomas Hopkins[6] Peake, Jr., b. 26 Jun 1926.
+ 1044 ii. Erwin Crockett[6] Peake, b. 20 Apr 1928.

505. Frances Elizabeth[5] Peake (Isaac Frank[4], Charlotte Frances[3], Charlotte[2], Charles[1]) was born 13 October 1905 in Union, South Carolina, was educated at Chicora College in Columbia, South Carolina. She taught school in Union and in Burlington, North Carolina. She married first, 27 March 1932, John McGee Fix, who was born 13 August 1900 and died 22 September 1941, son of John Meade and Carrie (Holt) Fix of Burlington, North Carolina. Frances Elizabeth Peake Fix married, second, on 23 April 1946, Carl Winfried Parsons, who was born 27 December 1900, Cairo, West Virginia, son of Albert Sheridan and Bertha Ellen (Tetchner) Parson. Carl W. Parsons and Frances Elizabeth now [1984] live in Ventura, California. Frances Elizabeth[5] had no children by either marriage.

506. Isaac Frank[5] Peake, Jr. (Isaac Frank[4], Charlotte Frances[3], Charlotte[2], Charles[1]) was born 11 September 1908 and Union, South Carolina, and attended Georgia Tech. He married, on 21 April 1934, in Charlotte, North Carolina, Mary Sue Ledford, who was born 15 August 1910, daughter of James Nelson and Ella Alice (Gantt) Ledford, of Charlotte. Isaac Frank[5] Peake, Jr., was employed by DuPont of Wilmington, Delaware, having lived in Old Hickory, Tennessee, Clinton, Iowa, and Wilmington, Delaware. Now retired, he lives in Tryon, North Carolina. They had one child:

+ 1045 i. Glenn David Peake, b. 31 Aug 1938.

507. Lucia Glennie[5] Peake (Glenn David[4], Charlotte Frances[3], Charlotte[2], Charles[1]) was born 22 September 1904 in Union, South Carolina and married Charles Lewis Noblitt of Spartanburg, South Carolina. There are four children:

+ 1046 i. Arvid Terry[6] Peake, b. 27 Mar 1924.
+ 1047 ii. Betty Lou[6] Noblitt, b. 12 Nov 1928.
+ 1048 iii. Elbert Graham[6] Noblitt, b. 2 Dec 1930.
  1049 iv. Jack Everett[6] Noblitt, b. 21 Nov 1932, Spartanburg, SC, m.
          22 Oct 1955, Patricia Margaret Vergenes, no issue.

508. Patricia Myra[5] Peake (Glenn David[4], Charlotte Frances[3], Charlotte[2], Charles[1]) was born 11 April 1907 in Union, South Carolina, and was married on 12 July 1930, in Spartanburg, South Carolina, to Paul Lee Reynolds, who was born 9 May 1902. One child:

+ 1050 Patricia Ann[6] Reynolds, b. 7 Oct 1933.

510. Hattie Elizabeth[5] Peake (John Lamartine[4], Charlotte Frances[3], Charlotte[2], Charles[1]) was born 5 June 1920 at Glenn Springs, South Carolina, married 23 December 1939, Walker William Kennedy, who was born 29 August 1910 in Pacolet, South Carolina, son of John Peter and Temmer Frances Kennedy. W. W. and Hattie Elizabeth[5] Peake Kennedy currently [1984] reside in Orlando, Florida. They had one child:

+ 1051 William Peake[6] Kennedy, b. 15 Feb 1944.

512. John Lamartine[5] Peake, Jr. (John Lamartine[4], Charlotte Frances[3], Charlotte[2], Charles[1]) was born 14 December 1928 in Glenn Springs, South Carolina, married 24 December 1948, in Glenn Springs, Marcia Evelyn Stone, who was born 20 February 1932, Woodruff, South Carolina, daughter of John Roscoe and Maude (Bobo) Stone. John L.[5] Peake, Jr., and wife Marcia currently [1984] live at Glenn Springs. Three children:

+ 1052 i. Jerald Lamartine[6] Peake, b. 28 Apr 1950 (twin).
+ 1053 ii. John Everette[6] Peake, b. 28 Apr 1950 (twin).
+ 1054 iii. Marcia Susan[6] Peake, b. 9 Dec 1952.

513. John Oliver[5] Barwick (Annie Lou[4], Sarah Ellen Medora[3], Charlotte[2], Charles[1]) was born in 1905 in Sumter, South Carolina, married 2 June 1931, Ellinor Gaillard Crawford, divorced 1937. (Ellinor married second Joe M. Bates.) They had one child:

+ 1055 Neil Gaillard[6] Barwick, b. 2 Feb 1934, after the remarriage
    of his mother, his name was legally changed to Neil Gaillard Bates.

519. Elizabeth[5] Carpenter (Elizabeth[4], Mary Ann Henrietta[3], Charlotte[2], Charles[1]) was born 29 July 1914 in Landrum, South Carolina, married 10 September 1932,

in Greenville, South Carolina, to Melvin Bellwood. They had four children:

1056 i. Melvin[6] Bellwood, Jr., b. 8 Nov 1934, Greenville, SC, m. Faye Adams, lives Orlando, FL.
1057 ii. Linda[6] Bellwood, b. 23 Feb 1943 (twin), Greenville, SC, m. T. C. Roberts.
1058 iii. Sandra[6] Bellwood, b. 23 Feb 1943 (twin), Greenville, SC, m. David Zywiczynaki.
1059 iv. Jimmy[6] Bellwood, b. 28 Jun 1948, Greenville, SC., m. Barbara _____.

521. Mary Evelyn[5] Randolph (William Isaac[4], Mary Ann Henrietta[3], Charlotte[2], Charles[1]) was born 27 November 1922 in Spartanburg, South Carolina, married 4 December 1949, at First Baptist Church, Spartanburg, to Clifford Calvin Hayslip. They had four children:

+ 1060 i. Clifford Calvin[6] Hayslip, Jr., b. 20 Aug 1951.
+ 1061 ii. Marsha Elizabeth[6] Hayslip, b. 30 Mar 1953.
1062 iii. Warren Randolph[6] Hayslip, b. 7 Jul 1954.
1063 iv. Norman Richard[6] Hayslip, b. 17 May 1956.

522. Paige Chapin[5] Gregory (Claude Chapin[4], John Wesley[3], Charlotte[2], Charles[1]) was born 27 November 1900 in Santuc, South Carolina, and died 14 September 1961. He is buried at St. Augustine, Florida. He married Florence Mae Guilfoyle, who was born 12 September 1904, daughter of James Daniel and Muriel Mae (King) Guilfoyle. They had one child:

+ 1064 Muriel Joy[6] Gregory, b. 16 Dec 1930.

523. Martin Chapin[5] McKenzie (Anne Laura[4], John Wesley[3], Charlotte[2], Charles[1]) was born 10 May 1914 in Eastover, South Carolina, was educated at Christ School, Asheville, North Carolina, and Clemson University, in agricultural engineering. He married Emma White Leitner, and currently [1984] resides near Clemson, South Carolina. They had three children:

1065 i. Martin Chapin[6] McKenzie, Jr.
1066 ii. John W.[6] McKenzie.
1067 iii. Jamie E.[6] McKenzie.

525. Llewellyn Gregory[5] Pearce (Sarah Eleanor[4], John Wesley[3], Charlotte[2], Charles[1]) was born 31 March 1914 in Columbia, South Carolina and died there 21 September 1984. He was a graduate of USC, retired from the State-Record Company and was organist at Eastminster Presbyterian Church in Columbia. On 18 May 1946, he married Alice Witherspoon Barron, who was born 11 Feb 1920 in Charleston, South Carolina, daughter of Frank Eugene and Etta Gregorie (Trott) Barron. Alice was a graduate of Queen's College in Charlotte, North Carolina. They had two children:

+ 1068 i. Llewellyn Gregory[6] Pearce, Jr., b. 5 Oct 1948.
  1069 ii. Alice Barron[6] Pearce, b. 11 Aug 1953, Columbia, SC,
       graduate of Converse College, Spartanburg, SC, and
       received MS from Fla. State Univ.

527. Mary Emily[5] Pearce (Sarah Eleanor[4], John Wesley[3], Charlotte[2], Charles[1]) was born 17 July 1916 in Columbia, South Carolina, married 27 December 1936, Robert Fuller Johnson, who was born 28 February 1914 in Connewat, Ohio, and died 28 July 1944 in Union County, South Carolina, son of Hobert Ward and Bessie Wilma (Fuller) Johnson. Mary Emily[5] Pearce Johnson is traffic manager, TV operations, WLTX in Columbia. Two children:

+ 1070 i. Eleanor Wilma[6] Johnson, b. 12 Aug 1938.
+ 1071 ii. Ward Pearce[6] Johnson, b. 9 Dec 1941.

NOTES AND REFERENCES

1. Obituary notice in The Progress, issue of 25 Aug 1911.

2. Marriage notice in The Weekly Union Times, issue of 1 Mar 1889.

3. Data supplied by Ophelia Robbins Dalton, September 1984, to the author.

4. Marriage notice in The Progress, issue of 7 Apr 1911.

5. Marriage notice in The Weekly Union Times, issue of 11 Jan 1889.

6. Obituary notice in The Progress, issue of 30 May 1911.

SIXTH GENERATION

533. George W.[6] Thomas (Margaret[5], Sarah A.[4], Dr. Christopher[3], Sarah[2], Charles[1]) was born 15 October 1889 and died 15 August 1945. He married Della Coleman Jeter, who was born 14 April 1895, daughter of Clarence A. and May (Jeter) Jeter. Della Jeter Thomas resides in Union, South Carolina. They had one child:

+ 1072 Judith Ann[7] Thomas, b. 15 Dec 1935.

536. Annie[6] Willard (Sarah Glenn[5], Sarah A.[4], Dr. Christopher[3], Sarah[2], Charles[1]) was born in Union, South Carolina, and married Bud Boulware. Annie Willard Boulware died shortly after the birth of their only child:

1073 i. Annie[7] Boulware.

537. Bernice Gertrude[6] Willard (Sarah Glenn[5], Sarah A.[4], Dr. Christopher[3], Sarah[2], Charles[1]) was born 17 April 1885 in Union, South Carolina, and died 18 February 1971 in Spartanburg, South Carolina. She married William Henry May, who was born 28 February 1872 in Hickory, North Carolina, and died 30 July 1951 in Spartanburg, South Carolina. They had eight children:

+ 1074 i. Ruth[7] May, b. 31 Jul 1904.
+ 1075 ii. Edna Elizabeth[7] May, b. 22 Nov 1906.
  1076 iii. Kathleen Amelia[7] May, b. 8 Feb 1908, Union, SC., d.
    13 Feb 1973, Spartanburg, SC, owned "Kathleen May Antiques"
    in Spartanburg.
  1077 iv. Carl Henry[7] May, b. 17 Jun 1910, Union, SC, graduate
    of Wofford College, was a veteran of World War II, m. 8 May
    1937, Anne May Hendricks, b. 3 Apr 1910, Pickens, SC; no issue.
+ 1078 v. Dan W.[7] May, b. 28 Feb 1914.
+ 1079 vi. Sarah Glenn[7] May, b. 2 Apr 1916.
+ 1080 vii. Margaret Helen[7] May, b. 10 Jan 1919.
  1081 viii. George Washington[7] May, b. 19 Mar 1921, Spartanburg,
    SC, d. 18 Jan 1922, Spartanburg, SC., bur. Oakwood Cem.

538. Mary[6] (Mamie) Willard (Sarah Glenn[5], Sarah A.[4], Dr. Christopher[3], Sarah[2], Charles[1]) was born in Union, South Carolina, died in 1965 in Union. She married Robert (Bob) Vaughan. Three children:

+ 1082 i. Harper[7] Vaughan.
+ 1083 ii. Fred[7] Vaughan.
  1084 iii. Rivers[7] Vaughan, m. Violet Wilkins.

540. Thomas Hancock[6] Willard (Sarah Glenn[5], Sarah A.[4], Dr. Christopher[3], Sarah[2], Charles[1]) was born 29 October 1896 in Union, South Carolina, and died 26 April 1977 in Spartanburg, South Carolina. He was a sergeant in World War I. He married Grace Crawley, who was born 16 February 1903 in Spartanburg, South Carolina, and died there on 31 January 1978. Three children:

+ 1085 i. Dorothy[7] Willard.
  1086 ii. Edna Grace[7] Willard, m. _____ Blair.
  1087 iii. Thomas Hancock[7] Willard, Jr., b. 16 Apr 1926, Spartanburg, SC, killed in Word War II, 15 Mar 1945, buried in Flanders Field, and later brought to Greenlawn Cem.

541. James Guy[6] Thomas (Martha Elizabeth[5], Sarah A.[4], Dr. Christopher[3], Sarah[2], Charles[1]) was born 28 December 1891 and died 11 January 1974. He married Gertrude Wade of Chester County, South Carolina. They lived in Newport, North Carolina. They had one child:

+ 1088 Margaret O'Bannon[7] Thomas, b. 24 Jul 1930.

542. Rowland Farr[6] Thomas (Martha Elizabeth[5], Sarah A.[4], Dr. Christopher[3], Sarah[2], Charles[1]) was born 8 March 1897 and died 21 December 1976. He married Alma Wade of Chester County, South Carolina. They had one child:

+ 1089 Rowland Farr[7] Thomas, Jr., b. 17 Dec 1925.

544. Roberta[6] Hix (Jesse Robert[5], Martha Elizabeth[4], Dr. Christopher[3], Sarah[2], Charles[1]) was born in 1879 and died in 1971. She married J. Clough Wallace. Two children:

+ 1090 i. Dr. Winter Clough[7] Wallace.
  1091 ii. Roberta[7] Wallace, m. DuBose Boylston, no issue.

545. Jessie[6] Hix (Jesse Robert[5], Martha Elizabeth[4], Dr. Christopher[3], Sarah[2], Charles[1]) was born in 1881 and died in 1969. She married Matt Melvin O'Shields. Five children:

+ 1092   i. Matt[7] O'Shields.
  1093 ii. Philip Cook[?] (Pete) O'Shields, m. Mary Chamble, no issue.
+ 1094 iii. Dan Hix[7] O'Shields.
+ 1095 iv. Hurl Edgar[7] (Buck) O'Shields.
+ 1096   v. Jessie Hix[7] O'Shields.

550. Walter[6] Hix (Jesse Robert[5], Martha Elizabeth[4], Dr. Christopher[3], Sarah[2], Charles[1]) married Madeline McCombs, and had four children:

  1097   i. Walter[7] Hix, Jr., m. Jayne Smith.
+ 1098 ii. Elliott[7] Hix.
+ 1099 iii. Hurl[7] Hix.
+ 1100 iv. Martha[7] Hix.

551. Kathleen[6] Hix (Jesse Robert[5], Martha Elizabeth[4], Dr. Christopher[3], Sarah[2], Charles[1]) married Sam Barron, an attorney and later Judge of the Criminal and Civil Courts of Union County, South Carolina. They had five children:

  1101   i. Rebecca[7] Barron, m. James Montgomery Lane, lives
             Delray Beach, FL.
+ 1102 ii. Elma[7] Barron.
  1103 iii. Jesse Hix[7] Barron, lives Union, SC.
  1104 iv. Rev. Robert G.[7] Barron, m. Betty Smoot.
  1105   v. James Edward[7] Barron, d. 1945, aged 15.

552. Ruth[6] Hix (Jesse Robert[5], Martha Elizabeth[4], Dr. Christopher[3], Sarah[2], Charles[1]) married Grady Bethea, and they had one child:

+ 1106   i. Rebecca Jeanne[7] Bethea.

553. Joseph Alston[6] Hix (Jesse Robert[5], Martha Elizabeth[4], Dr. Christopher[3], Sarah[2], Charles[1]) was born 1900, died 1981, married Viola Mehaffey. They had one child:

  1107 i. Joseph Alston[7] Hix, Jr.

564. Paul H.[6] Young (Simpson[5], Jared W. E.[4], Thomas[3], Sarah[2], Charles[1]) was born 11 August 1906 and died 15 May 1965; he is buried Rosemont Cemetery in Union, South Carolina. He married Inez Hart, who was born 10 October 1904. One child:

1108   Marjorie[7] Young, born 27 November 1927, married 1 October 1949, Clarence Nichols. Marjorie Young Nichols has been Probate Judge of Union Co., SC, since 16 Jun 1981.

566. Martha Ann[6] (Mattie) Betenbaugh (John Calhoun[5], Martha Ellen W.[4], Thomas[3], Sarah[2], Charles[1]) was born 18 November 1889 in Union County, South Carolina, and died 10 March 1978 in Spartanburg, South Carolina. She married, on 16 January 1910, Lonnie Marcellous Littlejohn, who was born 15 February 1887 and died 19 December 1957. They are buried at Corinth Baptist Church, near Gaffney, South Carolina. Children:

+ 1109   i. Era Virginia[7] Littlejohn, b. 26 Sept 1912.
+ 1110   ii. Lavare Verbena[7] Littlejohn, b. 15 Jul 1916.
+ 1111   iii. Lonnie Vernon[7] Littlejohn, b. 5 May 1919.
+ 1112   iv. Edisto Edith[7] Littlejohn, b. 10 Aug 1921.
  1113   v. Alvin Pittman[7] Littlejohn, b. 15 Jul 1924.
  1114   vi. Ruth Devinnie[7] Littlejohn, b. 1 May 1915, d. 8 Sept 1915.
  1115   vii. Helen Louise[7] Littlejohn, b. & d. 6 Apr 1931.

567. William David[6] (Will) Betenbaugh (John Calhoun[5], Martha Ellen W.[4], Thomas[3], Sarah[2], Charles[1]) was born 16 May 1894 in Union County, South Carolina. He moved to High Point, North Carolina, in 1923 and married, 20 February 1926, Mamie Foster, who was born 15 May 1904 in Asheboro, North Carolina. Both still [1984] reside in High Point, North Carolina, and have two children:

+ 1116   i. William David[7] (Bill) Betenbaugh, Jr., b. 30 Jan 1927.
+ 1117   ii. Betty[7] Betenbaugh, b. 16 Nov 1930.

571. Charner Michael[6] Betenbaugh (John Calhoun[5], Martha Ellen W.[4], Thomas[3], Sarah[2], Charles[1]) was born 14 August 1907 in Union County, South Carolina, married 27 March 1937, Gladys Lucille Totten, who was born 28 January 1910, High Point, North Carolina. They had two children:

  1118   i. Charner Michael[7] Betenbaugh, Jr., b. & d. 30 Nov 1937 (premature), High Point, NC.
+ 1119   ii. Gordon Murray[7] Betenbaugh, b. 30 Jun 1941, Clinton, SC.

572. Alvin S.[6] Jolly (Elizabeth Ann[5], Martha Ellen W.[4], Thomas[3], Sarah[2], Charles[1]) was born 12 April 1886 in Union County, South Carolina and died 25 October 1964; he married Nina Belcher, born 8 June ___. They had three children:

+ 1120 i. Alvin S.[7] Jolly, Jr.
+ 1121 ii. Edward K.[7] Jolly, b. 9 Aug 1923.
    1122 iii. Christine[7] Jolly, b. 18 Jan 1928, m. Paul Anderson.

574. Thomas Claude[6] Jolly (Elizabeth Ann[5], Martha Ellen W.[4], Thomas[3], Sarah[2], Charles[1]) was born 11 November 1892 and died 13 November 1971; he is buried at Forest Lawn Cemetery in Union, South Carolina. He was superintendant of Union schools. He married Mary Spears, and had three children:

    1123 i. Thomas Claude[7] Jolly, III.
    1124 ii. Mary Ann[7] Jolly, m. _____ Mack.
    1125 iii. Michael S.[7] Jolly.

575. Herbert M.[6] Jolly (Elizabeth Ann[5], Martha Ellen W.[4], Thomas[3], Sarah[2], Charles[1]) was born 17 December 1896, married Eleanor Menger, and had two children:

    1126 i. Helen[7] Jolly, m. _____ Cates.
    1127 ii. Herbert M.[7] Jolly, Jr.

577. Leila Pearl[6] Jolly (Elizabeth Ann[5], Martha Ellen W.[4], Thomas[3], Sarah[2], Charles[1]) was born 17 August 1903 and married Thomas J. Hannon, who was born 8 June 1902. They live near Inman, South Carolina, and had one child:

+ 1128 Suzanne[7] Hannon.

590. Margaret[6] Betenbaugh (Powell[5], Martha Ellen W.[4], Thomas[3], Sarah[2], Charles[1]) was born 15 January 1916, married, first, Ralph Phillips, who was born 18 April 1914 and died 24 June 1968; married, second, 6 November 1971, George W. Brown, who was born 11 January 1912. Margaret and Ralph Phillips had one child:

+ 1129 Ralph[7] Phillips, Jr.

596. Cyril Charles[6] (Mike) Betenbaugh (Beaty[5], Martha Ellen W.[4], Thomas[3], Sarah[2], Charles[1]) was born 24 September 1915 in Union, South Carolina, and died there 12 July 1983. On 12 September 1945 he married Sara Strange, who lives in Columbia, South Carolina. Two children:

+ 1130 i. Charles Michael[7] Betenbaugh, b. 29 May 1953.
  1131 ii. Thomas Stanley[7] Betenbaugh, b. 11 Sept 1954.

597. Neal Harden[6] Betenbaugh (Beaty[5], Martha Ellen W.[4], Thomas[3], Sarah[2], Charles[1]) married Peggy Ida McGeachen, and they reside in San Francisco, California. Three children:

  1132 i. Carol Wendy[7] Betenbaugh, m. Jerry Allen Watson.
  1133 ii. Jill Ann[7] Betenbaugh, m. Philip James Conner.
  1134 iii. Sherry Lynn[7] Betenbaugh, m. Theodore Charles Czuprynski.

598. Hubert Stanley[6] Betenbaugh (Beaty[5], Martha Ellen W.[4], Thomas[3], Sarah[2], Charles[1]) married Bernadette Burnet, and they reside in Bakersfield, California. Five children:

  1135 i. Christina Marie[7] Betenbaugh.
  1136 ii. Paul Martin[7] Betenbaugh.
  1137 iii. Rita Ann[7] Betenbaugh.
  1138 iv. Susan[7] Betenbaugh.
  1139 v. Antoinette[7] Betenbaugh.

617. Leila Mae[6] Young (George Ernest[5], Thomas Jefferson[4], George McCrary[3], Mary[2], Charles[1]) was born 17 March 1920 in Union County, South Carolina, and married Wendell Phillip Bailey, who was born 14 February 1925. They reside [1984] in Asheville, North Carolina, and had five children:

  1140 i. Phillip Michael[7] Bailey, b. 13 Aug 1948.
  1141 ii. Stephen Thomas[7] Bailey, b. 24 Oct 1949, m. Nancy Williams.
  1142 iii. William Ernest[7] Bailey, b. 28 Jun 1951.
  1143 iv. Kenneth Wendell[7] Bailey, b. 19 Oct 1954.
  1144 v. Daniel Anthony[7] Bailey, b. 5 Feb 1958.

619. Jimmy^6 Gallman (Josie^5, James B.^{4}, George McCrary^3, Mary^2, Charles^1) married Madalane_____ . They had one child:

1145 i. Jimmy^7 Gallman.

620. George Heyward^6 Gallman (Josie^5, James B.^{4}, George McCrary^3, Mary^2, Charles^1) married Betty _____ . They had two children:

1146 i. George Heyward^7 Gallman, Jr.
1147 ii. Betty^7 Gallman.

626. Ellen Jo^6 Young (Leland Cunningham^5, James B.^{4}, George McCrary^3, Mary^2, Charles^1) married Waylon Cagle. They had four children:

1148 i. Karen Lynne^6 Cagle, m. George Arthur Wilson.
1149 ii. David^7 Cagle.
1150 iii. Vickie^7 Cagle.
1151 iv. Bonnie^7 Cagle.

627. Morris^6 (Bud) Young (Leland Cunningham^5, James B.^{4}, George McCrary^3, Mary^2, Charles^1) married Barbara Brown, and they had one child:

1152 i. Gerald David^7 Young, m. Emma Ruth Bright.

631. Annie Laurie^6 Young (James Heyward^5, James B.^{4}, George McCrary^3, Mary^2, Charles^1) married Fred Palmer, 22 August 1947. They had two children:

1153 i. Frederick H.^{7} Palmer, b. 25 Oct 1949, d. 31 Aug 1953.
1154 ii. James Elwood^7 Palmer, m. Amanda Renwick.

634. Margaret^6 Caldwell (Sallie^5, Katherine^4, George McCrary^3, Mary^2, Charles^1) married James R. Roundtree. They had three children:

1155 i. Judy^7 Roundtree.
1156 ii. James R.^{7} Roundtree, Jr.
1157 iii. John^7 Roundtree.

639. Jean^6 Sanders (Julia A.^{5}, Katherine^4, George McCrary^3, Mary^2, Charles^1) married Everette H. Hughes. They had one child:

1158 i. Douglas H.[7] Hughes.

640. Catherine[6] Sanders (Julia A.[5], Katherine[4], George McCrary[3], Mary[2], Charles[1]) married Fred O. Lawson, Sr. They had one child:

+ 1159 Fred O.[7] Lawson, Jr.

647. Arthur Russell[6] Collins, Jr. (Dr.) (Mable[5], Katherine[4], George McCrary[3], Mary[2], Charles[1]) married 13 June 1959, Loye Camille Jones. They live at Myrtle Beach, South Carolina, and had one child:

1160 i. Gary Russell[7] Collins, b. 24 May 1960.

649. Walter Bishop[6] Alverson (William Giles[5], Katherine[4], George McCrary[3], Mary[2], Charles[1]) married Elsie Lee Gregory. They had one child:

1161 i. Walter Bishop[7] Alverson, Jr.

651. Claudia Sue[6] Greer (Mattie[5], Rachel Ann[4], George McCrary[3], Mary[2], Charles[1]) was born 18 September 1904 and died 29 October 1981. On 3 July 1921, she married James Douglas Vanderford, who was born 28 February 1896 and died 16 March 1973. They had five children:

1162 i. James Douglas[7] Vanderford, Jr., b. 23 Jun 1922, d. 28 Jun 1976, m. Varnell _____.
1163 ii. Lydia Louise[7] Vanderford, b. 13 May 1923, d. 29 Sept 1957, m. Charlie Thompson.
1164 iii. Myrtic Allen[7] Vanderford, b. 19 Jan 1925, m. 23 Apr 1947, John E. Harrison, at Ridgeland, SC.
1165 iv. Wesley Balwin[7] Vanderford, b. 24 Mar 1926, Palm Beach, FL., m. Doris _____, in Mexico.
1166 v. Dan Marion[7] Vanderford, b. 11 Nov 1950, Savannah, GA., m. 22 Feb 1969, Diana Sharon Bernardes, Tampa, FL.

652. Charner Jason[6] (Buddy) Greer (Mattie[5], Rachel Ann[4], George McCrary[3], Mary[2], Charles[1]) was born 1 May 1907 and died 29 December 1983 in Stanley, North Carolina. He married Della Carver and had three children:

1167 i. Terry[7] Greer.
1168 ii. Johnnie Faye[7] Greer.
1169 iii. Jo Ann[7] Greer.

1186 i. John Mobly[7] Lowe.
1187 ii. Cynthia Dianne[7] Lowe, b. 26 Dec 1946, m. ___ Thompson.

657. Lydia Loretta[6] Greer (Mattie[5], Rachel Ann[4], George McCrary[3], Mary[2], Charles[1]) was born 14 December 1922 and married, first, _____ Johnson; second, Wesley Wilder. She had seven children:

    1188 i. Lydia Louise[7] Johnson.
    1189 ii. Dorothy[7] Johnson.
    1190 iii. Truman[7] Johnson.
    1191 iv. Linda[7] Johnson.
    1192 v. Wesley[7] Wilder.
    1193 vi. Johnnie[7] Wilder.
    1194 vii. Sandra[7] Wilder.

658. Mattie Hazel[6] Greer (Mattie[5], Rachel Ann[4], George McCrary[3], Mary[2], Charles[1]) was born 7 December 1926, and was married on 2 March 1946 to General Lee Brewington. They had six children:

    1195 i. Louise B. Tesner[7] Brewington, b. 14 Dec 1946.
+ 1196 ii. Michael Lee[7] Brewington, b. 16 Feb 1948.
    1197 iii. Butler DePass[7] Brewington, b. 2 Jan 1949.
+ 1198 iv. Sadie Marie[7] Brewington, b. 24 Aug 1959.
    1199 v. Penny Patricia[7] Brewington, b. 29 Mar 1962.
    1200 vi. Troy Dean[7] Brewington, m. 15 Jun 1983, Cynthia
        Denise Smith.

661. Cornelia[6] May (Pearl[5], Rachel Ann[4], George McCrary[3], Mary[2], Charles[1]) was born 18 March 1909 in Union County, South Carolina, and died there 20 March 1974. She married in New York City, Robert F. Stevens. They had one child:

1201 i. Ronald[7] Stevens, b. 1950.

662. Pearl Frances[6] May (Pearl[5], Rachel Ann[4], George McCrary[3], Mary[2], Charles[1]) was born 25 October 1911 and died 3 January 1978. She married on 29 September 1929, John T. Sanders, who was born 23 April 1900 and died 31 August 1957. They had five children:

+ 1202   i. Rachel Ann[7] Sanders, b. 23 Feb 1930.
  1203   ii. Heyward Berton[7] Sanders, b. 13 Jan 1933, m. 28 Dec
             1958, Mary Ann Hamm, b. 16 Oct 1934, no issue.
+ 1204 iii. John Wallace[7] Sanders, b. 10 Feb 1937.
+ 1205   iv. Cornelia Pearl[7] Sanders, b. 9 Aug 1939.
  1206   v. Ned Arthur[7] Sanders, b. 8 Jul 1942, d. 17 Jun 1961.

663. Gary Hope[6] Holcomb (Rufus[5], Rachel Ann[4], George McCrary[3], Mary[2], Charles[1]) was born 30 November 1916 in Union, South Carolina, married 8 August 1942 in Laurens, South Carolina, to Hazel Elizabeth Howard, who was born 24 February 1920, near Campobello, South Carolina, daughter of Horace Milton and Mollie (Jackson) Howard. Gary Holcomb was co-owner of Sunshine Cleaners, Clinton, South Carolina, from 1946 until 1983. They had two children:

  1207   i. Brent Howard[7] Holcomb, b. 4 May 1950, Clinton, SC,
             B. Music, Furman Univ., 1972; M. A., UNC Chapel Hill, 1975;
             genealogist, organist-choirmaster at Our Saviour Lutheran
             Church, West Columbia, since 1975; resides Columbia, SC (the author).
+ 1208   ii. Barry Milton[7] Holcomb, b. 19 Sept 1954.

665. Rufus T.[6] Holcomb, Jr. (Rufus[5], Rachel Ann[4], George McCrary[3], Mary[2], Charles[1]) was born 31 January 1924 in Union, South Carolina, married 13 October 1945 to Frances Simpson, of Charlotte, North Carolina, who was born 16 January 1927. They still [1984] reside in Charlotte and had two children:

+ 1209   i. Russell Dwight[7] Holcomb, b. 22 Jan 1947.
  1230   ii. Mark Arnold[7] Holcomb, b. 3 Jul 1957, d. 16 Sept 1979.

666. Jessie Marie[6] Holcomb (Rufus[5], Rachel Ann[4], George McCrary[3], Mary[2], Charles[1]) was born 10 July 1932 in High Point, North Carolina. She married, first, on 14 October 1955, Cole Blease Crook, who was born in 1912 and died in 1958; married, second, on 14 June 1962, Donald McCombs, who died in 1962. Both Cole Blease Crook and Donald McCombs are buried at Yarborough Chapel Methodist Church, near Cross Anchor, South Carolina. Jessie Marie[6] married, third, on 11 May 1965, Wayne E. Wolfe, and they have one child:

  1231 i. Lori Ann[7] Wolfe, b. 18 Feb 1966, Greenville, SC.

Gary H. Holcomb, Hazel (Howard) Holcomb, Brent Holcomb,
and Barry Holcomb

1969

668. Sidney Earl[6] (June Bugg) Holcombe (Kennis[5], Rachel Ann[4], George McCrary[3], Mary[2], Charles[1]) was born 25 April 1918 and died 3 October 1980, married Margaret Gregory. Children:

    1232 i. June Carolyn[7] Holcombe, m. ___ Abee.
    1233 ii. Patricia Dianne[7] Holcombe, m. Robert[6] Betenbaugh, #958.
    1234 iii. Kenneth[7] Holcombe.
+ 1235 iv. Michael Dennis[7] Holcombe.

669. Sara Frances[6] Holcombe (Kennis[5], Rachel Ann[4], George McCrary[3], Mary[2], Charles[1]) was born 11 April 1920, married 1 January 1939, Martin Luther Epps, born 5 April 1910. They had one child:

+ 1236 John Lawrence[7] Epps, b. 3 Jun 1943.

670. Annie[6] Holcombe (Kennis[5], Rachel Ann[4], George McCrary[3], Mary[2], Charles[1]) married John D. Long, Sr., and had one child:

    1237 Mac Beth[7] Long.

671. Virginia[6] (Jenny) Holcombe (Kennis[5], Rachel Ann[4], George McCrary[3], Mary[2], Charles[1]) married Elliott Smith, and had two children:

    1238 i. Eddie[7] Smith.
    1239 ii. Susan[7] Smith.

672. Jesse Rufus[6] Hawkins (Casey[5], Rachel Ann[4], George McCrary[3], Mary[2], Charles[1]) married Marie Brown, and had two children:

    1240 i. Gail[7] Hawkins, d. in infancy.
    1241 ii. Jesse Rufus[7] Hawkins, Jr., m. Cheryl _____.

673. Casey Conrad[6] Hawkins (Casey[5], Rachel Ann[4], George McCrary[3], Mary[2], Charles[1]) married, first, Daisy _____, and had one child; married, second, Alice McCloud, and had three children:

    1242 i. Mary Ruth[7] Hawkins, m. Robert Jacobs.
    1243 ii. James[7] Hawkins, m. Phyllis Lankford.
    1244 iii. Casey Conrad[7] Hawkins, Jr.
    1245 iv. Deborah May[7] Hawkins, m. John Wayne Risher.

674. Wanda June[6] Hawkins (Casey[5], Rachel Ann[4], George McCrary[3], Mary[2], Charles[1]) married, first, Fred Bowman Breeden, second Boyd Haney. Children:

1246 i. Sharon Dianne[7] Breeden (adopted), m. Willie Steve Vittatoe.
1247 ii. Brenda Joyce[7] Breeden.

675. Billie Sue[6] Hawkins (Casey[5], Rachel Ann[4], George McCrary[3], Mary[2], Charles[1]) married Thurman Brown, and had two children:

1248 i. Sandra Sue[7] Brown, m. Lewis Allan Whisnant.
1249 ii. Glenda June[7] Brown.

676. Sarah Lou[6] Hawkins (Casey[5], Rachel Ann[4], George McCrary[3], Mary[2], Charles[1]) was born 12 December 1931, married Burton Eugene Harvey on 7 April 1950. They had six children:

+ 1250 i. Donna June[7] Harvey, b. 18 Jun 1951.
+ 1251 ii. Kathy Jean[7] Harvey, b. 7 May 1953.
+ 1252 iii. Lou Ann[7] Harvey, b. 1 Feb 1955.
+ 1253 iv. Karen Virginia[7] Harvey, b. 15 Dec 1957.
  1254 v. Burton Clyde[7] Harvey, b. 20 Jan 1961.
  1255 vi. Paula Marie[7] Harvey, b. 23 Apr 1963.

677. Paul David[6] Hawkins (Casey[5], Rachel Ann[4], George McCrary[3], Mary[2], Charles[1]) married Jimmy Sue Stafford, and had two children:

1256 i. James Paul[7] (Rusty) Hawkins.
1257 ii. Paula Suzette[7] Hawkins.

678. Don Gary[6] Hawkins (Casey[5], Rachel Ann[4], George McCrary[3], Mary[2], Charles[1]) married Novella Ann Smallen, and had one child:

1258 Robin Elaine Hawkins.

680. Helen[6] Holcombe (Thomas[5], Rachel Ann[4], George McCrary[3], Mary[2], Charles[1]) was born 29 January 1922 in Union, South Carolina, married Edward Austin. She married, second, on 10 September 1984, Lewis LeMaster. Children:

+ 1259 i. Elizabeth[7] Austin, b. 30 Jan 1938.
+ 1260 ii. Patricia Ann[7] Austin, b. 3 Jan 1942.
  1261 iii. Samuel Edward[7] (Ted) Austin, b. 27 Aug 1949, m.

Mary Jo Maggin.

682. Willie Edward[6] Greer, Jr. (May Inez[5], Rachel Ann[4], George McCrary[3], Mary[2], Charles[1]) was born 6 March 1939 in Union, South Carolina, married 11 August 1963, Nina Sinclair. Children:

    1262 i. Edward Albert[7] (Al) Greer, b. 9 Apr 1968.
    1263 ii. Suzanne Minita[7] Greer, b. 28 Dec 1971.

683. Catherine[6] Holcombe (Sidney[5], Rachel Ann[4], George McCrary[3], Mary[2], Charles[1]) married Charles Greer. Children:

    1264   i. Martha Ann[7] Greer, m. _____ Rogers.
    1265 ii. Larry[7] Greer.
    1266 iii. Mike[7] Greer.

687. Martha Juanita[6] (Shirley) Holcombe (Sidney[5], Rachel Ann[4], George McCrary[3], Mary[2], Charles[1]) married Billy Palmer. Children:

    1267   i. Sidney Harold[7] Palmer, m. Jerry Ann Holt.
+ 1268 ii. Billie Allen[7] Palmer.
+ 1269 iii. Jerry Wayne[7] Palmer.
    1270 iv. Daren Eugen[7] Palmer, d. in infancy.

688. Curtis[6] Holcombe (Sidney[5], Rachel Ann[4], George McCrary[3], Mary[2], Charles[1]) married Nadine Mease. Children:

    1271 i. Kenneth Hayward[7] Holcombe.
    1272 ii. Tony Stewart[7] Holcombe.

690. Ione[6] Sinclair (Kathleen[5], Conquest[4], George McCrary[3], Mary[2], Charles[1]) married Grady Nichols, and had two children:

    1273 i. Eugene[7] Nichols.
    1274 ii. Michael[7] Nichols.

695. J. C.[6] Jolly (Grace[5], Conquest[4], George McCrary[3], Mary[2], Charles[1]) married Louise Gwinn, and had one child:

+ 1275 Stanley[7] Jolly.

698. Reubin^6 Jolly (Mattie Irene^5, Jackson^4, George McCrary^3, Mary^2, Charles^1) married Lucille McGowan.   Children:

   1276 i. Grace^7 Jolly.
   1277 ii. Joyce$_7$ Jolly.
   1278 iii. R. H.^{7} Jolly.
   1279 iv. John$_7$ Jolly.
   1280 v. Jane$_7$ Jolly.
   1281 vi. Nancy^7 Jolly.

699. Ben^6 Jolly (Mattie Irene^5, Jackson^4, George McCrary^3, Mary^2, Charles^1) married Faye Wilkins.   Children:

   1282 i. Frances^7 Jolly.
+ 1283 ii. Ben^7 Jolly.

700. Lois^6 Jolly (Mattie Irene^5, Jackson^4, George McCrary^3, Mary^2, Charles^1) married Robert (Bob) Wilson.   Children:

   1284 i. Bobby W.$_7^7$ Wilson.
   1285 ii. Janie Sue^7 Wilson.
   1286 iii. Helen^7 Wilson.

704. Ralph^6 Jolly (Mattie Irene^5, Jackson^4, George McCrary^3, Mary^2, Charles^1) married Katherine Vaughan.   Children:

   1287 i. Steven$_7^7$ Jolly.
+ 1288 ii. Debbie$_7$ Jolly.
   1289 iii. Robin^7 Jolly, m. ___ Metevier.

705. Roy^6 Jolly (Mattie Irene^5, Jackson^4, George McCrary^3, Mary^2, Charles^1) married Alice Ingle.   Children:

   1290 i. Roy$^7_7$ Jolly, Jr.
   1291 ii. Terry^7 Jolly.
   1292 iii. Patty Sue^7 Jolly.
   1293 iv. Jo Ann^7 Jolly.

706. Margaret^6 Jolly (Mattie Irene^5, Jackson^4, George McCrary^3, Mary^2, Charles^1) married Kenneth Gregory.   Children:

1294 i. Wayne^7 Gregory.
1295 ii. David^7 Gregory.

707. Mary Nell^6 Jolly (Mattie Irene^5, Jackson^4, George McCrary^3, Mary^2, Charles^1) married Ernest Crawford, Jr. Children:

1296 i. Gwendolyn Nell^7 Crawford.
1297 ii. Ernest Milton^7 Crawford.

709. Charlie B.^{6} Jolly (Mattie Irene^5, Jackson^4, George McCrary^3, Mary^2, Charles^1) married Doris Waldrop. One child:

1298 Wayne^7 Jolly.

713. Hazel^6 Young (Thomas E.^{5}, Jackson^4, George McCrary^3, Mary^2, Charles^1) married Detroit Berry. Children:

1299 i. Carolyn^7 Berry.
1300 ii. Kenneth^7 Berry.
1301 iii. Davie^7 Berry.

716. Peggy^6 Young (Ernest Arthur^5, Jackson^4, George McCrary^3, Mary^2, Charles^1) married James Quinn. Children:

+ 1302 i. Peggy Lynn^7 Quinn.
1303 ii. James^7 Quinn, Jr., m. Becky _____.

717. Reeda^6 Young (Ernest Arthur^5, Jackson^4, George McCrary^3, Mary^2, Charles^1) married Earl Jones Smith. One child:

1304 i. Earl Jones^7 Smith, Jr.

718. Ernest Arthur^6 (Sonny) Young (Ernest Arthur^5, Jackson^4, George McCrary^3, Mary^2, Charles^1) married June Barker. One child:

+ 1305 i. Connie^7 Young.

719. James^6 Bailey (Ethel^5, Robert^4, George McCrary^3, Mary^2, Charles^1) married, first, Frances Harris; married, second, Resse _____. Children:

133

+ 1306 i. Carol^7 Bailey
+ 1307 ii. Karen^7 Bailey.
 1308 iii. Deborah Dianne^7 Bailey, m. Ronald Lynn Harris.
 1309 iv. Robert^7 Bailey.
 1310 v. Jimmy^7 Bailey (only child by Resse).

720. Fred Richard^6 Bailey (Ethel^5, Robert^4, George McCrary^3, Mary^2, Charles^1) married, first, Alma Harris; married, second, Ermease _____. Children by Alma Harris:

+ 1311 i. Margaret^7 Bailey.
+ 1312 ii. Marvin^7 Bailey.
+ 1313 iii. Sue^7 Bailey.

721. Dolly^6 Bailey (Ethel^5, Robert^4, George McCrary^3, Mary^2, Charles^1) married Smith Leitner. One child:

 1314 i. Elaine^7 Leitner, m. Jimmy Lee Eubanks.

722. Louise^6 Bailey (Ethel^5, Robert^4, George McCrary^3, Mary^2, Charles^1) married Wallace Trakas. One child:

+ 1315 i. Terry^7 Trakas.

723. Mabel Alice^6 Bailey (Ethel^5, Robert^4, George McCrary^3, Mary^2, Charles^1) married Floyd Longshore. One child:

 1316 i. Dennis^7 Longshore.

724. Frances^6 Bailey (Ethel^5, Robert^4, George McCrary^3, Mary^2, Charles^1) married Calvin Nelson. Children:

+ 1317 i. James^7 Nelson.
 1318 ii. Beth^7 Nelson.
 1319 iii. Virgine^7 Nelson.
 1320 iv. George^7 Nelson.

725. Ann^6 Bailey (Ethel^5, Robert^4, George McCrary^3, Mary^2, Charles^1) married J. B. Sanders. Children:

1321 i. Merrie Robin[7] Sanders, m. Bobbie Bailey.
+ 1322 ii. Pennie[7] Sanders.

727. Betty[6] Keisler (Pauline[5], Robert[4], George McCrary[3], Mary[2], Charles[1]) was born 15 May 1925, married 29 August 1969, to Sims Johns. One child:

1323 i. Teresa Lynne[7] Johns, b. 5 Aug 1960.

732. Roger Dale[6] Bailey (Helen[5], Robert[4], George McCrary[3], Mary[2], Charles[1]) was born 4 May 1947 in Union, South Carolina, married 3 April 1976, at Gaffney, South Carolina, Judy Lemaster, who was born 22 April 1951. Children:

1324 i. Catherine Dale[7] Bailey, b. 19 Jun 1976, Spartanburg, SC.
1325 ii. Nancy Brooke[7] Bailey, b. 8 Jun 1982, Spartanburg, SC.

733. Frances[6] (Polly) Kelly (Adella Frances[5], Christopher C.[4], Sarah[3], Mary[2], Charles[1]) was born 6 December 1891 in Union, South Carolina, and died 22 May 1975 in Charleston, South Carolina. She married 4 November 1915 in Spartanburg, South Carolina, Edwin Jesse Thornhill. Children:

1326 i. Edwin Jesse[7] Thornhill, Jr.
1327 ii. Frances[7] Thornhill.

734. John Granberry[6] Kelly (Adella Frances[5], Christopher C.[4], Sarah[3], Mary[2], Charles[1]) was born 7 March 1893 in Cowpens, South Carolina, and died 27 April 1975 in Orangeburg, South Carolina; he is buried in Rock Hill, South Carolina. He married 8 April 1916, at Holly Hill, South Carolina, Cherry Lou Harvey. Children:

1328 i. Cherry Dell[7] Kelly.
1329 ii. Elizabeth[7] Kelly.
1330 iii. John Granberry[7] Kelly, Jr.
1331 iv. Julie Hart[7] Kelly.

735. William Houston[6] Kelly (Adella Frances[5], Christopher C.[4], Sarah[3], Mary[2], Charles[1]) married, first, Marion Dantzler; married, second, Mary Wolfe. Children:

1332 i. Billie[7] Kelly.
1333 ii. Houston[7] Kelly.
1334 iii. William[7] Kelly (only child by Mary Wolfe).

736. Samuel Sartor[6] Kelly (Adella Frances[5], Christopher C.[4], Sarah[3], Mary[2], Charles[1]) married Winifred Sherrill, at Statesville, North Carolina. Children:

1335 i. Winifred[7] Kelly.
1336 ii. Melvin Bookman[7] Kelly.

737. Thomas Edwin[6] Kelly (Adella Frances[5], Christopher C.[4], Sarah[3], Mary[2], Charles[1]) was born 24 August 1900 in Greenville, South Carolina, and died 5 March 1962 in Beaufort, North Carolina. He is buried in Morehead, North Carolina. He married in November 1926 in Beaufort, North Carolina, Clyde Neal. Children:

1337 i. Thomas Edwin[7] Kelly, Jr.
1338 ii. Frances[7] Kelly.
1339 iii. Julia[7] Kelly.

738. Claude Christopher[6] Sartor, Jr. (Claude Christopher[5], Christopher C.[4], Sarah[3], Mary[2], Charles[1]) was born 19 October 1902 in Union County, South Carolina, and died 27 December 1972 in Spartanburg, South Carolina. He married Allie Whitton. One child:

1340 i. Claude Christopher[7] Sartor, III (Dr.).

739. Milton Humphries[6] Sartor (Claude Christopher[5], Christopher C.[4], Sarah[3], Mary[2], Charles[1]) was born 20 June 1908 in Union, South Carolina, and died there 15 January 1963. He married Virginia Huntsinger (1906-1975). One child:

1341 i. Kathleen[7] Sartor.

741. Mary Cornelia[6] (Mamie) Sartor (Claude Christopher[5], Christopher C.[4], Sarah[3], Mary[2], Charles[1]) was born 21 July 1914 in Union, South Carolina, married 24 June 1939 to John Daniel Avant. They reside [1984] in Columbus, Ohio. Children:

1342 i. John D.[7] Avant.
1343 ii. Mary Sartor[7] Avant.

742. James Louis[6] Gilliam (Sarah Frances[5], James Christopher[4], Sarah[3], Mary[2], Charles[1]) married Imogene Salley, of Salley, South Carolina. Children:

+ 1344 i. James Louis[7] Gilliam, Jr.
+ 1345 ii. Eleanor Frances[7] Gilliam.
+ 1346 iii. Eugene Fant[7] Gilliam.

744. Lillian Zena[6] Gilliam (Sarah Frances[5], James Christopher[4], Sarah[3], Mary[2], Charles[1]) married Dewey Lee Oakman, of Spartanburg, South Carolina. One child:

+ 1347 i. June Gilliam[7] Oakley.

745. David Fant[6] Gilliam, Jr. (Sarah Frances[5], James Christopher[4], Sarah[3], Mary[2], Charles[1]) married Dorothy Query, of Wellford, South Carolina. One child:

+ 1348 Lucy Fant[7] Gilliam.

746. Rachel Sartor[6] Gilliam (Sarah Frances[5], James Christopher[4], Sarah[3], Mary[2], Charles[1]) was born 26 June 1910, married 18 June 1938, Robert Cyrus Williams, who was born 16 December 1905. One child:

+ 1349 Robert Cyrus[7] Williams, Jr., b. 26 Sept 1945.

747. Ruth Cornelia[6] Gilliam (Sarah Frances[5], James Christopher[4], Sarah[3], Mary[2], Charles[1]) was born 6 May 1913, Union, South Carolina, married 13 August 1936, William Poole Lancaster, of Spartanburg, South Carolina, born 3 July 1915, died 13 January 1970. Children:

+ 1350 i. Jane Fant[7] Lancaster, b. 17 Jul 1941.
+ 1351 ii. William Poole[7] Lancaster, Jr., b. 12 Oct 1943.

753. Edward Marcus[6] White (Carrie Sartor[5], Caroline[4], Sarah[3], Mary[2], Charles[1]) was born 2 April 1941, married Linda Williams. Children:

137

1352 i. Vickie[7] White, b. 14 Nov 1962, Ozark, AL.
1353 ii. Robert Edward[7] White, b. 2 Apr 1970, Rock Hill, SC.
1354 iii. Candice Lyn[7] White, b. 11 Nov 1974, Rock Hill, SC.

755. Edith[6] Flynn (Edith[5], Emma[4], Sarah[3], Mary[2], Charles[1]) married James Gilmore Butler. One child:

+ 1355 James Gilmore[7] Butler, Jr.

756. Frances[6] Flynn (Edith[5], Emma[4], Sarah[3], Mary[2], Charles[1]) married Paul S. Mims. Children:

1356 i. Larkin[7] Mims.
1357 ii. Linda[7] Mims.
1358 iii. Paul S.[7] Mims.

757. Philip Dunn[6] Flynn, Jr. (Edith[5], Emma[4], Sarah[3], Mary[2], Charles[1]) married _____. Children:

+ 1359 i. Philip Dunn[7] Flynn, III.
1360 ii. Nancy[7] Flynn, m. ____ Hope.

758. Edward Dunn[6] Flynn (Edith[5], Emma[4], Sarah[3], Mary[2], Charles[1]) married _____. Children:

1361 i. Edward Dunn[7] Flynn, Jr.
1362 ii. Paul Watson[7] Flynn.
1363 iii. Ann[7] Flynn.

759. John Sartor[6] Flynn (Edith[5], Emma[4], Sarah[3], Mary[2], Charles[1]) married _____. Children:

1364 i. Nora Alston[7] Flynn.
1365 ii. Anne Macon[7] Flynn.

764. Grover Cleveland[6] Gregory (Sarah Ellen[5], Adelade[4], John Thomas[3], William[2], Charles[1]) was born 13 November 1884, died 9 July 1960. He married in January 1914, Lollie Brooklyn Jolly, who was born 23 July 1893 and died 19 November 1977. Both are buried at Hebron Baptist Church in Union County, South Carolina. Children:

+ 1366 i. Anita[7] Gregory, b. 16 Dec 1914.
  1367 ii. Annie Grey[7] Gregory, b. 3 Mar 1917, d. 16 Jun 1979.
  1368 iii. Douglass Leroy[7] Gregory, b. 6 Aug 1919, d. 10 Apr 1921.
+ 1369 iv. Claude Cleveland[7] Gregory, b. 6 Dec 1921.
  1370 v. Mary Jo[7] Gregory, b. 5 Dec 1926.
+ 1371 vi. John Wilson[7] Gregory, b. 29 Nov 1934.

766. Eugene[6] Gregory (Sarah Ellen[5], Adelade[4], John Thomas[3], William[2], Charles[1]) was born 2 May 1889, Union County, South Carolina, died in April 1976 in High Point, North Carolina. He married 28 June 1908, Donna Ellen Turner, who was born 16 May 1887. Children:

+ 1372 i. Charlotte Elizabeth[7] Gregory, b. 17 May 1911.
+ 1373 ii. Rachel[7] Gregory, b. 21 May 1916.
+ 1374 iii. Joseph Loyd[7] Gregory, b. 4 Sept 1918.
+ 1375 iv. Leland Cozine[7] Gregory, b. 28 Mar 1920.
  1376 v. Cornelius Earl[7] Gregory, b. 2 Jan 1921, m. Frances Grogan.
  1377 vi. Carolyn[7] Gregory, b. 21 Jan 1922, m. James Driver.

779. Paul[6] Jolly (Caroline Lorena[5], Adelade[4], John Thomas[3], William[2], Charles[1]) was born in 1904, and married on 25 December 1925, Sallie Greer, who was born 7 September 1908 and died in 1962, daughter of Charner Lester Greer and his wife Mattie Vaughan. Child:

1378 i. Paul Edgar[7] Jolly.

786. Robert Christopher[6] Greer (Louisa[5], Adelade[4], John Thomas[3], William[2], Charles[1]) was born 6 March 1891 in Jonesville, South Carolina, and died 31 December 1971 in Dayton, Ohio. He is buried in the Morrow Cemetery in Warren County, Ohio. He married Eva Grace Bobo, who was born 29 June 1888 and died 8 January 1948 in Augusta, Georgia, and is buried Hebron Baptist Church, Union County, South Carolina. Children:

1379 i. Robert[7] Greer, b. 1917, d. 1954, bur. Hebron
        Baptist Church.
1380 ii. Augustus[7] Greer, b. 1921, d. 21 Jul 1960.
1381 iii. William[7] Greer, b. 22 Dec ____, m. Margie Gunter.
1382 iv. Betty Sue[7] Greer.
1383 v. Mary Payne[7] Greer, m. 1st Leroy Baker, 2nd Fred B.
        Innis, 3rd Ed Grietner.
1384 vi. Kenneth[7] Greer.

1385 vii. Melvin[7] Greer.
1386 viii. Paul Hobson[7] Greer, b. 7 Feb 1932 (twin), m. Opal
     (Adams) Sproles.
+ 1387 ix. Richard Thomas[7] Greer, b. 7 Feb 1932 (twin).

787. Clarence Eugene[6] Greer (Louisa[5], Adelade[4], John Thomas[3], William[2], Charles[1]) was born in 1893 and married Minnie Toney. Children:

1388 i. Helen[7] Greer, m. William Hall.
1389 ii. Robert[7] Greer, m. Betty ____.
1390 iii. Imogene[7] Greer, m. ____ Morris.
1391 iv. Benny[7] Greer, m. Dana Morris.

802. Adelaide[6] Willard (Jackson Lee[5], Adelade[4], John Thomas[3], William[2], Charles[1]) was born in 1902, married James Roy Workman, and lives in Clinton, South Carolina. This excellent lady has been known to the author all of his life. She was always known to be a good neighbor, and the author had many discussions with her about relatives, family, from his early years. One child:

1392 i. James Roy[7] Workman, Jr.

804. John[6] Willard (Jackson Lee[5], Adelade[4], John Thomas[3], William[2], Charles[1]) was born in 1906, died in 1965 and married Lucille Gentry. One child:

+ 1393 Hazel[7] Willard.

806. Sarah Lee[6] Willard (Jackson Lee[5], Adelade[4], John Thomas[3], William[2], Charles[1]) was born in 1920, married David Glenn, and lives in Clinton, South Carolina. Children:

+ 1394 i. Sarah Willard[7] Glenn, b. 1941.
+ 1395 ii. William David[7] Glenn, b. 1944.

807. Lillian[6] Whisenant (Mary Lou[5], Mary Ann[4], John Thomas[3], William[2], Charles[1]) married John Cathcart. One child:

1396 i. Miriam[7] Cathcart.

811. Ed[6] Whisenant (Belle[5], Sarah[4], John Thomas[3], William[2], Charles[1]) married Augusta (Gussie) Dillon. Children:

+ 1397 i. Ed[7] Whisenant, Jr.
 1398 ii. Louise[7] Whisenant (twin) d. in childhood.
+ 1399 iii. Isabelle[7] Whisenant (twin).

815. Sallie[6] Edwards (Bernice[5], Sarah[4], John Thomas[3], William[2], Charles[1]) was born 18 November 1893 in Union County, South Carolina, and died 31 August 1972 in Union County. She married, on 20 March 1910, James Greer, son of George Washington (Bush) Greer and his wife Martha Dean McDaniel. He was born 12 September 1889 and died 16 September 1952. They had eleven children (all born Union County):

+ 1400   i. Lena Lucille[7] Greer, b. 25 Dec 1910.
 1401 ii. Willie Edward[7] Greer, b. 19 Feb 1912, m. May Inez[5]
        Holcombe Vaughan (see #294 for descendants).
 1402 iii. James[7] Greer, Jr., b. 28 Aug 1913, d. Sept. 1913.
 1403 iv. James Russell[7] Greer, b. 5 Aug 1914, d. 14 Apr 1941,
        m. 5 Mar 1937, Julia Ivey.
 1404   v. Paul Sarratt[7] Greer, b. 23 Oct 1916, m. 15 Oct 1946,
        Marguerite Crawford.
+ 1405 vi. Nina Louise[7] Greer, b. 16 Oct 1918.
 1406 vii. Charles Manley[7] Greer, b. 22 May 1920, m. 21 Nov 1945,
        Julia Ivey Greer.
 1407 viii. Margaret Mae[7] Greer, b. 13 Apr 1922, m. 22 Jan 1944,
        Charles Moore, Jr.
 1408 ix. Clarence Earl[7] Greer, b. 5 May 1924, m. 26 May 1945,
        m. Athaleen Ivey.
 1409   x. John Lewis[7] Greer, b. 1 May 1927, m. 16 Feb 1950,
        Betty Jo Bailey, who was Probate Judge of Union County
        from 28 February 1964 until 26 June 1981.
 1410 xi. Hubert Dean[7] Greer, b. 19 Jul 1934, m. 15 Feb 1958,
        Linda Harmon.

823. Lewis Crawford[6] Edwards (Bernice[5], Sarah[4], John Thomas[3], William[2], Charles[1]) was born 16 November 1906 in Union County, South Carolina, and died 30 December 1977 in Rock Hill, South Carolina. He married, on 15 September 1931 at Rock Hill, Mary Gill Steele, who was born 2 August 1908. One child:

+ 1411 James Lewis[7] Edwards, b. 24 December 1941.

833. Robert Monroe[6] McDaniel (Robert Lee[5], Medora[4], John Thomas[3], William[2], Charles[1]) married Ruth Shillinglaw. Children:

+ 1412 i. Margaret Ann[7] McDaniel.
+ 1413 ii. Janet Elizabeth[7] McDaniel.
+ 1414 iii. Rebecca Maclyn[7] McDaniel.

840. Ida Florence[6] Vaughan (Lucy Smith[5], Medora[4], John Thomas[3], William[2], Charles[1]) was born 24 December 1897 and died 30 December 1973; she married on 19 January 1919, William M. Bradburn, who was born 25 December 1896 and died 11 May 1962. Both are buried at Rosemont Cemetery in Union, South Carolina. Children:

+ 1415 i. Rubye Eileen[7] Bradburn, b. 3 Oct 1919.
  1416 ii. William Wallace[7] Bradburn, b. 14 Oct 1920, d. 2 Dec 1920.
+ 1417 iii. Hay Fant[7] Bradburn, b. 22 Oct 1921.
  1418 iv. Rex Switzer[7] Bradburn, b. 14 Feb 1928, d. 28 Mar 1929.

841. Annie Estelle[6] Vaughan (Lucy Smith[5], Medora[4], John Thomas[3], William[2], Charles[1]) was born 1 March 1899 in Union County, South Carolina and died 7 January 1979 in Wilmington, North Carolina; she married on 26 April 1914, Foster Cromer. Children:

  1419 i. Margaret[7] Cromer, m. Curt Treadway.
+ 1420 ii. Catherine[7] Cromer.
  1421 iii. Elizabeth[7] Cromer.

844. Lindsey[6] Vaughan (Lucy Smith[5], Medora[4], John Thomas[3], William[2], Charles[1]) was born 6 November 1903, died 29 July 1976, married Agnes Brown. Children were twins:

  1422 i. Lindsey[7] Vaughan, Jr., b. June 1939.
  1423 ii. Lillian[7] Vaughan, b. June 1939.

845. Katie Louise[6] Vaughan (Lucy Smith[5], Medora[4], John Thomas[3], William[2], Charles[1]) was born 7 April 1908, married, first, Hoyt Haydock; second, John T. Sanders; third, John Graham. Children:

  1424 i. Everett[7] Haydock.
  1425 ii. Florence[7] Haydock, m. Ed Murphy.
  1426 iii. James[7] Haydock.

848. Helen Ruth[6] Jolly (Mary Ann[5], Medora[4], John Thomas[3], William[2], Charles[1]) was born 11 May 1919 and died 10 April 1964; she married Clyde Hughes. Children:

+ 1427 i. Mary Ann[7] Hughes, b. 1942.
  1428 ii. John Lewis[7] Hughes, b. 1946.
  1429 iii. Harold Clyde[7] Hughes, b. 1956.

851. Jack Wylie[6] Humphries (Evelyn Frances[5], John Wylie[4], John Thomas[3], William[2], Charles[1]) was born 14 November 1911 and died 12 April 1943. He married on 22 July 1933, Estelle Bailey, who was born 29 June 1910. Children:

+ 1430 i. Wylie Bailey[7] Humphries, b. 8 Jul 1934.
  1431 ii. Jack Sterling[7] Humphries, b. 8 Sept 1936, m. 4 Feb
      1965, Elizabeth Payne Stevens, b. 17 Apr 1921.
+ 1432 iii. Sherrelle Clyde[7] Humphries, b. 31 May 1938.

852. Roy Humphries[6] Kirven (Olive[5], John Wylie[4], John Thomas[3], William[2], Charles[1]) was born 20 May 1904, and married on 9 February 1935, Edward (Ted) Riggs, who was born 16 April 1913. Children:

  1433 i. Roy Humphries[7] Kirven, Jr., b. 17 Nov 1935, d. 21 Nov 1952.
+ 1434 ii. William Edward[7] Kirven, b. 5 Sept 1942.
+ 1435 iii. Elizabeth Ann[7] Kirven, b. 8 Jul 1945.
  1436 iv. Robert Lee[7] Kirven, b. 5 Aug 1953.

853. Bertha E.[6] Kirven (Olive[5], John Wylie[4], John Thomas[3], William[2], Charles[1]) was born 8 December 1905, and died 22 May 1926, married 19 July 1925, Wade Lawrence Stokes. One child:

  1437 i. William Lawrence[7] Stokes, b. 22 May 1926.

855. Edith Mae[6] Kirven (Olive[5], John Wylie[4], John Thomas[3], William[2], Charles[1]) was born 26 October 1911 and married James William Pilkington. Children:

+ 1438 i. Edward Earl[7] Pilkington.
+ 1439 ii. George Montgomery[7] Pilkington.
+ 1440 iii. Betty Lou[7] Pilkington.

856. Frances Williamson[6] Humphries (Robert Ray[5], John Wylie[4], John Thomas[3], William[2], Charles[1]) was born 9 December 1919, married 6 June 1947, the Rev. Robert Hampton Price, who was born 3 December 1913, son of John Randolph Price and wife Elcana Virginia Smith. Two children:

+ 1441 i. Robert Randolph[7] Price, b. 25 Aug 1949.
  1442 ii Ray Hampton Price, b. 29 Oct 1952, m. 29 Aug 1981,
       Sarah Ann Rankin, b. 2 Apr 1954, dau. of John Robert Rankin
       and wife Doris Strobel, of AL.

858. Elizabeth[6] Taylor (Bessie[5], John Wylie[4], John Thomas[3], William[2], Charles[1]) was born 3 March 1910 and married on 25 July 1936, married Copeland Smarr. Children:

+ 1443 i. Albert Copeland[7] Smarr, b. 4 Sept 1940.
+ 1444 ii. Ronald Taylor Smarr, b. 7 Apr 1942.

859. Harry Ray[6] Taylor (Bessie[5], John Wylie[4], John Thomas[3], William[2], Charles[1]) was born 8 August 1912; he married on 23 September 1939, Frances Kelly. Children:

+ 1445 i. Kaye Kelly[7] Taylor, b. 19 Jul 1942.
+ 1446 ii. Sara Ann Taylor, b. 20 Apr 1947.

860. William Marion[6] Taylor (Bessie[5], John Wylie[4], John Thomas[3], William[2], Charles[1]) was born 23 August 1914, married 29 January 1947, Margaret Pearl Bennett, who was born 16 October 1924. Children:

  1447 i. James Albert[7] Taylor, b. 5 Nov 1949.
+ 1448 ii. Margaret Ann[7] Taylor, b. 1 Jan 1951.
  1449 iii. David Marion Taylor, b. 2 Aug 1956.
  1450 iv. Linda Jane Taylor, b. 23 May 1963.
  1451 v. Allen Joseph Taylor, b. 11 Apr 1966.

861. Frances Alberta[6] Taylor (Bessie[5], John Wylie[4], John Thomas[3], William[2], Charles[1]) was born 20 June 1916, married 23 July 1938, Henry Norris Garrett. Children:

+ 1452   i. Robert Henry$_7^7$ Garrett, b. 11 Jun 1939.
+ 1453 ii. Francis Taylor$_7$ Garrett, b. 13 Mar 1943.
+ 1454 iii. Janice Othella^7 Garrett, b. 4 Oct 1946.

862. Martha Victoria^6 Taylor (Bessie^5, John Wylie^4, John Thomas^3, William^2, Charles^1) was born 30 April 1918, married 12 February 1938, Benjamin Guthrie Stackhouse. Children:

1455   i. John Albert^7 Stackhouse, b. 2 Jan 1946, m. 13 Dec 1975,
       Ena West Hardy.
+ 1456 ii. Ben Jefferson^7 Stackhouse, b. 8 Jun 1952.

863. Mary Lenora^6 Taylor (Bessie^5, John Wylie^4, John Thomas^3, William^2, Charles^1) was born 30 April 1918, married 1 August 1936, Luther Zeno Wilson. Children:

+ 1457   i. Martha Beth$^7_7$ Wilson, b. 13 May 1939.
+ 1458 ii. Marion Lynda^7 Wilson, b. 13 Jul 1942.

864. Doris Ruth^6 Taylor (Bessie^5, John Wylie^4, John Thomas^3, William^2, Charles^1) was born 19 October 1931, married 20 September 1952, William Lee Henderson. Children:

+ 1459   i. Doris Susan^7 Henderson, b. 5 Aug 1953.
1460 ii. Lee Taylor^7 Henderson, b. 18 Feb 1958.

865. Mary Alice^6 Rice (Lona Mae^5, John Wylie^4, John Thomas^3, William^2, Charles^1) was born 28 July 1917 in Union County, South Carolina and died 1 August 1973 in Clinton, South Carolina. On 16 May 1944 she married Arthur Lee Benjamin, who was born 2 June 1915 and died 3 July 1978 in Clinton. Both are buried at Rosemont Cemetery in Clinton. One child:

1461   Arthur Lee^7 Benjamin, Jr., b. 13 Oct 1950, m. 10 Aug 1977,
       Sharon Gossett.

866. Helen^6 Rice (Lona Mae^5, John Wylie^4, John Thomas^3, William^2, Charles^1) was born 19 February 1919 and married on 8 October 1938, Herbert Allen Brown. Children:

145

1462 i. Rebecca Ann[7] Brown, b. 11 Oct 1939, m. 11 Jun 1959,
    John L. Finnigan.
1463 ii. Herbert Allen[7] Brown, b. 4 Mar 1943, m. 14 Aug 1963,
    Sara Jane Clark.
1464 iii. Terry Clough[7] Brown, b. 2 Feb 1945, m. 10 Aug 1968,
    Linda Sue Homes.
1465 iv. Brenda Sharon[7] Brown, b. 30 Oct 1948, m. 8 Jun 1966,
    Homer Dee Wright.

867. William[6] Rice (Lona Mae[5], John Wylie[4], John Thomas[3], William[2], Charles[1]) was born 8 August 1920 and was married on 15 May 1947 to Broddie Riddle. Children:

1466 i. Harriet Ann[7] Rice, b. 4 May 1949, m. 30 Aug 1968,
    William Johnson Goforth.
1467 ii. William Stanley[7] Rice, b. 4 Nov 1952, m. 5 Sept 1981,
    Nancy Morris.

868. Louise[6] Rice (Lona Mae[5], John Wylie[4], John Thomas[3], William[2], Charles[1]) was born 18 October 1922 and was married on 11 October 1941 to James Lewis Grady. Children:

1468 i. James[7] Grady, b. 26 Dec 1942, m. 22 Feb 1961,
    Helen Margaret Kysur.
1469 ii. Alice Frances[7] Grady, b. 21 Nov 1944, m. 31 May 1962,
    William Herold Beam.
1470 iii. Peggy Ann[7] Grady, b. 30 Mar 1948, m. 2 Apr 1967,
    Robert Asque Watson.
1471 iv. Katie Louise[7] Grady, b. 4 Aug 1950, m. 3 Aug 1970,
    Robert Timothy Allen.

869. Donald[6] Rice (Lona Mae[5], John Wylie[4], John Thomas[3], William[2], Charles[1]) was born 5 May 1924 and was married on 12 August 1952 to Dorothy Nell Hanna. Children:

1472 i. Donald Paul[7] Rice, b. 11 Aug 1955.
1473 ii. Debra Jean[7] Rice, b. 12 Feb 1958, m. 3 Jun 1980,
    Ronald Wayne Roberson.
1474 iii. Shirley Dianne[7] Rice, b. 11 Mar 1961.
1475 iv. David Kenneth[7] Rice, b. 20 Nov 1962.
1476 v. Darlene Annett[7] Rice, b. 8 Jun 1964.

870. Harriett Lucille[6] Rice (Lona Mae[5], John Wylie[4], John Thomas[3], William[2], Charles[1]) was born 11 January 1926 and married on 15 October 1949 to William Albert Byars. One child:

    1477 Amanda Othella[7] Byars, b. 8 Feb 1958, m. 13 Jun 1976, Edmund Wilson Prince.

871. Cornelia Othela[6] Rice (Lona Mae[5], John Wylie[4], John Thomas[3], William[2], Charles[1]) was born 19 May 1928, was married on 3 November 1951 to William Odus Young, and lives in Clinton, South Carolina. Children:

    1478 i. William Ronald[7] (Ronnie) Young, b. 20 Jun 1953, m. 14 Jul 1973, Katherine Elizabeth McLendon.
    1479 ii. Odus McDowell[7] (Mac) Young, b. 16 Jun 1955, m. 25 Jul 1981, Frances Ann Barnett.
    1480 iii. Pamela Marie[7] Young, b. 3 Apr 1960, m. 21 Aug 1982, Ernest Walker Crosby.

872. James McDowell[6] Rice (Lona Mae[5], John Wylie[4], John Thomas[3], William[2], Charles[1]) was born 18 October 1933 and was married on 7 December 1955 to Renata Nicklus. Children:

    1481 i. William Herold[7] Rice, b. 2 Jan 1955, m. 1 Oct 1981, Lori Lyn Sanders.
    1482 ii. Anita Jane[7] Rice, b. 2 Aug 1956.
    1483 iii. Mary Susan[7] Rice, b. 7 Aug 1958, m. 26 Aug 1979, Mark Scott Barns.
    1484 iv. Elsie Louise[7] Rice, b. 26 Nov 1960, m. 18 Jul 1980, Rick Malpass.
    1485 v. Connie Frances[7] Rice, b. 24 Aug 1962.

873. Charles Hilliard[6] Humphries, III (Charles Hilliard[5], Charles Hilliard[4], Absalom B.[3], William[2], Charles[1]) was born 29 May 1945 and married Sarah Sprouse. Children:

    1486 i. Charles Brian[7] Humphries, b. 27 Aug 1974.
    1487 ii. Robert Alan[7] Humphries, b. 25 May 1976.
    1488 iii. Sarah Elizabeth[7] Humphries, b. 1 Dec 1979.

877. Ralph Joyner[6] Humphries (Julian Maxwell[5], Charles Hilliard[4], Absalom B.[3], William[2], Charles[1]) was born 24 January 1952 and married Patricia Bacalis. Child:

1489 i. Emily Meredith[7] Humphries, b. 20 Jan 1981.

878. Susan Claire[6] Humphries (Julian Maxwell[5], Charles Hilliard[4], Absalom B.[3], William[2], Charles[1]) was born 5 July 1954 and married Richard Ballard Simmon. Children:

1490 i. Jennifer Claire[7] Simmon, b. 16 Oct 1976.
1491 ii. Matthew Ballard[7] Simmon, b. 2 Dec 1979.

879. Robert Maxwell[6] Love (Norma[5], Charles Hilliard[4], Absalom B.[3], William[2], Charles[1]) was born 3 August 1947 and married Linda Faye Counts. Children:

1492 i. Jason Robert[7] Humphries, b. 27 Jun 1975.
1493 ii. Jennifer Sue[7] Humphries, b. 8 May 1979.

880. Julia Elizabeth[6] Love (Norma[5], Charles Hilliard[4], Absalom B.[3], William[2], Charles[1]) was born 8 April 1950 and married Fred May Thrailkill, Jr. Children:

1494 i. Margaret Sue[7] Thrailkill, b. 1 Dec 1975.
1495 ii. Robert Benjamin[7] Thrailkill, b. 24 Aug 1979.

882. George Badger[6] Humphries, Jr. (George Badger[5], Charles Hilliard[4], Absalom B.[3], William[2], Charles[1]) was born 24 March 1947 in Augusta, Georgia and married Aliene Shields. They currently [1984] live in Columbia, South Carolina. Children:

1496 i. George Badger[7] Humphries, III, b. 29 Jun 1973, Birmingham, AL.
1497 ii. Charles Shields[7] Humphries, b. 30 Jun 1975, Winston-Salem, NC.

883. Claude Maxwell[6] Humphries (George Badger[5], Charles Hilliard[4], Absalom B.[3], William[2], Charles[1]) was born 16 December 1953 and married Diane Hammond. They live in Johnston, South Carolina. Child:

1498   Claude Maxwell[7] Humphries, Jr., b. 16 Dec 1981,
        Columbia, SC.

884. Elizabeth Ann[6] Paschal (Olive[5], Charles Hilliard[4], Absalom B.[3], William[2], Charles[1]) was born 24 August 1954 and married Tony Lee Creswell. Children:

1499   i. Leigh Ann[7] Paschal, b. 28 Jun 1977.
1500 ii. Ryan John[7] Paschal, b. 30 Oct 1978.
1501 iii. Erin Bethany[7] Paschal, b. 24 Sept 1981.

888. Myrtle Coline[6] Smith (Coline[5], Frances Catherine[4], Mary E.[3], William[2], Charles[1]) was born 7 June 1899 in Union, South Carolina. On 8 June 1921, she married George Edwin Simmons, who was born 1 January 1894 and died 25 September 1984, son of James Howard Simmons and wife Alice Mifford. Myrtle Coline Smith is a graduate of Lander College in Greenwood, South Carolina, and was a public school teacher in South Carolina, Texas, and Missouri, and was chairman of pediatrics, Presbyterian Hospital Auxiliary in Charlotte, North Carolina. George Edwin Simmons was a graduate of Wofford College in Spartanburg, South Carolina, and was retired as executive director of YMCA in Charlotte, North Carolina. Myrtle Smith Simmons lives in Spartanburg, South Carolina. One child:

+ 1502 Coline Elizabeth[7] Simmons, b. 15 Jun 1929.

890. Frances Lake[6] Edwards (Joseph Eugene[5], Frances Catherine[4], Mary E.[3], William[2], Charles[1]) was born 29 May 1919, and married on 7 December 1941, Marett Larkin Outz, who was born 2 March 1919 at Fairplay, South Carolina, son of Joe Outz and his wife Nora Belle Marett. Frances Edwards is a graduate of Winthrop College, and was a public school teacher. Marett L. Outz is a grduate of Clemson University, and a retired real estate salesman. Children:

+ 1503   i. Jane Larkin[7] Outz, b. 24 Sept 1943.
  1503 ii. John Marett[7] Outz, b. 2 Sept 1947.
+ 1504 iii. Laura Rebecca[7] Outz, b. 17 Mar 1954.

891. Joseph Eugene[6] Edwards, Jr. (Joseph Eugene[5], Frances Catherine[4], Mary E.[3], William[2], Charles[1]) was born 23 October 1920 in Union County, South Carolina

and married on 21 June 1943, Frances Mae Ferguson, who was born 19 January 1925, daughter of Burrel Hampton Ferguson and wife Ellen Cogdell. Children:

+ 1505 i. Jean Ferguson[7] Edwards, b. 29 Mar 1945.
+ 1506 ii. Martha Ellen[7] Edwards, b. 15 Mar 1948.
  1507 iii. Robert Michael[7] Edwards, b. 13 Nov 1949, m.
       7 Oct 1972, Susie Gilliland, b. 8 Apr 1951, Union, SC.
+ 1508 iv. Susan Lake[7] Edwards, b. 11 Feb 1954.

892. Martha Louise[6] Edwards (Joseph Eugene[5], Frances Catherine[4], Mary E.[3], William[2], Charles[1]) was born 29 May 1923 in Union, South Carolina, and married 1 June 1946, Jack Vincent Buerkle, who was born 9 August 1923, son of Henry Adam Buerkle. Children:

  1509 i. Stephen Vincent[7] Buerkle, b. 18 Dec 1951, Iowa City, IA.
  1510 ii. Melanie Lake[7] Buerkle, b. 27 Jun 1959, New Haven, Conn.

893. Mannie Lee[6] Edwards (George Douglas[5], Frances Catherine[4], Mary E.[3], William[2], Charles[1]) was born 13 March 1912 in Union County, South Carolina, and married on 25 October 1932, Leon Lawson Mabry, who was born 7 February 1910, son of Richard Vernon Mabry and wife Ida Permelia Lawson. Mannie Lee Edwards is a graduate of Winthrop College, and was a deputy sheriff of Lee County, Florida. They currently [1984] live in Union, South Carolina. Child:

  1511 i. Bobby Lee[7] Mabry, b. 12 Aug 1933, attended Clemson College,
     and UCLA.

894. Johnathan Franklin[6] Edwards (George Douglas[5], Frances Catherine[4], Mary E.[3], William[2], Charles[1]) was born 21 November 1925 in Union County, South Carolina and married on 22 December 1962, Frances Emma Orr, who was born 30 May 1928 in Transylvania County, North Carolina, daughter of Depew Harrison Orr and wife Emma Elsada Lyday. Johnathan Edwards is a graduate of Wofford College in Spartanburg, South Carolina, and Frances Emma Orr is a graduate of Carson-Newman College in Jefferson City, Tennessee, and has a Master of Religious Education degree from Southern Baptist Theological Seminary in Louisville, Kentucky. Children:

1512 i. Lillie Emma[7] Edwards, b. 18 Mar 1964.
1513 ii. Johnathan Franklin[7] Edwards, Jr., b. 24 Oct 1966.

895. Frances[6] Simpson (Leila[5], Frances Catherine[4], Mary E.[3], William[2], Charles[1]) was born 15 June 1921 in Clinton, South Carolina, and married on 20 May 1944, Kitt Rion McMaster, Jr., who was born 20 May 1918, and died 13 September 1970, and is buried Associate Reformed Presbyterian Cemetery in Winnsboro, South Carolina. He was the son of Kitt Rion McMaster and wife Nelle Elliott. Frances Simpson is a graduate of the University of South Carolina. Children:

+ 1514 i. Ellen Simpson[7] McMaster, b. 15 Feb 1946.
1515 ii. Kitt Rion[7] McMaster, III, b. 18 Nov 1947.

913. Joy Elizabeth[6] Humphries (John S.[5], John [4], Charles H.[3], William[2], Charles[1]) was born 25 December 1905 in Pritchett, Upshur County, Texas, and married on 17 February 1922 at Gilmer, Texas, Lindsey Clore Honeycutt, who was born 10 February 1901 in Tyler, Texas, and died 30 December 1971 in Kansas City, Missouri. Children:

1516 i. Reba Rose[7] Honeycutt, b. 14 Sept 1923, Tyler, TX,
         m. 22 May 1938, Audrey H. Adams.
1517 ii. Billy Joe[7] Honeycutt, b. 25 Aug 1926, Tyler, TX,
         m. 24 Aug 1950, Virginia Oisterirch.
1518 iii. Gene Austin[7] Honeycutt, b. 7 Jul 1928, Big Sandy,
         Upshur Co., TX, m. 17 Feb 1947, Pauline Schanevelt.
1517 iv. Audrey Theodore[7] Honeycutt, b. 12 Sept 1930,
         Tyler, TX, m. 23 Jun 1957, Donna Jean Strunk.
+ 1518 v. Lindsey Clore[7] Honeycutt, Jr., b. 21 Oct 1933.

916. Paul Heyward[6] Burgess (Lawrence[5], Frances[3], Katherine[3], William[2], Charles[1]) married Rose Finger. Child:

+ 1519 Paul Heyward[7] Burgess, Jr.

920. Cleo[6] Burgess (Joseph[5], Frances[4], Katherine[3], William[2], Charles[1]) married James D. Bass, lives in Clinton, South Carolina. Child:

+ 1520 James D.[7] (Jimmy) Bass.

922. LaVerne[6] Burgess (Joseph[5], Frances[4], Katherine[3], William[2], Charles[1]) married John Thomas (Jake) Brown. Child:

+ 1521 Susan[7] Brown.

923. Roy[6] Burgess (Joseph[5], Frances[4], Katherine[3], William[2], Charles[1]) married Ruth Johnson. Child:

1522 i. Roy[7] Burgess, Jr.

934. Wilcie Mae[6] Thompson (Nannie[5], Frances[4], Katherine[3], William[2], Charles[1]) married Kay Farr. Children:

1523 i. Kay Thompson[7] Farr.
1524 ii. Lisa Kay[7] Farr.

935. Rubye[6] Thompson (Nannie[5], Frances[4], Katherine[3], William[2], Charles[1]) married Marion Surrett. Child:

1525 i. Barbara[7] Surrett, m. Taft Dantzler.

939. Boyce Malcolm[6] Vise (Della[5], Susan Fair[4], Katherine[3], William[2], Charles[1]) was born 4 August 1900 and married on 13 November 1925, Lunette Kirby, who was born 12 October 1907. They live on Lake Murray, near Irmo, South Carolina. Child:

1526 i. Ernest[7] Vise, b. 12 Jun 1932.

940. Jeannette[6] Vise (Della[5], Susan Fair[4], Katherine[3], William[2], Charles[1]) was born 22 August 1905, died 15 May 1967, married Richard Welch. Child:

+ 1527 Jean[7] Welch.

942. Herman Douglas[6] Betenbaugh (James Sanders[5], Susan Fair[4], Katherine[3], William[2], Charles[1]) was born 27 December 1905 and died 6 June 1972. He married Lillie Linderman, who was born 11 September 1918. Children:

+ 1528   i. James Sanders[7] Betenbaugh, II, b. 24 Jul 1938.
+ 1529 ii. Patricia Ann[7] Betenbaugh, b. 9 Aug 1939.
+ 1530 iii. William Douglas[7] Betenbaugh, b. 23 Jul 1941.

1531   iv. Herman Donald[7] Betenbaugh, b. 14 Nov 1948 (for
        descendants, see #1311).
1532   v. Thomas Michael[7] Betenbaugh, b. 5 Jul 1947, d. 17 Aug 1966.
1533   vi. Martha Susan[7] Betenbaugh, b. 23 Dec 1950, d. 6 Oct 1972.
+ 1534 vii. John Roper[7] Betenbaugh, b. 20 Dec 1951.
+ 1535 viii. David Robin[7] Betenbaugh, b. 22 Aug 1953.

950. Hazel[6] Betenbaugh (Morris Douglas[5], Susan Fair[4], Katherine[3], William[2], Charles[1]) was born 18 February 1922 and died 1 February 1972; she married Ralph Robinson. Children:

1536   i. Janet Sue[7] Robinson, b. 6 May 1948.
1537 ii. Ralph Douglas[7] Robinson, b. 1 Nov 1952.

952. Walter Russell[6] Betenbaugh, Jr. (Walter Russell[5], Susan Fair[4], Katherine[3], William[2], Charles[1]) married, first, Frank Eline; married, second, Susan _____. Children:

1538   i. Linda[7] Betenbaugh (by Frank Eline).
1539 ii. David[7] Betenbaugh (by Susan).

962. Ezell Manly[6] Willard (Humphries[5], Janie[4], Katherine[3], William[2], Charles[1]) was born 10 November 1910 and died 3 June 1962. He married Grace Godshall on 8 February 1942. Children:

1540   i. Ezell Manly[7] Willard, Jr., b. 2 Mar 1943.
1541 ii. Humphries Eugene[7] Willard, b. 4 Oct 1946.

965. Helen Ruth[6] Willard (Humphries[5], Janie[4], Katherine[3], William[2], Charles[1]) was born 9 October 1918 and married on 26 August 1945, John Tatom Bradley, who died 29 October 1980. Children:

+ 1542   i. Helen Tate[7] Bradley, b. 3 Dec 1946.
  1543 ii. Caroline Ladd[7] Bradley, b. 24 Jul 1955,
        m. 4 Jun 1977, Dr. Larry Herm Smith.

978. Herbert Earl[6] Wilson (Letitia Mary Jane[5], Elizabeth Levenia[4], Charles G. W.[3], Thomas[2], Charles[1]) was born 3 January 1895 in Darlington, South Carolina and died 30 April 1969 in Columbia, South Carolina. He married, first, Anna Gault, by whom he had one child. They were divorced. He married, second,

Mildred Elizabeth Lindler, born 24 October 1922, who married after his death, Frank Turnipseed. Children:

+ 1544 i. Gaynelle[7] Wilson, b. 16 Oct 1919.
+ 1545 ii. Jean Lindler[7] Wilson, b. 5 Oct 1953.
  1546 iii. Sherri Lynn[7] Wilson, b. 23 Dec 1958, m.
       5 Aug 1980, Charlie Whyde.

979. Mary Elizabeth[6] Wilson (Letitia Mary Jane[5], Elizabeth Levenia[4], Charles G. W.[3], Thomas[2], Charles[1]) was born 23 October 1897 in Darlington, South Carolina and died 1 January 1961 in Lakeland, Florida. She married on 23 May 1918, Joseph Franklin Wright, who was born 8 June 1869 and died 16 January 1942 in Cordova, North Carolina. She married, second, on 20 January 1947, in Grand Rapids, Michigan, Vinton Arnold Mill, who was born 15 November 1887 and died 24 July 1973. Joseph Franklin Wright is buried at Grove Hill Cemetery in Darlington. Mary Elizabeth Wilson Wright Mill is buried at Greenlawn Cemetery in Columbia, South Carolina. Children:

+ 1547 i. Joseph Franklin[7] Wright, Jr., b. 9 Mar 1920.
+ 1548 ii. Mary Doris[7] Wright, b. 25 Jul 1922.

980. James Bertram[6] (Bert) Wilson (Letitia Mary Jane[5], Elizabeth Levenia[4], Charles G. W.[3], Thomas[2], Charles[1]) was born 25 July 1899 in Darlington, South Carolina, and died in April 1972. He married Ada Wright, who was born 15 January 1903. Bert is buried at Woodlawn Cemetery in Greenville, South Carolina. Children:

+ 1549 i. Dorothy[7] Wilson.
  1550 ii. James Bertram[7] Wilson, Jr., m. Doris _____.
+ 1551 iii. Betty[7] Wilson.
+ 1552 iv. Madeline[7] Wilson.

981. Virgil William[6] Wilson (Letitia Mary Jane[5], Elizabeth Levenia[4], Charles G. W.[3], Thomas[2], Charles[1]) was born 2 September 1901 in Darlington, South Carolina and died 19 September 1960 in East Rockingham, North Carolina. He married on 28 December 1923, in Columbia, South Carolina, Mable Merritt, who was born 30 March _____, who currently [1984] lives there. He married, second,

24 February 1934, at Rockingham, North Carolina, Pearl Hazel Moore, who was born 26 July 1917. Children:

1553 i. Virgil William[7] Wilson, Jr., b. 25 Jun 1926, Columbia, SC.
+ 1554 ii. Manley Merritt[7] Wilson, b. 10 Feb 1930, Columbia, SC.
+ 1555 iii. Sybil Joyce[7] Wilson, b. 7 May 1937, Cordova, NC.
+ 1556 iv. Joseph Earl[7] Wilson, b. 24 Jan 1939, Cordova, NC.

982. Robert Stevenson[6] Wilson (Letitia Mary Jane[5], Elizabeth Levenia[4], Charles G. W.[3], Thomas[2], Charles[1]) was born 1 September 1903 in Darlington, South Carolina, died there in April 1924. He married Ella Kline. Child:

1557 i. James Edward[7] Wilson.

983. Oscar LaFaye[6] Wilson (Letitia Mary Jane[5], Elizabeth Levenia[4], Charles G. W.[3], Thomas[2], Charles[1]) was born 10 December 1905 in Darlington, South Carolina and died 6 September 1971. He is buried at Greenlawn Cemetery in Columbia, South Carolina. He married Ruth Martin. Child:

+ 1558 i. James Reed[6] Wilson, b. 30 Apr 1930.

984. Myrtle Leona[6] Wilson (Letitia Mary Jane[5], Elizabeth Levenia[4], Charles G. W.[3], Thomas[2], Charles[1]) was born 1 October 1909 in Darlington, South Carolina and married on 25 December 1936, Nicholas Vanderwall, who was born 9 March 1903 in New Era, Michigan, and died 1 October 1956 in Columbia, South Carolina. He is buried at Greenlawn Cemetery in Columbia. Children:

+ 1559 i. Gaynelle Doris[7] Vanderwall, b. 11 Aug 1938.
+ 1560 ii. Mary Margaret[7] Vanderwall, b. 17 Aug 1942.

986. Woodrow Frank[6] Wilson (Letitia Mary Jane[5], Elizabeth Levenia[4], Charles G. W.[3], Thomas[2], Charles[1]) was born 1 December 1915 in Darlington, South Carolina. He married on 9 May 1937 in West Columbia, South Carolina, Elizabeth Wise, who was born 21 September 1917 and died 3 June 1972 in Columbia. She is buried Greenlawn Cemetery in Columbia. Child:

1561 Woodrow Frank[7] Wilson, Jr., b. 3 Jan 1943, m. Patricia Miles.

987. Emerson Edward[6] Wilson (Letitia Mary Jane[5], Elizabeth Levenia[4], Charles G. W.[3], Thomas[2], Charles[1]) was born 11 October 1917 in Darlington, South Carolina and died 15 March 1964 in Columbia, South Carolina. He is buried in Elmwood Cemetery in Columbia. He married, 16 November 1938, in Columbia, Lois Moody, who was born 4 September 1921. Lois Moody Wilson, married, second, Carl Williams. Children:

+ 1562 i. Barbara Ann[7] Wilson, b. 6 Nov 1939.
+ 1563 ii. Catherine[7] Wilson, b. 4 Apr 1943.

988. Ella Louise[6] Hatchell (Lue Ella[5], Elizabeth Levenia[4], Charles G. W.[3], Thomas[2], Charles[1]) was born 6 April 1906 and married, first, on 28 October 1922, James Henry[6] Humphries, #1006 (John Duncan[5], Charles G. W.[4], Thomas Henry Durant[3], Thomas[2], Charles[1]), who was born 12 December 1903 and died 6 October 1932 in Darlington, South Carolina. She married, second, John McLaurin Keith. Children:

+ 1564 i. David Melvin[7] Humphries, b. 4 Aug 1923.
  1565 ii. Maurice Duncan[7] Humphries, b. 4 Jun 1927,
          d. 13 Apr 1969, m. Mae Garner.
  1566 iii. Meddie Lou[7] Humphries, m. 1st Jack Waymire,
          2nd Ed Brendle.
  1567 iv. Mollie Joyce[7] Keith, m. Alston Campbell.

992. Meres Evelyn[6] Hatchell (Lue Ella[5], Elizabeth Levenia[4], Charles G. W.[3], Thomas[2], Charles[1]) was born 31 March 1918 in Darlington, South Carolina, and married on 1 October 1933, Jessie Charlie Kenneth Davis, who was born 11 September 1914 and died 27 December 1970 in Darlington. Children:

  1568 i. Elizabeth Eva Lou[7] Davis, b. 30 Apr 1936, m.
          1st Jack Cole Jr., 2nd James D. Lane.
  1569 ii. Marian Evelyn[7] Davis, b. 3 April 1938, m.
          Thomas Earl Leaird.

994. Cecil Edgar[6] Lambert (Charles Franklin[5], Elizabeth Levenia[4], Charles G. W.[3], Thomas[2], Charles[1]) was born 15 June 1920 in Darlington, South Carolina, and died there 2 March 1977. He is buried there in the Grove Hill Cemetery. He married, on 24 November 1940, Margaret June Clements, who was born 20

April 1921 in Florence, South Carolina. Children:

+ 1570 i. Franklin Harold[7] Lambert, b. 26 May 1946.
+ 1571 ii. Carol Frances[7] Lambert, b. 9 Mar 1950.
+ 1572 iii. Jo Cecile[7] Lambert, b. 23 Dec 1956.

995. Monroe Terry[6] Lambert (Charles Franklin[5], Elizabeth Levenia[4], Charles G. W.[3], Thomas[2], Charles[1]) was born 25 January 1922 in Darlington, South Carolina, and married on 1 May 1942, Eva Mae Weinburg, who was born 5 December 1924 in Darlington County, and died 1 August 1981 in Florence, South Carolina. She is buried Grove Hill Cemetery in Darlington. Children:

  1573 i. Monroe Terry[7] Lambert, Jr., b. 9 Dec 1949, m.
         17 Oct 1969, Mary Elizabeth Byrd.
  1574 ii. Charles Allen[7] Lambert, b. 1 Jan 1956.

996. Gena Ray[6] Lambert (Charles Franklin[5], Elizabeth Levenia[4], Charles G. W.[3], Thomas[2], Charles[1]) was born 14 December 1925 and married Gene Wayland Cook. Child:

+ 1575 Sara Kathleen[7] Cook, b. 8 Jan 1947.

1022. Marion Eugene[6] Bishop (Lucille[5], Henry B.[4], Absalom C. C.[3], Thomas[2], Charles[1]) married Rebecca Gault. Child:

  1576 i. Tommy[7] Bishop, b. 19 Nov 1966.

1023. Terry Wilson[6] Humphries (Woodrow Wilson[5], Henry B.[4], Absalom C. C.[3], Thomas[2], Charles[1]) married on 21 June 1968, Margie Lee O'Shields. Children:

  1577 i. Wendy Darlene[7] Humphries, b. 20 Jan 1970.
  1578 ii. Tiffany Dianne[7] Humphries, b. 18 Oct 1973.
  1579 iii. Benji Wilson[7] Humphries, b. 10 Apr 1979.

1025. Carroll G.[6] Hughes (Louise[5], Lettie[4], Absalom C. C.[3], Thomas[2], Charles[1]) married Connie Kay Bannister. Children:

  1580 i. Elizabeth[7] Hughes.
  1581 ii. Leslie[7] Hughes.

1026. Phillip L.[6] Hughes (Louise[5], Lettie[4], Absalom C. C..[3], Thomas[2], Charles[1]) married Glenda Swygert. Child:

    1582 i. Phillip L.[7] Hughes, Jr.

1027. June Mavis[6] Lawson (John Minter[5], Lettie[4], Absalom C. C..[3], Thomas[2], Charles[1]) married David L. Brown. Child:

    1583 i. Laronne[7] Brown.

1028. Ann[6] Lawson (John Minter[5], Lettie[4], Absalom C. C..[3], Thomas[2], Charles[1]) married Frank Chestnut. Child:

    1584 i. Donald[7] Chestnut.

1030. K. Donnan[6] Lawson (Guy H.[5], Lettie[4], Absalom C. C..[3], Thomas[2], Charles[1]) married Irene Sightler. Children:

    1585 i. Marion[7] Lawson.
    1586 ii. Michael[7] Lawson.

1032. Glenda Jo[6] Lawson (John Minter[5], Lettie[4], Absalom C. C..[3], Thomas[2], Charles[1]) married Charles Cannon. Children:

    1587 i. Scott[7] Cannon.
    1588 ii. Mark[7] Cannon.

1033. John Leroy[6] Allen, Jr. (Lena Victoria[5], Lettie[4], Absalom C. C..[3], Thomas[2], Charles[1]) married Deborah van Sciver. Child:

    1589 i. John Christopher[7] Allen.

1034. William Conrad[6] Allen (Lena Victoria[5], Lettie[4], Absalom C. C..[3], Thomas[2], Charles[1]) married, first, Brenda Farmer, and second, Thelma Rodgers. Children:

    1590 i. William Conrad[7] Allen, Jr. (by Brenda).
    1591 ii. Michael Jeffery[7] Allen (by Thelma).
    1592 iii. Winifred Lee[7] Allen (by Thelma).
    1593 iv. David Edmond[7] Allen (by Thelma).

1037. Frank Ernell[6] Peake, Jr. (Frank Ernell[5], Isaac Frank[4], Charlotte Frances[3], Charlotte[2], Charles[1]) was born 12 February 1924 in Rock Hill, South Carolina, and married 26 December 1951, at Roseburg, Oregon, Jane Macnider, who was born 17 December 1923. Frank E. Peake, Jr., is a graduate of Duke University, and in 1982, was living in Fairfax, Virginia. Children:

+ 1594   i. Leslie Drew[7] Peake, b. 6 Feb 1953, Fairfax, VA.
   1595 ii. Cheryl Anne[7] Peake, b. 2 Apr 1955, Fairfax, VA.

1038. Robert Sanders[6] Peake (Frank Ernell[5], Isaac Frank[4], Charlotte Frances[3], Charlotte[2], Charles[1]) was born 20 October 1926 in Columbia, South Carolina and married on 26 November 1955 in Cambridge, Massachusetts, Constance Warren Jenks, daughter of Henry A. and Constance (Bouveau) Jenks. Robert S. Peake is a graduate of Duke University, and in 1982 was living in Durham, North Carolina. Children:

   1596   i. Cynthia Warren[7] Peake, b. 25 Feb 1957, Durham, NC,
              graduate of UNC Chapel Hill (1979).
   1597 ii. Diane Sanders[7] Peake, b. 10 Jan 1959, Durham, NC,
              graduate of Vanderbilt University (1981), m. 31 Jul 1982,
              Dennis Keith Taggart.

1039. William Derrick[6] Peake (Frank Ernell[5], Isaac Frank[4], Charlotte Frances[3], Charlotte[2], Charles[1]) was born 11 June 1929, Columbia, South Carolina, married Leah Ruth Banks, who was born 1 March 1930 in Burnsville, North Carolina, daughter of Plato Marion and Mary (Young) Banks of Yancey County, North Carolina. William D. Peake is a graduate of Clemson University, and is a practicing architect in Fairfax, Virginia. Children:

+ 1598   i. Derrick Sanders[7] Peake, b. 11 Jul 1954, Washington, DC.
+ 1599 ii. Judith Ann[7] Peake, b. 10 Mar 1956, Arlington, VA.
   1600 iii. Martha Frances[7] Peake, b. 5 Aug 1957, Arlington, VA.
   1601 iv. David Franklin[7] Peake, b. 22 Apr 1965, Arlington, VA.

1040. Jean Neely[6] Peake (Keith Cockrell[5], Isaac Frank[4], Charlotte Frances[3], Charlotte[2], Charles[1]) was born 7 May 1926 in Rock Hill, South Carolina, and married in June 1952, in National Cathedral, Washington, D. C., Edgar Farr Russell, Jr., who was born 9 May 1927, Washington, D. C., son of Edgar Farr and

Ida Rebecca (Frazier) Russell. Children:

1602 i. Edgar Farr[7] Russell, III, b. 14 Jan 1954,
Washington, D. C., graduate of Georgetown Univ. (1977).
1603 ii. Frazier Neely Southey[7] Russell, b. 19 Sept 1957,
Washington, D. C., graduate of NYU (1979).

1043. Thomas Hopkins[6] (Hop) Peake, Jr. (Thomas Hopkins[5], Isaac Frank[4], Charlotte Frances[3], Charlotte[2], Charles[1]) was born 26 June 1926 in Union, South Carolina, married 28 November 1959, at Oakland Avenue Presbyterian Church, Rock Hill, South Carolina, to Margaret Louise Simril, who was born 6 September 1928 in Rock Hill, daughter of Hugh Loraine and Louise Evans Simril. Hop is a graduate of Clemson University (1947) and Margaret is a graduate of Winthrop College (1949), and they reside currently [1984] at Trinity, North Carolina. Hop Peake has contributed the data on the descendants of Charlotte[2] Humphries Gregory for this volume. Children:

+ 1604 i. Evans McMurray[7] Peake, b. 5 Oct 1961, Charlotte, NC.
1605 ii. Gregory Charles[7] (Greg) Peake, b. 18 Mar 1964,
Charlotte, NC.

1044. Erwin Crockett[6] Peake (Thomas Hopkins[5], Isaac Frank[4], Charlotte Frances[3], Charlotte[2], Charles[1]) was born 20 April 1928 in Union, South Carolina, attended Clemson College, and was graduated from the U. S. Naval Academy (1951). He married, first, Sylvia Deming, in Las Vegas, Nevada, divorced. He married, second, on 6 July 1963, in White Sands, New Mexico, Marilyn Stoneburg, daughter of Carl Joseph and Mabel Irene (Schreyer) Stoneburg of Klamath Falls, Oregon. In 1982, they were living in Albuquerque, New Mexico. Children:

1606 i. Lisa Rochelle[7] Peake, b. 20 Sept 1958 (dau. of Marilyn
by a previous marriage, legally adopted by Erwin Crockett
Peake), m. 26 Jul 1980, Kenneth John Duling, b. 28 Jan 1956.
1607 ii. Andrew Erwin[7] Peake, b. 16 Nov 1965, Redlands, CA.
1608 iii. Janine Michelle[7] Peake, b. 29 Jan 1969, White Sands, NM.

1045. Glenn David[6] Peake (Isaac Frank[5], Isaac Frank[4], Charlotte Frances[3], Charlotte[2], Charles[1]) was born 31 August 1938 in Old Hickory, Tennessee, and married Martha Woods, who was born 28 August 1941 in Dothan, Alabama, daughter of Dr. Thomas Baxter and Mariam (Christmas) Woods. Glenn David Peake is a graduate of Georgia Tech (1961). In 1982, they were living in Atlanta, Georgia. Children:

1609 i. Glenn David[7] Peake, Jr., b. 19 Aug 1966, Wilmington, DE.
1610 ii. Thomas Franklin[7] Peake, b. 1969, Atlanta, GA.

1046. Arvid Terry[6] Peake (Lucia Glennie[5], Glenn David[4], Charlotte Frances[3], Charlotte[2], Charles[1]) was born 27 March 1924 in Spartanburg, South Carolina, and married Mary Kate Hines in February 1947. Children:

1611 i. Micheal Terry[7] Peake, b. 28 Mar 1948.
1612 ii. Richard Glenn[7] Peake, b. 13 Apr 1951.
1613 iii. Jeffeory Lynn[7] Peake, b. 14 Aug 1953.

1047. Betty Lou[6] Noblitt (Lucia Glennie[5], Glenn David[4], Charlotte Frances[3], Charlotte[2], Charles[1]) was born 12 November 1928 in Spartanburg, South Carolina, and married 8 October 1948, Harry R. Crocker. Children:

1614 i. Linder Kay[7] Crocker, b. 6 Nov 1952.
1615 ii. Christy Lynn[7] Crocker, b. 16 Sept 1956.

1048. Elbert Graham[6] Noblitt (Lucia Glennie[5], Glenn David[4], Charlotte Frances[3], Charlotte[2], Charles[1]) was born 2 December 1930 in Spartanburg, South Carolina and married 12 April 1952, Thelma May Brewington. Child:

1616 i. Vickey Paulette[7] Noblitt, b. 17 May 1953.

1050. Patricia Ann[6] Reynolds (Patricia Myra[5], Glenn David[4], Charlotte Frances[3], Charlotte[2], Charles[1]) was born 7 October 1933 in Spartanburg, South Carolina, and married on 12 April 1953, Fred Andrew Lamb. Child:

1617 i. Donna Michelle[7] Lamb, b. 9 Apr 1954, Spartanburg, SC.

1051. William Peake[6] Kennedy (Hattie Elizabeth[5], John Lamartine[4], Charlotte Frances[3], Charlotte[2], Charles[1]) was born 15 February 1944 in Charleston, South Carolina, and married on 28 June 1967, Beverly Cowaird Berry, who was born 18 March 1943 in Orlando, Florida. William Peake Kennedy is a graduate of USC in pharmacy, operates Thayer's Drug Store in Orlando. Children:

1618 i. Ashely Elizabeth[6] Kennedy, b. 20 Jul 1970, Orlando, FL.
1619 ii. Courtney Berry[7] Kennedy, b. 10 Aug 1973, Orlando, FL.

1052. Jerald Lamartine[6] Peake (John Lamartine[5], John Lamartine[4], Charlotte Frances[3], Charlotte[2], Charles[1]) was born 28 April 1950 in Glenn Springs, South Carolina, and married on 25 November 1969, Shirley Jean Simmons, who was born 24 June 1950, daughter of Robert Eugene and Virginia Ruth (Townsend) Simmons. In 1982, they were living in Glenn Springs. Children:

1620 i. Andrew Jeremy[7] Peake, b. 1 Oct 1975.
1621 ii. Thomas Stephen[7] Peake, b. 21 Mar 1979.

1053. John Everette[6] Peake (John Lamartine[5], John Lamartine[4], Charlotte Frances[3], Charlotte[2], Charles[1]) was born 28 April 1950 in Glenn Springs, South Carolina, and married on 6 August 1980 Regina Lynn Mitchem, who was born 6 September 1950, daughter of Marion Julius Mitchem and Virginia McDaniel of Wellford, South Carolina. Children:

1622 i. Jonathon Chad[7] Peake, b. 20 Feb 1975.
1623 ii. (name unknown), b. 1980.

1054. Marcia Susan[6] Peake (John Lamartine[5], John Lamartine[4], Charlotte Frances[3], Charlotte[2], Charles[1]) was born 9 December 1952 in Glenn Springs, South Carolina, and married on 22 July 1971 Walter Eugene Cherry, Jr., who was born 20 January 1951, son of Walter Eugene Cherry and Jennivieve Houston Cherry Gosnell. Child:

1624 Jason Blalock[7] Cherry, b. 30 Jan 1976.

1055. Neil Gaillard[6] Bates (John Oliver[5], Annie Lou[4], Sarah Ellen Medora[3], Charlotte[2], Charles[1]) was born 2 February 1934 in Sumter, South Carolina, was graduated from the U. S. Naval Academy (1957), and was married on 1 February 1958 in Tallahassee, Florida, to Malinda Ann Marshall, who was born 3 July 1937, daughter of William A. and Virginia (Thornton) Marshall. In 1982, they were living in St. Matthews, South Carolina. Children:

1625 i. Malinda Catherine[7] Bates, b. 26 Nov 1958, Byran, TX,
     graduate of Columbia College (1981).
1626 ii. Teresa Crawford[7] Bates, b. 20 Jun 1962, Hamilton, Bermuda.

1060. Clifford Calvin[6] Hayslip, Jr. (Mary Evelyn[5] William Isaac[4], Mary Ann Henrietta[3], Charlotte[2], Charles[1]) was born 20 August 1951 in Spartanburg, South Carolina, has one child:

1627 i. Alva Catherine[7] Hayslip, b. 13 February 1977.

1061. Marsha Elizabeth[6] Hayslip (Mary Evelyn[5] William Isaac[4], Mary Ann Henrietta[3], Charlotte[2], Charles[1]) was born 30 March 1953 in Spartanburg, South Carolina, married _____ Cantrell. Children:

1628 i. Matthew Hayslip[7] Cantrell, b. 13 Jan 1977.
1629 ii. Marian Walker[7] Cantrell, b. 21 Jun 1979.

1064. Muriel Joy[6] Gregory (Martin Chapin[5], Anne Laura[4], John Wesley[3], Charlotte[2], Charles[1]) was born 16 December 1930, in Jacksonville, Florida, and married Laurance Arville Petit, Jr., who was born 24 December 1925 in Moline, Illinois, son of Laurance Arville and Mabel Josephine (Larson) Petit. Muriel is a graduate of Hillsborough Community College in Tampa, Florida, and Laurance is a graduate of the University of Miami in Coral Gables, Florida. In 1982, they were living in St. Petersburg, Florida. Children:

1630 i. Laurance Gregory[7] Petit, b. 31 Jul 1952, Miami, FL,
     m. 7 Jun 1980, Teri Linda Bendit.
+ 1631 ii. Gail Lauren[7] Petit, b. 16 Jun 1954.
1632 iii. Douglas Conrad[7] Petit, b. 6 Sept 1957, Coral Gables, FL.

1068. Llewellyn Gregory[6] (Greg) Pearce, Jr. (Llewellyn Gregory[5], Sarah Eleanor[4], John Wesley[3], Charlotte[2], Charles[1]) was born 5 October 1948 in Columbia, South Carolina, and married on 22 July 1972 in Hartsville, South Carolina, to Johnny Beverly (Beasley) Chapman, who was born 30 March 1950 in Florence, South Carolina, daughter of Ben Thomas Beasley Jr. and Mary Louise (Edens) Beasley Chapman. Greg is a graduate of Presbyterian College in Clinton, South Carolina (1970) and Beverly is a graduate of Winthrop College (1972). They currently

[1984] live in Columbia, South Carolina. Children:

1633   i. Louise Barron[7] Pearce, b. 6 Sept 1971, Columbia, SC.
1634 ii. Llewellyn Gregory[7] Pearce, III, b. 24 Jun 1981, Columbia, SC.

1070. Eleanor Wilma[6] Johnson (Mary Emily[5], Sarah Eleanor[4], John Wesley[3], Charlotte[2], Charles[1]) was born 12 August 1938 in Columbia, South Carolina, was married on 2 September 1960, Theodore Jefferson Blizard, who was born 5 June 1935 in Mount Airy, North Carolina, son of Thomas Jefferson and Glenna Ellen (Pierce) Blizard. They reside [1984] in Columbia. Children:

1635   i. Theodore Jefferson[7] Blizard, Jr., b. 2 Aug 1966.
1636 ii. Elizabeth Pearce[7] Blizard, b. 24 Sept 1967, Columbia, SC.

1071. Ward Pearce[6] Johnson (Mary Emily[5], Sarah Eleanor[4], John Wesley[3], Charlotte[2], Charles[1]) was born 9 December 1941 in Columbia, South Carolina, was married, first, on 31 October 1965, Maxine Pulliam. He married, second, on 25 May 1976, Deborah Elaine Dimmery, born 6 September 1951, Columbia, South Carolina, daughter of Bill B. and Dorothy (Taylor) Dimmery. They currently [1984] live in Columbia. Children:

1637   i. Elinor Chapin[7] Johnson, b. 21 Feb 1969, Columbia, SC.
1638 ii. Mary Louise[7] Johnson, b. 20 Jun 1972, Columbia, SC.
1639 iii. Matthew Ward[7] Johnson, b. 18 June 1980, Columbia, SC.

SEVENTH GENERATION

1072. Judith Ann[7] Thomas (George W.[6], Margaret[5], Sarah A.[4], Dr. Christopher[3], Sarah[2], Charles[1]) was born 15 December 1935 and married John Dillon Eversman, Jr., of Flat Rock, North Carolina. Judith is a graduate of Winthrop College, and teaches school in Union, South Carolina. Children:

1640 i. John Dillon[8] Eversman, III, b. 1 Feb 1962.
1641 ii. Lynn Thomas[8] Eversman, b. 9 Jun 1964.

1074. Ruth[7] May (Bernice Gertrude[6], Sarah Glenn[5], Sarah A.[4], Dr. Christopher[3], Sarah[2], Charles[1]) was born 31 July 1904 in Spartanburg, South Carolina, and married 30 April 1922, Walter Vernon Cooper, who was born 21 January 1907 in Spartanburg, South Carolina, and died 25 February 1962 in West Palm Beach, Florida. Child:

+ 1642 Constance Marian[8] Cooper, b. 8 Oct 1923, Spartanburg, SC.

1075. Edna Elizabeth[7] May (Bernice Gertrude[6], Sarah Glenn[5], Sarah A.[4], Dr. Christopher[3], Sarah[2], Charles[1]) was born 22 November 1906 in Union, South Carolina, and was married on 27 November 1931 to Charles DuBose DeLorme, who was born 6 December 1906 in Charleston, South Carolina, and died there 15 September 1952. Edna May DeLorme is a graduate of Converse College, and did graduate work at Wofford College, Clemson University, the University of South Carolina, and Randolph-Macon Women's College. She has taught in Beaufort High School, Beaufort, North Carolina, and Spartanburg High School. Child:

+ 1643 Charles DuBose[8] DeLorme, Jr., b. 2 Dec 1939, Spartanburg, SC.

1078. Dan W.[7] May (Bernice Gertrude[6], Sarah Glenn[5], Sarah A.[4], Dr. Christopher[3], Sarah[2], Charles[1]) was born 28 February 1914 in Spartanburg, South Carolina, and was married on 30 August 1940 to Betty Jeanette Jenkins, who was born 17 June 1922 in Shelby, North Carolina, and teaches third grade in Flat Rock, North Carolina. Child:

+ 1644 Daniel Jenkins[8] May, b. 30 May 1942.

1079. Sarah Glenn[7] May (Bernice Gertrude[6], Sarah Glenn[5], Sarah A.[4], Dr. Christopher[3], Sarah[2], Charles[1]) was born 2 April 1916 in Spartanburg, South Carolina, and died 27 October 1957. She married on 3 June 1939, James Franklin Deal, who was born 15 August 1912 in Iredell County, North Carolina, and died in 1971 in Hickory, North Carolina. Children:

+ 1645 i. James Franklin[8] Deal, Jr., b. 20 Aug 1940, Hickory, NC.
  1646 ii. Beverly Ann[8] Deal, b. 24 Mar 1944, Hickory, NC.

1080. Margaret Helen[7] May (Bernice Gertrude[6], Sarah Glenn[5], Sarah A.[4], Dr. Christopher[3], Sarah[2], Charles[1]) was born 10 January 1919 in Spartanburg, South Carolina, was married on 6 September 1942, to Edward Pool, who was born 4 July 1914 in Greenville, South Carolina. Margaret is a graduate of Furman University and taught at Methodist College, Fayettteville, North Carolina. Edward Pool is owner of Pool's Freight Line, Greenville. Children:

+ 1647 i. Edward May[8] Pool, b. 16 Mar 1944, Spartanburg, SC.
+ 1648 ii. Margaret Helen[8] Pool, b. 28 Apr 1946, Greenville, SC.
+ 1649 iii. Kathleen Elizabeth[8] Pool, b. Greenville, SC.

1082. Harper[7] Vaughan (Mary[6], Sarah Glenn[5], Sarah A.[4], Dr. Christopher[3], Sarah[2], Charles[1]) married Bruce Bowen. Children:

  1650 i. Robert[8] Vaughan.
  1651 ii. Anthony[8] Vaughan, m. ___ Jenkins.
  1652 iii. Ann[8] Vaughan.

1083. Fred[7] Vaughan (Mary[6], Sarah Glenn[5], Sarah A.[4], Dr. Christopher[3], Sarah[2], Charles[1]) had one child:

  1653 i. Freda[8] Vaughan.

1085. Dorothy[7] Willard (Thomas Hancock[6], Sarah Glenn[5], Sarah A.[4], Dr. Christopher[3], Sarah[2], Charles[1]) married Joe Macon Hightower, son of Ernest Edward Hightower and wife Myrtle Charlotte Sudduth. Children:

+ 1654 i. Sadie Joyce[8] Hightower.
+ 1655 ii. Myrtle Jeane[8] Hightower.
  1656 iii. Joe Macon[8] (Jody) Hightower, Jr.

1089. Rowland Farr[7] Thomas, Jr. (Rowland Farr[6], Martha Elizabeth[5], Sarah A.[4], Dr. Christopher[3], Sarah[2], Charles[1]) was born 17 December 1925 and married Ramona Davis. He received degrees from Wofford College in Spartanburg, South Carolina, and East Caroline College in Kinston, North Carolina, and is training director of George-Pacific Corporation in Atlanta, Georgia. Children:

  1657 i. Rowland Glenn[8] Thomas, b. 3 Jul 1954.
+ 1658 ii. Jeannette Suzanne[8] Thomas, b. 27 Jun 1956.

1090. Dr. Winter Clough[7] Wallace (Roberta[6], Jesse Robert[5], Martha Elizabeth[4], Dr. Christopher[3], Sarah[2], Charles[1]) married Mildred F. Taylor, of Rutherfordton, North Carolina. Child:

+ 1659 Jane[8] Wallace.

1092. Matt[7] O'Shields (Jessie[6], Jesse Robert[5], Martha Elizabeth[4], Dr. Christopher[3], Sarah[2], Charles[1]) married Mary Clara Reid, and had one child. He married second Eva Dale Morrison. Child:

  1660 i. Patrick Reid[8] O'Shields.

1094. Dan Hix[7] O'Shields (Jessie[6], Jesse Robert[5], Martha Elizabeth[4], Dr. Christopher[3], Sarah[2], Charles[1]) married Dorothy Wilson. Children:

  1661 i. Ronald[8] O'Shields.
  1662 ii. Wade Hampton[8] O'Shields.
  1663 iii. Dan[8] O'Shields.

1095. Hurl Edgar[7] (Buck) O'Shields (Jessie[6], Jesse Robert[5], Martha Elizabeth[4], Dr. Christopher[3], Sarah[2], Charles[1]) married Myrtle Merrit. Children:

  1664 i. Lynn O'Shields, m. William Legrand, Jr.
  1665 ii. Susan O'Shields, m. Kenneth Pryor.
  1666 iii. Steven O'Shields.

1697 i. Sheryl[8] Betenbaugh, b. 14 Feb 1963.
1698 ii. Timothy Shawn[8] Betenbaugh, b. 5 May 1965.

1117. Betty[7] Betenbaugh (William David[6], John Calhoun[5], Martha Ellen W.[4], Thomas[3], Sarah[2], Charles[1]) was born 16 November 1930 and married Delmar Burch Auman. Children:

1699 i. Richard Curtis[8] Auman, b. 16 Oct 1951, m. Kathy Ackers.
+ 1700 ii. Robin Marie[8] Auman, b. 20 Nov 1956.
1701 iii. John Andrew[8] Auman, b. 17 Jan 1965.

1119. Gordon Murray[7] Betenbaugh (Charner Michael[6], John Calhoun[5], Martha Ellen W.[4], Thomas[3], Sarah[2], Charles[1]) was born 30 June 1941 in Clinton, South Carolina, and married on 5 June 1965, Helen Reckenzaun. Both are graduates of Westminister Choir College in Princeton, New Jersey, and are church musicians. Children:

1702 i. Melanie Louise[8] Betenbaugh, b. 7 Jul 1970.
1703 ii. Jennifer Elaien[8] Betenbaugh, b. 19 Dec 1972.

1120. Alvin S.[7] Jolly, Jr. (Alvin S.[6], Elizabeth Ann[5], Martha Ellen W.[4], Thomas[3], Sarah[2], Charles[1]) married Dorothy Harlan. Child:

1704 i. Alvin S.[8] Jolly, III, m. Melissa _____.

1121. Edward K.[7] Jolly (Alvin S.[6], Elizabeth Ann[5], Martha Ellen W.[4], Thomas[3], Sarah[2], Charles[1]) was born 9 August 1923 and married Dorothy ____. Children:

1705 i. Debra[8] Jolly, b. 5 Nov 1953.
1706 ii. Edward K.[8] Jolly, Jr. b. 17 Jan 1957.
1707 iii. Benjamin[8] Jolly, b. 25 May 1968.

1128. Suzanne[7] Hannon (Leila[6], Elizabeth Ann[5], Martha Ellen W.[4], Thomas[3], Sarah[2], Charles[1]) married John R. New. Children:

1708 i. Marc[8] New.
1709 ii. Jim[8] New.

1129. Ralph[7] Phillips, Jr. (Margaret[6], Powell H.[5], Martha Ellen W.[4], Thomas[3], Sarah[2], Charles[1]) married, first, Michelle McLennan, and had two children. He

170

married, second, on 18 December 1981, Barbara Blackwood. Children:

    1710 i. Elizabeth Ann[8] Phillips, b. 8 Feb 1968.
    1711 ii. Evelyn Ashley[8] Phillips, b. 18 Dec 1974.

1130. Charles Michael[7] Betenbaugh (Cyril[6], Beaty[5], Martha Ellen W.[4], Thomas[3], Sarah[2], Charles[1]) was born 29 May 1953 and married Laura Frazier. Children:

    1712 i. Michelle[8] Betenbaugh.
    1713 ii. Michael[8] Betenbaugh.
    1714 iii. Andy[8] Betenbaugh.

1159. Fred O.[7] Lawson, Jr. (Catherine[6], Julia A.[5], Katherine[4], George McCrary[3], Mary[2], Charles[1]) married Brenda Brooks. Children:

    1715 i. Stephen Brooks[8] Lawson, b. 14 Feb 1959.
    1716 ii. Julia Catherine[8] Lawson, b. 1 Mar 1960.

1182. Sarah Frances[7] Greer (George Wesley[6], Mattie[5], Rachel Ann[4], George McCrary[3], Mary[2], Charles[1]) was born 28 September 1940 and married on 18 February 1961, James Arnold Brockman (divorced 1970). She married, second, on 8 November 1981, Franklin D. Brown. Children:

    1717 i. William Jeffrey[8] Brockman, b. 18 Aug 1962.
 - 1718 ii. Susan Ann[8] Brockman, b. 16 May 1965.

1183. Joyce Ann[7] Greer (George Wesley[6], Mattie[5], Rachel Ann[4], George McCrary[3], Mary[2], Charles[1]) was born 1 December 1942 and married on 3 June 1960, Robert Eugene Smith. Children:

    1719 i. Cynthia Denise[8] Smith, b. 23 Dec 1961.
    1720 ii. Robert Wesley[8] Smith, b. 27 Oct 1963.

1185. Sandra Faye[7] Greer (George Wesley[6], Mattie[5], Rachel Ann[4], George McCrary[3], Mary[2], Charles[1]) was born 12 September 1946 and married on 12 February 1966, Daniel Conway Burnett (divorced). She married, second, on 4 August 1973, David Lee Cain. Child:

1721 i. Kris Novella[8] Burnett, b. 20 Apr 1970.

1196. Michael Lee[7] Brewington (Mattie Hazel[6], Mattie[5], Rachel Ann[4], George McCrary[3], Mary[2], Charles[1]) was born 16 Feburary 1948 and married Karen Bogan. Children:

1722 i. Michael Lance[8] Brewington, b. 16 Feb 1972.
1723 ii. Mark Allen[8] Brewington, b. 26 May 1974.

1198. Sadie Marie[7] Brewington (Mattie Hazel[6], Mattie[5], Rachel Ann[4], George McCrary[3], Mary[2], Charles[1]) was born 14 August 1959 and married 7 December 1973, Jerry Erwin. Children:

1724 i. Michelle Dawn[8] Erwin, b. 14 Jul 1976.
1725 ii. Jerry Dennis[8] Erwin, b. 14 Mar 1979.
1726 iii. Sharon[8] Erwin, b. 17 Jun 1980.

1202. Rachel Ann[7] Sanders (Pearl[6], Pearl[5], Rachel Ann[4], George McCrary[3], Mary[2], Charles[1]) was born 23 February 1930 in Union, South Carolina, and was married on 25 December 1947, to Paul Henry Smith, who was born 6 July 1928. They live [1984] near Union. Children:

+ 1727 i. Paul Hayward[8] Smith, b. 28 Apr 1951.
  1728 ii. Linda Susan[8] Smith, b. 28 Jun 1953 (twin), m. 6
           Oct 1973, Jackie Edward Parks, b. 14 Sept 1951.
+ 1729 iii. Brenda Kaye[8] Smith, b. 28 Jun 1953 (twin).

1204. John Wallace[7] Sanders (Pearl[6], Pearl[5], Rachel Ann[4], George McCrary[3], Mary[2], Charles[1]) was born 10 February 1937, Union, South Carolina and married on 6 December 1958, Peggy Wood, who was born 7 April 1939. Children:

1730 i. Sabra Renee[8] Sanders, b. 7 Jan 1962.
1731 ii. Kimberly Ann[8] Sanders, b. 22 Nov 1964.
1732 iii. Dana Maria[8] Sanders, b. 17 Sept 1971.

1205. Cornelia Pearl[7] Sanders (Pearl[6], Pearl[5], Rachel Ann[4], George McCrary[3], Mary[2], Charles[1]) was born 9 August 1939 in Union, South Carolina, and married on 21 April 1958, Edward O'Shields, who was born 26 February 1935 in Buffalo, South Carolina. Children:

+ 1733 i. Julie Ann[8] O'Shields, b. 11 Nov 1958.
  1734 ii. Mark Edward[8] O'Shields, b. 19 Jul 1961, m. 22 Sept
         1984, Tammie Lynn Huggins.
  1735 iii. David Lynn[8] O'Shields, b. 9 Aug 1962.

1208. Barry Milton[7] Holcomb (Gary H.[6], Rufus[5], Rachel Ann[4], George McCrary[3], Mary[2], Charles[1]) was born 19 September 1954 in Clinton, South Carolina, and married on 7 August 1977, in Atlanta, Georgia, Margaret Carol Eddings, who was born 4 January 1956. Barry is a graduate of Presbyterian College, and is doing graduate work at Converse College. He is a supervisor at Whitten Center in Clinton, South Carolina. His wife Carol is a secretary, and organist at Broad Street Methodist Church in Clinton. Children:

  1736 i. Nathanael Christopher[8] (Nathan) Holcomb, b. 27 Feb 1980.
  1737 ii. Adria Denise[8] Holcomb, b. 27 May 1983.

1209. Russell Dwight[7] Holcomb (R. T.[6], Rufus[5], Rachel Ann[4], George McCrary[3], Mary[2], Charles[1]) was born 22 January 1947 in Charlotte, North Carolina, married Mary Jane Priest, and they reside in Fresno, California. Children:

  1738 i. Teresa[8] Holcomb, b. 28 Jun 1969.
  1739 ii. Eric[8] Holcomb, b. 11 May 1973.

1235. Michael Dennis[7] Holcombe (Sidney Earl[6], Kennis[5], Rachel Ann[4], George McCrary[3], Mary[2], Charles[1]) married Barbara Phipps. Children:

  1740 i. Jennie Lou[8] Holcombe.
  1741 ii. Teresa[8] Holcombe.

1236. John Lawrence[7] Epps (Sara Frances[6], Kennis[5], Rachel Ann[4], George McCrary[3], Mary[2], Charles[1]) was born 3 June 1943 in Union, South Carolina, and married Sally Edwards, who was born 10 July 1936. Children:

  1742 i. James Bradford[8] (Barry) Epps, b. 10 Sept 1964.
  1743 ii. June Ann[8] Epps, b. 12 May 1967.

1250. Donna June[7] Harvey (Sarah Lou[6], Casey[5], Rachel Ann[4], George McCrary[3], Mary[2], Charles[1]) was born 18 June 1951 and married on 30 July 1971, Jerry Ray Praytor. Children:

Barry Holcomb, Carol (Eddings) Holcomb, Nathan and Adria

1984

1744 i. Jeremy Lee[8] Praytor, b. 22 Jan 1972.
1745 ii. Jason Ray[8] Praytor, b. 3 May 1974.

1251. Kathy Jean[7] Harvey (Sarah Lou[6], Casey[5], Rachel Ann[4], George McCrary[3], Mary[2], Charles[1]) was born 7 May 1973 and married on 13 June 1970, Herbert George Burkhalter, Jr. Children:

1745 i. Matthew Jay[8] Burkhalter, b. 19 May 1973.
1746 ii. Tracy Heather[8] Burkbalter, b. 18 Nov 1975.

1252. Lou Ann[7] Harvey (Sarah Lou[6], Casey[5], Rachel Ann[4], George McCrary[3], Mary[2], Charles[1]) was born 1 February 1955 and married 20 September 1973, Roger Clay Wagoner. Children:

1748 i. Eric Roger[8] Wagoner, b. 16 Mar 1975.
1749 ii. Cynthia Diane[8] Wagoner, b. 31 May 1978.

1253. Karen Virginia[7] Harvey (Sarah Lou[6], Casey[5], Rachel Ann[4], George McCrary[3], Mary[2], Charles[1]) was born 15 December 1957 and married on 14 October 1975, Larry Dean Billings. Children:

1750 i. Kristina Jolene[8] Billings, b. 30 Oct 1975.
1751 ii. Russell Eugene[8] Billings, b. 15 November 1977.

1259. Elizabeth[7] Austin (Helen[6], Thomas[5], Rachel Ann[4], George McCrary[3], Mary[2], Cbarles[1]) was born 30 January 1938 and married Lamar A. Miller. Children:

1752 i. Mark Edward[8] Miller, b. 7 Aug 1959, Union Co., SC.
1753 ii. Samuel Thomas[8] Miller, b. 2 Sept 1962, Griffin, GA.

1260. Patricia Ann[7] Austin (Helen[6], Thomas[5], Rachel Ann[4], George McCrary[3], Mary[2], Charles[1]) was born 3 January 1942 and married Kenneth H. Kingsmore. Child:

1754 Scott Ashley[8] Kingsmore, b. 29 Mar 1969, Del Rio, TX.

1268. Billie Allen[7] Palmer (Martha[6], Sidney[5], Rachel Ann[4], George McCrary[3], Mary[2], Charles[1]) married Kathy O'Shields. Children:

1755 i. Christopher Allen^8 Palmer.
1756 ii. Misty Gale^8 Palmer.

1269. Jerry Wayne^7 Palmer (Martha^6, Sidney^5, Rachel Ann^4, George McCrary^3, Mary^2, Charles^1) married Ann Richburg. Child:

1757 i. William Clayton^8 Palmer.

1275. Stanley^7 Jolly (J. C.^{6}, Grace^5, Conquest^4, George McCrary^3, Mary^2, Charles^1) married Rita Lowry. Children:

1758 i. Joseph Stanton^8 Jolly.
1759 ii. Amy^8 Jolly.
1760 iii. Lee^8 Jolly.

1283. Ben^7 Jolly (Ben^6, Mattie Irene^5, Jackson^4, George McCrary^3, Mary^2, Charles^1) married Barbara Ann Vaughan. Child:

1761 i. Sandy^8 Jolly.

1288. Debbie^7 Jolly (Ralph^6, Mattie Irene^5, Jackson^4, George McCrary^3, Mary^2, Charles^1) married Gene Schmidt. Children:

1762 i. Ericka^8 Schmidt.
1763 ii. Katie^8 Schmidt.

1302. Peggy Lynn^7 Quinn (Peggy^6, Ernest Arthur^5, Jackson^4, George McCrary^3, Mary^2, Charles^1) married Sammy Hicks Summer. Child:

1764 i. Sammy Lynne^8 Summer.

1305. Connie^7 Young (Ernest Arthur^6, Ernest Arthur^5, Jackson^4, George McCrary^3, Mary^2, Charles^1) married Jim Rieves, Houston, Texas. Child:

1765 i. Jami^8 Rieves.

1306. Carol^7 Bailey (James^6, Ethel^5, Robert^4, George McCrary^3, Mary^2, Charles^1) married Darrell Pack. Children:

1766 i. Darrell^8 Pack.
1767 ii. Caroline^8 Pack.
1768 iii. James Bolt^8 Pack.

1307. Karen^7 Bailey (James^6, Ethel^5, Robert^4, George McCrary^3, Mary^2, Charles^1) married Roy Stanley Gallman. Child:

1769 i. Brandi^8 Gallman.

1311. Margaret^7 Bailey (Fred Richard^6, Ethel^5, Robert^4, George McCrary^3, Mary^2, Charles^1) married Herman Donald^7 Betenbaugh, #1531, (Herman^6, James Sanders^5, Susan Fair^4, Katherine^3, William^2, Charles^1) who was born 14 November 1948. Children:

1770 i. Donald Richard^8 Betenbaugh, b. 23 Apr 1968.
1771 ii. Donna Sue^8 Betenbaugh, b. 23 Jan 1970.
1772 iii. Kimbrely Dawn^8 Betenbaugh, b. 13 Sept 1979.

1312. Marvin^7 Bailey (Fred Richard^6, Ethel^5, Robert^4, George McCrary^3, Mary^2, Charles^1) married Toni _____. Children:

1773 i. Leslie^8 Bailey.
1774 ii. Joelle^8 Bailey.

1313. Sue^7 Bailey (Fred Richard^6, Ethel^5, Robert^4, George McCrary^3, Mary^2, Charles^1) married Joe Adams. Children:

1775 i. Michael^8 Adams.
1776 ii. Michelle^8 Adams.
1777 iii. Paul^8 Adams.

1315. Terry^7 Trakas (Louise^6, Ethel^5, Robert^4, George McCrary^3, Mary^2, Charles^1) married first William Thomas Stover, second Ronald Johnson. Children:

1778 i. Brooks^8 Stover.
1779 ii. Kyle^8 Stover.

1317. James^7 Nelson (Frances^6, Ethel^5, Robert^4, George McCrary^3, Mary^2, Charles^1) married Peggy _____. Children:

1780 i. Michelle[8] Nelson.
1781 ii. Dolly[8] Nelson.

1322. Pennie[7] Sanders (Ann[6], Ethel[5], Robert[4], George McCrary[3], Mary[2], Charles[1]) married Anthony Duckett. Child:

1782 i. Tiffany[8] Duckett.

1344. James Louis[7] Gilliam, Jr. (James Louis[6], Sarah Frances[5], James Christopher[4], Sarah[3], Mary[2], Charles[1]) was born in Union, South Carolina, married Elizabeth Frey, of Lynchburg, Virginia. Children:

1783 i. James Louis[8] Gilliam, III.
1784 ii. Thomas Conrad[8] Gilliam.
1785 iii. Ann Elizabeth[8] Gilliam.

1345. Eleanor Frances[7] Gilliam (James Louis[6], Sarah Frances[5], James Christopher[4], Sarah[3], Mary[2], Charles[1]) was born in Union, South Carolina, married Samuel Edgar Anderson. Children:

+ 1786 i. Jean Salley[8] Anderson.
  1787 ii. Elizabeth Reid[8] Anderson.

1346. Eugene Fant[7] Gilliam (James Louis[6], Sarah Frances[5], James Christopher[4], Sarah[3], Mary[2], Charles[1]) was born in Spartanburg, South Carolina, married Bernice Stanton, of Florence, South Carolina, and lived in Columbia, South Carolina. He was Vice-President of the Old Charleston Insurance Company.

1347. June Gilliam[7] Oakley (Lillian Zena[6], Sarah Frances[5], James Christopher[4], Sarah[3], Mary[2], Charles[1]) married Claude Earle Thomas, and they live in Waco, Texas. Children:

1788 i. Christopher Lee[8] Oakley.
1789 ii. Matthew Earle[8] Oakley.
1790 iii. Andrew Beauregard[8] Oakley.

1348. Lucy Fant[7] Gilliam (David Fant[6], Sarah Frances[5], James Christopher[4], Sarah[3], Mary[2], Charles[1]) married David W. Mauterer, of Columbia, South Carolina. Children:

1791 i. Elizabeth Shadduck[8] Mauterer.
1792 ii. Graham Warren[8] Mauterer.

1349. Robert Cyrus[7] Williams, Jr. (Dr.) (Rachel Sartor[6], Sarah Frances[5], James Christopher[4], Sarah[3], Mary[2], Charles[1]) was born 26 September 1945 and married on 9 June 1968, Patricia Diane Hammill. They reside [1984] in Hickory, North Carolina. Child:

1793 i. Amy Caroline[8] Williams, b. 17 Nov 1974.

1350. Jane Fant[7] Lancaster (Ruth Cornelia[6], Sarah Frances[5], James Christopher[4], Sarah[3], Mary[2], Charles[1]) was born 17 July 1941 in Spartanburg, South Carolina, and married on 6 November 1965, Donald Louis Boney, who was born 27 June 1940 in Fitzgerald, Georgia. They reside [1984] in Atlanta, Georgia. Children:

1794 i. Sarah Poole[8] Boney, b. 1 Aug 1970, Atlanta, GA.
1795 ii. John Thomas[8] Boney, b. 11 Jun 1973, Decatur, GA.

1351. William Poole[7] Lancaster (Ruth Cornelia[6], Sarah Frances[5], James Christopher[4], Sarah[3], Mary[2], Charles[1]) married Martha Ann Crockett, of Bluefield, West Virginia, and resides in Charleston, South Carolina, where he is Associate Minister of First (Scots) Presbyterian Church.

1355. James Gilmore[7] Butler, Jr. (Edith[6], Edith[5], Emma[4], Sarah[3], Mary[2], Charles[1]) has one child:

1796 i. James Gilmore[8] Butler, III.

1359. Philip Dunn[7] Flynn, III (Philip Dunn[6], Edith[5], Emma[4], Sarah[3], Mary[2], Charles[1]) has three children:

1797 i. Philip Dunn[8] Flynn, IV.
1798 ii. Sean[8] Flynn.
1799 iii. Lauren[8] Flynn.

1366. Anita[7] Gregory (Grover[6], Sarah Ellen[5], Adelade[4], John Thomas[3], William[2], Charles[1]) was born 16 December 1914 and married on 6 March 1936, Clarence Berry Sanders. They live [1984] in Union, South Carolina. Children:

+ 1800 i. Donald Ray[8] Sanders, b. 1 Jun 1937.
+ 1801 ii. Mary Ann[8] Sanders, b. 4 Mar 1939.

1369. Claude Cleveland[7] Gregory (Grover[6], Sarah Ellen[5], Adelade[4], John Thomas[3], William[2], Charles[1]) was born 6 December 1921 and married Virginia May. Children:

1802 i. Claude Cleveland[8] Gregory, Jr., b. 11 Mar 1962.
1803 ii. Debra Jean[8] Gregory, b. 29 Jun 1966, m. 1984, Chester Duty.

1371. John Wilson[7] Gregory (Grover[6], Sarah Ellen[5], Adelade[4], John Thomas[3], William[2], Charles[1]) was born 29 November 1934 and married Joann Hartle. They adopted one child:

1804 John Richard[8] (Ricky) Gregory, b. 19 May 1975.

1372. Charlotte Elizabeth[7] Gregory (Eugene[6], Sarah Ellen[5], Adelade[4], John Thomas[3], William[2], Charles[1]) was born 17 May 1911 and married Carl Lanier. Children:

1805 i. Malcolm Keith[8] Lanier, b. 19 Dec 1937.
1806 ii. Martha Jean[8] Lanier, b. 13 Mar 1945.

1373. Rachel[7] Gregory (Eugene[6], Sarah Ellen[5], Adelade[4], John Thomas[3], William[2], Charles[1]) was born 21 May 1916 and married Charles Homer Prevost. Children:

1807 i. Sylvia Sue[8] Prevost, b. 12 Mar 1937, m. Ellis Brinson.
1808 ii. Brenda LaLane[8] Prevost, b. 22 Jun 1940, m. D. T. Myers.
1809 iii. Charles Gregory[8] Prevost, b. 23 Jun 1942, m. Judy Green.

1374. Joseph Loyd[7] Gregory (Eugene[6], Sarah Ellen[5], Adelade[4], John Thomas[3], William[2], Charles[1]) was born 4 September 1918 and married Otha Elnore Ellege. Children:

1810 i. Wayne Ray[8] Gregory, b. 25 Nov 1940.
1811 ii. Alma Joyce[8] Gregory, b. 29 Jan 1950.
1812 iii. Jerry Lee[8] Gregory, b. 23 Aug 1956.

1375. Leland Cozine[7] Gregory (Eugene[6], Sarah Ellen[5], Adelade[4], John Thomas[3], William[2], Charles[1]) was born 28 March 1920 and married Triva Inez Swalm, who was born 8 June 1916. Children:

1813　i. Barbara Jean[8] Gregory, b. 15 Nov 1939, m. E. T. Collins.
1814　ii. Donna Kay[8] Gregory, b. 22 Dec 1946, m. John David Harper.

1387. Richard Thomas[7] Greer (Robert Christopher[6], Louisa[5], Adelade[4], John Thomas[3], William[2], Charles[1]) was born 7 February 1932, in Washington, D. C., and married on 10 November 1951, Betty Louise Girton. One child:

+ 1815　Richard Thomas[8] Greer, Jr., b. 10 Aug 1953.

1393. Hazel[7] Willard (John[6], Jackson Lee[5], Adelade[4], John Thomas[3], William[2], Charles[1]) married William B. Shank. Children:

1816　i. William B.[8] Shank, Jr.
1817　ii. John Calvin[8] Shank.
1818　iii. Sharon Leigh[8] Shank.

1394. Sarah Willard[7] (Sally) Glenn (Sara Lee[6], Jackson Lee[5], Adelade[4], John Thomas[3], William[2], Charles[1]) was born in 1941 and married Kenneth Woodard. Child:

1819　i. Christina[8] Woodard.

1395. William David[7] (Billy) Glenn (Sara Lee[6], Jackson Lee[5], Adelade[4], John Thomas[3], William[2], Charles[1]) married Kay Caldwell. Children:

1820　i. William Jayson[8] Glenn.
1821　ii. David Graig[8] Glenn.

1397. Ed[7] Whisenant, Jr. (Ed[6], Belle[5], Sarah[4], John Thomas[3], William[2], Charles[1]) married Sylvia McAbee. Children:

1822　i. Eddie[8] Whisenant.
1823　ii. Mark[8] Whisenant.

1399. Isabelle[7] Whisenant (Ed[6], Belle[5], Sarah[4], John Thomas[3], William[2], Charles[1]) married David Dempsey. Children:

1824 i. David^8 Dempsey.
1825 ii. Susie^8 Dempsey.
1826 iii. Julia^8 Dempsey.
1827 iv. Cynthia^8 Dempsey.

1400. Lena Lucille^7 Greer (Sally^6, Bernice^5, Sarah^4, John Thomas^3, William^2, Charles^1) was born 25 December 1910 in Union County, South Carolina, and married on 22 February 1930, Fred Wallace Ivey, who was born 29 June 1907 in Union County. Children:

+ 1828 i. Mary Jeanette^8 Ivey, b. 9 Feb 1931.
  1829 ii. Margaret Salley^8 Ivey, b. & d. 12 Oct 1938.
+ 1830 iii. James Wallace^8 Ivey, b. 18 Nov 1940.

1405. Nina Louise^7 Greer (Sally^6, Bernice^5, Sarah^4, John Thomas^3, William^2, Charles^1) was born 16 October 1918 in Union County, South Carolina, and married Charles William Wilson, who was born 31 July 1923. Children:

+ 1831 i. Charles William^8 Wilson, Jr., b. 9 Jul 1952.
  1832 ii. James Greer^8 Wilson, b. 16 Sept 1953.
+ 1833 iii. Beth Marlene^8 Wilson, b. 14 Oct 1956.

1411. James Lewis^7 Edwards (Lewis^6, Bernice^5, Sarah^4, John Thomas^3, William^2, Charles^1) was born 24 December 1941 in Rock Hill, South Carolina, and married on 24 July 1965, Anne Elizabeth Reed, who was born 12 June 1944 in Columbia, South Carolina. They live in Clinton, South Carolina, where James L. Edwards is an attorney. Children:

1834 i. Rebecca Lynn^8 Edwards, b. 19 May 1967, Offutt AFB,
        Douglas, NE.
1835 ii. Lewis Reed^8 Edwards, b. 7 May 1972, Greenwood, SC.
1836 iii. James Todd^8 Edwards, b. 15 Jan 1975, Greenwood, SC.
1837 iv. Suzanne Steele^8 Edwards, b. 23 Jun 1978, Greenwood, SC.

1412. Margaret Ann^7 McDaniel (Robert Monroe^6, Robert Lee^5, Medora^4, John Thomas^3, William^2, Charles^1) married John Fouche Brownlaw, III. Children:

1838 i. John Fouche^8 Brownlaw, IV.
1839 ii. Robert McDaniel^8 Brownlaw.
1840 iii. Walter Edward^8 Brownlaw.

1413. Janet Elizabeth[7] McDaniel (Robert Monroe[6], Robert Lee[5], Medora[4], John Thomas[3], William[2], Charles[1]) married Paul Schurr. Children:

    1841 i. Susan McDaniel[8] Schurr.
    1842 ii. Jaime Elizabeth[8] Schurr.
    1843 iii. Paul Benjamin[8] Schurr.

1414. Rebecca Maclyn[7] McDaniel (Robert Monroe[6], Robert Lee[5], Medora[4], John Thomas[3], William[2], Charles[1]) married Mayon Weeks. Children:

    1844 i. Justin Jerome[8] Weeks.
    1845 ii. Jason Monroe[8] Weeks.
    1846 iii. Joshua McDaniel[8] Weeks.
    1847 iv. Jeffery Kennon[8] Weeks.

1415. Rubye Eileen[7] Bradburn (Ida Florence[6], Lucy Smith[5], Medora[4], John Thomas[3], William[2], Charles[1]) was born 3 October 1919 in Union County, South Carolina, married on 4 July 1941, Lee Paul Nabors, who was born 8 January 1915 in Union County. Children:

+ 1848 i. Larraine Paula[8] Nabors, b. 29 Apr 1945.
- 1849 ii. Pamela[8] Nabors, b. 10 Nov 1951.

1417. Hay Fant[7] Bradburn (Ida Florence[6], Lucy Smith[5], Medora[4], John Thomas[3], William[2], Charles[1]) was born 22 October 1921 in Union, South Carolina, and married on 19 June 1948 in Hernando, Mississippi, Vivian Johnson, who was born 27 February 1921 in White County, Arkansas. Children:

    1850 i. James William[8] Bradburn, b. 21 Aug 1951, Bay Co., FL.,
            m. 4 Oct 1980, Kathleen Andrew.
    1851 ii. Janet[8] Bradburn, b. 27 Sept 1953, Lowndes Co., GA.

1420. Catherine[7] Cromer (Annie Estelle[6], Lucy Smith[5], Medora[4], John Thomas[3], William[2], Charles[1]) married L. R. Frost. Children:

+ 1852 i. Lewis[8] Frost.
    1853 ii. Lindsey[8] Frost.
    1854 iii. Elsie[8] Frost.

1427. Mary Ann[7] Hughes (Helen Ruth[6], Mary Ann[5], Medora[4], John Thomas[3], William[2], Charles[1]) was born in 1942 and married Charles E. Fox. Children:

    1855 i. Mary Elizabeth[8] Fox, b. Aug 1970.
    1856 ii. Caroline Helen[8] Fox, b. 23 Dec 1973.

1430. Wylie Bailey[7] Humphries (Jack Wylie[6], Evelyn Frances[5], John Wylie[4], John Thomas[3], William[2], Charles[1]) was born 8 July 1934 and married on 7 February 1958, Patricia Ann Thompson, who was born 20 July 1936. Children:

    1857 i. James King[8] Humphries, b. 19 Dec 1958.
    1858 ii. Thomas Wylie[8] Humphries, b. 16 Jan 1961.
    1859 iii. Alan Patrick[8] Humphries, b. 17 Jun 1963.
    1360 iv. David Anthony[8] Humphries, b. 12 Apr 1968.

1432. Sherrelle Clyde[7] Humphries (Jack Wylie[6], Evelyn Frances[5], John Wylie[4], John Thomas[3], William[2], Charles[1]) was born 31 May 1938 and married on 21 February 1959, Henry A. Revell, who was born 17 January 1936. Children:

    1861 i. Celeste Aleen[8] Revell, b. 5 Oct 1963.
    1862 ii. Jack Alfred[8] Revell, b. 9 Jun 1968.

1434. William Edward[7] Kirven (Roy Humphries[6], Olive[5], John Wylie[4], John Thomas[3], William[2], Charles[1]) was born 5 September 1942 and married Bettye M. _____, who was born 21 September 1945. Child:

    1863 i. Kelly M.[8] Kirven, b. 29 Jun 1972.

1435. Elizabeth Ann[7] Kirven (Roy Humphries[6], Olive[5], John Wylie[4], John Thomas[3], William[2], Charles[1]) was born 8 July 1945 and married on 19 January 1969, Jim Boggs. Child:

    1864 i. Lesley D.[8] Boggs, b. 19 Nov 1971.

1438. Edward Earl[7] Pilkington (Edith Mae[6], Olive[5], John Wylie[4], John Thomas[3], William[2], Charles[1]) married Karen _____. Children:

    1865 i. Scott[8] Pilkington.
    1866 ii. Gregory[8] Pilkington.

1439. George Montgomery[7] (Monty) Pilkington (Edith Mae[6], Olive[5], John Wylie[4], John Thomas[3], William[2], Charles[1]) married Sonie _____. Children:

    1867 i. Monica[8] Pilkington.
    1868 ii. Keith[8] Pilkington.

1440. Betty Lou[7] Pilkington (Edith Mae[6], Olive[5], John Wylie[4], John Thomas[3], William[2], Charles[1]) married Larry Willis. Children:

    1869 i. Duane[8] Willis.
    1870 ii. Lori[8] Willis.

1441. Robert Randolph[7] Price (Frances[6], Robert Ray[5], John Wylie[4], John Thomas[3], William[2], Charles[1]) was born 25 August 1949 and married on 11 July 1981, Virginia Norman Neb, who was born 20 April 1950, daughter of Logan B. Neb and Edna Lee (Roberts) Neb of Louisville, Kentucky. Child:

    1871 i. Mark Hampton[8] Price, b. 16 May 1984, Raleigh, NC.

1443. Albert Copeland[7] Smarr (Elizabeth[6], Bessie[5], John Wylie[4], John Thomas[3], William[2], Charles[1]) was born 4 September 1940 and married on 25 May 1974, Lois Shirer. Children:

    1872 i. Emily Elizabeth[8] Smarr, b. 25 May 1977.
    1873 ii. Carolyn Marie[8] Smarr, b. 30 Jun 1979.

1444. Ronald Taylor[7] Smarr (Elizabeth[6], Bessie[5], John Wylie[4], John Thomas[3], William[2], Charles[1]) was born 7 April 1942 and married on 7 April 1961, Kay Henderson. He married, second, on 10 January 1964, Alvena Miller. Children:

    1874 i. Kevin Dale[8] Smarr, b. 3 Jan 1962.
    1875 ii. Ronald Taylor[8] Smarr Jr., b. 8 Nov 1968.
    1876 iii. Tressa Elizabeth[8] Smarr, b. 6 Mar 1971.

1445. Kaye Kelly[7] Taylor (Harry Ray[6], Bessie[5], John Wylie[4], John Thomas[3], William[2], Charles[1]) was born 19 July 1942 and married on 16 August 1964, Donald House. Children:

1877 i. Andrew Ray^8 House, b. 6 Jan 1967.
1878 ii. Jeffrey Tate^8 House, b. 7 Feb 1969.
1879 iii. Leigh Taylor^8 House, b. 6 May 1973.
1880 iv. Amy Kaye^8 House, b. 15 Jun 1977.

1446. Sara Ann^7 Taylor (Harry Ray^6, Bessie^5, John Wylie^4, John Thomas^3, William^2, Charles^1) was born 20 April 1947 and married on 4 April 1971, Keane La Fontain. Children:

1881 i. Mark Keane^8 La Fontain, b. 17 May 1974.
1882 ii. Kevin Taylor^8 La Fontain, b. 7 Nov 1977.

1448. Margaret Ann^7 Taylor (William Marion^6, Bessie^5, John Wylie^4, John Thomas^3, William^2, Charles^1) was born 1 January 1951 and married on 24 June 1973, Hugh Tolan Bailey. Children:

1883 i. Brenton Hugh^8 Bailey, b. 24 Dec 1977.
1884 ii. Kristen Taylor^8 Bailey, b. 18 Aug 1980.
1885 iii. Vance Marion^8 Bailey, b. 21 Jan 1982.

1452. Robert Henry^7 Garrett (Frances Alberta^6, Bessie^5, John Wylie^4, John Thomas^3, William^2, Charles^1) was born 11 June 1939 and married on 5 November 1961, Judy Poplin. Child:

1886 i. Deborah Kaye^8 Garrett, b. 10 Aug 1962.

1453. Francis Taylor^7 Garrett (Frances Alberta^6, Bessie^5, John Wylie^4, John Thomas^3, William^2, Charles^1) was born 13 March 1943 and married on 12 June 1966, Mary Ella Ross. Children:

1887 i. Timothy Taylor^8 Garrett, b. 17 Feb 1968.
1888 ii. Robin Ross^8 Garrett, b. 27 Nov 1970.

1454. Janice Othella^7 Garrett (Frances Alberta^6, Bessie^5, John Wylie^4, John Thomas^3, William^2, Charles^1) was born 4 October 1946 and married on 29 August 1965, Tommy Messex. Children:

1889 i. Tommy Derrick^8 Messex, b. 12 Nov 1966.
1890 ii. Travis Garrett^8 Messex, b. 26 Mar 1970.
1891 iii. Wramie Frances^8 Messex, b. 14 March 1974.

1456. Ben Jefferson[7] Stackhouse (Martha Victoria[6], Bessie[5], John Wylie[4], John Thomas[3], William[2], Charles[1]) was born 8 June 1952 and married on 8 February 1975, Mary Lou Bulger. Child:

1892 i. Autumn Leigh[8] Stackhouse, b. 9 Feb 1977.

1457. Martha Beth[7] Wilson (Mary Lenora[6], Bessie[5], John Wylie[4], John Thomas[3], William[2], Charles[1]) was born 13 May 1939 and married 20 September 1960, Peter John Stathakos. They adopted one child:

1893 i. Andrew Peter[8] Stathakos, b. 29 Sept 1972.

1458. Marion Lynda[7] Wilson (Mary Lenora[6], Bessie[5], John Wylie[4], John Thomas[3], William[2], Charles[1]) was born 13 July 1942 and married on 24 June 1962, Wayne Hobson Munn. Child:

1894 i. Monica Wilson[8] Munn, b. 20 Jun 1969.

1459. Doris Susan[7] Henderson (Doris Ruth[6], Bessie[5], John Wylie[4], John Thomas[3], William[2], Charles[1]) was born 5 August 1953 and married Thurmond Duke. Children:

1895 i. Elizabeth Grace[8] Duke, b. 28 Apr 1979.
1896 ii. Benjamin Scott[8] Duke, b. 28 Jun 1982.

1502. Coline Elizabeth[7] Simmons (Myrtle[6], Coline[5], Frances Catherine[4], Mary E.[3], William[2], Charles[1]) was born 15 June 1929 in St. Louis, Missouri, and married on 11 August 1956, Barnwell Rhett Chamberlain, Jr., who was born 10 April 1930 in Charlotte, North Carolina. Coline received the AB degree from Wellesley College, 1951, AM, University of Michigan, 1955, and Ph. D., from UNC Chapel Hill, 1979. Barnwell Rhett Chamberlain Jr., holds an AB from Duke University, 1955, and is with the Employment Security Commission, in Raleigh, North Carolina. They reside in Durham, North Carolina. Child:

1897 i. Edwin Rhett[8] Chamberlain, b. 20 Jan 1959, Charlotte, NC.

1503. Jane Larkin[7] Outz (Frances[6], Joseph Eugene[5], Frances Catherine[4], Mary E.[3], William[2], Charles[1]) was born 24 September 1943 in Union, South Carolina, and married on 20 May 1970 in Laurens, South Carolina, James Hoke Askew, who was born 29 March 1943 in Chipley (now Pine Mountain), Georgia. Children:

    1898 i. Joy Larkin[8] Askew, b. 8 Dec 1971, LaGrange, GA.
    1899 ii. Julie Elizabeth[8] Askew, b. 7 Jul 1974, LaGrange, GA.
    1900 iii. Nancy Jane[8] Askew, b. 29 Jun 1976, LaGrange, GA.

1504. Laura Rebecca[7] Outz (Frances[6], Joseph Eugene[5], Frances Catherine[4], Mary E.[3], William[2], Charles[1]) was born 17 March 1954 in Seneca, South Carolina, and married on 26 July 1975 in Laurens, South Carolina, Duane Dennie, who was born 29 June 1953 in Landstuhl, Germany. Child:

    1901 i. Laura Elizabeth[8] Dennie, b. 13 Jun 1980, Columbia, SC.

1505. Jean Ferguson[7] Edwards (Joseph Eugene[6], Joseph Eugene[5], Frances Catherine[4], Mary E.[3], William[2], Charles[1]) was born 29 March 1945 in Union, South Carolina, and married on 4 September 1965, Jerry Ralph Byrd, who was born 30 May 1943 in Greenville, South Carolina. Children:

    1902 i. Christy Michelle[8] Byrd, b. 12 Mar 1973, Greenville, SC.
    1903 ii. Melissa Edwards[8] Byrd, b. 30 Sept 1974, Greenville, SC.

1506. Martha Ellen[7] Edwards (Joseph Eugene[6], Joseph Eugene[5], Frances Catherine[4], Mary E.[3], William[2], Charles[1]) was born 15 March 1948 in Union, South Carolina, married, first, Gerald O. Gault (divorced); she married, second, on 28 June 1974, Joel Ringgold Stegall, who was born 7 April 1939 in Hertford, North Carolina. Children:

    1904 i. Jennifer Lake[8] Gault, b. 29 Mar 1970, Asheville, NC.
    1905 ii. Tamara Lynn[8] Gault, b. 31 Aug 1971, Asheville, NC.

1508. Susan Lake[7] Edwards (Joseph Eugene[6], Joseph Eugene[5], Frances Catherine[4], Mary E.[3], William[2], Charles[1]) was born 11 February 1954 in Union, South Carolina, and married on 10 May 1975, to Theron Donald Duncan, who was born 12 September 1955 in Union. Children:

1906 i. Joseph Trakas[8] Duncan, b. 10 Jan 1980, Spartanburg, SC.
1907 ii. Reggie Wilson[8] Duncan, b. 2 Apr 1981, Spartanburg, SC.

1514. Ellen Simpson[7] McMaster (Frances[6], Leila[5], Frances Catherine[4], Mary E.[3], William[2], Charles[1]) was born 15 February 1946 in Clinton, South Carolina, and married on 29 June 1968 in Winnsboro, South Carolina, Dr. John Vinson Nicholson, Jr., who was born 7 March 1945 in Winnsboro. She is a music teacher in Winnsboro, and organist-choir director at St. John's Episcopal Church in Winnsboro. Children:

1908 i. Elliott McMaster[8] Nicholson, b. 21 Sept 1972, Charleston, SC.
1909 ii. John Palmer[8] Nicholson, b. 19 Jun 1976, Columbia, SC.

1518. Lindsey Clore[7] Honeycutt, Jr. (Joyce Elizabeth[6], John S.[5], John[4], Charles H.[3], William[2], Charles[1]) was born 21 October 1933 in Tyler, Texas, and married on 15 July 1967 in Kansas City, Missouri, Glenda Jean James, who was born 18 January 1945 in Jackson, Missouri. Children:

1910 i. Jacqueline Louise[8] Honeycutt, b. 1 Feb 1971, Kansas City, MO.
1911 ii. Jennifer Lynn[8] Honeycutt, b. 1 Oct 1975, Kansas City, MO.

1519. Paul Heyward[7] Burgess, Jr. (Paul[6], Lawrence[5], Frances[4], Katherine[3], William[2], Charles[1]) married Phyllis Kelly. and is employed at Whitten Center in Clinton, South Carolina. Child:

1912 i. Paul Heyward[8] Burgess, III.

1520. James D.[7] (Jimmy) Bass (Cleo[6], Joseph[5], Frances[4], Katherine[3], William[2], Charles[1]) married Betty Pace. Child:

1913 i. Brett[8] Bass.

1521. Susan[7] Brown (LaVerne[6], Joseph[5], Frances[4], Katherine[3], William[2], Charles[1]) married Reed Hoke. Children:

1914 i. Cindy[8] Hoke.
1915 ii. John Thomas[8] Hoke.

1527. Jean^7 Welch (Jeannette^6, Della^5, Susan Fair^4, Katherine^3, William^2, Charles^1) married Whit Plowden. Children:

   1916 i. Cynthia Jean^8 Plowden, m. _____ Goldberg.
+ 1917 ii. Richard W.^{8} Plowden.
   1918 iii. Gerald W.^{8} (Jerry) Plowden.

1528. James Sanders^7 Betenbaugh, II (Herman^6, James Sanders^5, Susan Fair^4, Katherine^3, William^2, Charles^1) was born 24 July 1938 and married first, Jackie Garrison; he married second, Judy _____. Children:

   1919 i. James Sanders^8 Betenbaugh, III, b. 17 Sept 1958.
   1920 ii. Lisa^8 Betenbaugh, b. Aug 1959.
   1921 iii. Carl Alyin^8 Betenbaugh, b. Apr 1961.
   1922 iv. Michael^8 Betenbaugh, b. Sept 1963.
   1923 v. Adam^8 Betenbaugh (twin), b. Sept 1975.
   1924 vi. Jennifer^8 Betenbaugh (twin), b. Sept. 1975.
   1925 vii. Kirkland^8 Betenbaugh, b. Oct 1980 (by Judy).

1529. Patricia Ann^7 Betenbaugh (Herman^6, James Sanders^5, Susan Fair^4, Katherine^3, William^2, Charles^1) was born 9 August 1939 and married Carol E. Sanders, who was born 30 May 1940. Children:

+ 1926 i. Kathryn Diane^8 Sanders, b. 14 Nov 1958.
   1927 ii. Carol E.^{8} Sanders, Jr., b. 9 Oct 1961.
   1928 iii. Kenneth Wayne^8 Sanders, b. 5 Jun 1964.

1530. William Douglas^7 Betenbaugh (Herman^6, James Sanders^5, Susan Fair^4, Katherine^3, William^2, Charles^1) was born 23 July 1941 and married Eunice Fulbright. Children:

   1929 i. Carolyn Teresa^8 Betenbaugh, b. 15 Sept 1964.
   1930 ii. William Douglas^8 Betenbaugh, b. 11 Dec 1967.

1534. John Roper^7 Betenbaugh (Herman^6, James Sanders^5, Susan Fair^4, Katherine^3, William^2, Charles^1) was born 20 December 1951 and married Wanda Payne. Children:

   1931 i. Misty Michelle^8 Betenbaugh, b. 5 Jul 1974.
   1932 ii. John Michael^8 Betenbaugh, b. 23 Feb 1979.

1535. David Robin[7] Betenbaugh (Herman[6], James Sanders[5], Susan Fair[4], Katherine[3], William[2], Charles[1]) was born 22 August 1953 and married Mary Lee West. Children:

1933 i. David Robin[8] Betenbaugh, Jr., b. 26 Apr 1971.
1934 ii. Cynthia Lynn[8] Betenbaugh, b. 4 Sept 1972.

1542. Helen Tate[7] Bradley (Helen Ruth[6], Humphries[5], Janie[4], Katherine[3], William[2], Charles[1]) was born 3 December 1946 and married in Union, South Carolina, on 4 August 1972, Dr. Louis Dean Majette. Children:

1935 i. Bradley Lynn[8] Majette, b. 26 Jul 1975.
1936 ii. Helen Claire[8] Majette, b. 24 Apr 1980.
1937 iii. John Fox[8] Majette, b. 28 Jun 1983.

1544. Gaynelle[7] Wilson (Herbert Earl[6], Letitia Mary Jane[5], Elizabeth Levenia[4], Charles G. W.[3], Thomas[2], Charles[1]) was born 16 October 1919 in Columbia, South Carolina, and married Ralph Cuthbertson. Children:

1938 i. Herbert[8] Cuthbertson.
1939 ii. Ralph[8] Cuthbertson, Jr.
1940 iii. Anna Beth[8] Cuthbertson.
1941 iv. Gaynelle[8] Cuthbertson.

1545. Jean Lindler[7] Wilson (Herbert Earl[6], Letitia Mary Jane[5], Elizabeth Levenia[4], Charles G. W.[3], Thomas[2], Charles[1]) was born 5 October 1953 in Columbia, South Carolina, and married Richard Lee Brockington. Children:

1942 i. Richard Alan[8] Brockington (twin).
1943 ii. Rion Lee[8] Brockington (twin).

1547. Joseph Franklin[7] Wright, Jr. (Mary Elizabeth[6], Letitia Mary Jane[5], Elizabeth Levenia[4], Charles G. W.[3], Thomas[2], Charles[1]) was born 9 March 1920 in Darlington, South Carolina, and married on 23 December 1941, Alicia Valeria Young, who was born 28 March 1921 in Columbia, South Carolina. Children:

1944 i. Alicia Anne[8] Wright, b. 7 Aug 1947, Sanford, NC, m. 10 May 1969, William Hooper Holt.
1945 ii. Debra Dale[8] Wright, b. 24 Aug 1952, Sanford, NC, m. 25 Jul 1977, Melvine Alan Roberson.

1548. Mary Doris[7] Wright (Mary Elizabeth[6], Letitia Mary Jane[5], Elizabeth Levenia[4], Charles G. W.[3], Thomas[2], Charles[1]) was born 25 July 1922 in Darlington, South Carolina, and married on 23 July 1942 at Rockingham, North Carolina, James Eldred Edwards, who was born 18 February 1919 in Cordova, North Carolina. Children:

+ 1946 i. Jerry Lynn[8] Edwards, b. 11 Jul 1943, Corpus Christi, TX.
+ 1947 ii. Daniel Bryan[8] Edwards, b. 21 Aug 1948, Grand Rapids, MI.
+ 1948 iii. Karen Elizabeth[8] Edwards, b. 10 Aug 1953, Grand Rapids, MI.
+ 1949 iv. James Vinton[8] Edwards, b. 23 Oct 1954, East Grand Rapids, MI.

1549. Dorothy[7] Wilson (James Bertram[6], Letitia Mary Jane[5], Elizabeth Levenia[4], Charles G. W.[3], Thomas[2], Charles[1]) married Leonard Liner. Children:

1950 i. Mary[8] Liner, m. Hugh Gilchrist.
1951 ii. Libby[8] Liner.

1551. Betty[7] Wilson (James Bertram[6], Letitia Mary Jane[5], Elizabeth Levenia[4], Charles G. W.[3], Thomas[2], Charles[1]) married Charlie Johnson. Children:

+ 1952 i. Joni[8] Johnson.
  1953 ii. Scottie[8] Johnson.

1552. Madeline[7] Wilson (James Bertram[6], Letitia Mary Jane[5], Elizabeth Levenia[4], Charles G. W.[3], Thomas[2], Charles[1]) married _____ Stoudemire. Child:

1954 i. Tracy[8] Stoudemire.

1554. Manley Merritt[7] Wilson (Virgil William[6], Letitia Mary Jane[5], Elizabeth Levenia[4], Charles G. W.[3], Thomas[2], Charles[1]) was born 10 February 1930 in Columbia, South Carolina, and married Betty _____. Children:

1955 i. Martha Ann[8] Wilson, m. Herby Nixon.
1956 ii. Manley M.[8] Wilson, m. Diane _____.
1957 iii. Earl[8] Wilson.

1555. Sybil Joyce[7] Wilson (Virgil William[6], Letitia Mary Jane[5], Elizabeth Levenia[4], Charles G. W.[3], Thomas[2], Charles[1]) was born 7 May 1937 in Cordova, North Carolina, and married on 29 December 1957, Jimmy Dean Baldwin.

Children:

+ 1958 i. Marcia Denise[8] Baldwin, b. 12 Jan 1961.
  1959 ii. Kay Dean[8] Baldwin, b. 14 Feb 1967.

1556. Joseph Earl[7] Wilson (Virgil William[6], Letitia Mary Jane[5], Elizabeth Levenia[4], Charles G. W.[3], Thomas[2], Charles[1]) was born 24 January 1939 in Cordova, North Carolina, and married on 9 June 1956 at Wilmington, North Carolina, Alice Diane Yost. Children:

  1960 i. Gary Lyn[8] Wilson, b. 18 Jun 1960.
  1961 ii. Gerald Kevin[8] Wilson, b. 8 Jun 1964.

1558. James Reed[6] Wilson (Oscar LaFaye[6], Letitia Mary Jane[5], Elizabeth Levenia[4], Charles G. W.[3], Thomas[2], Charles[1]) was born 30 April 1930 in Columbia, South Carolina, and married on 21 August 1953, Barbara Ann Hutto, who was born 6 August 1934. Children:

  1962 i. Rebecca Lynn[8] Wilson, b. 29 Dec 1954, m. 17 May 1975,
          David Allen Lowder.
  1963 ii. Susan Elaine[8] Wilson, b. 7 Feb 1958, m. John Cotton.
  1964 iii. James Reed[8] Wilson, Jr., b. 31 Jan 1959.
  1965 iv. Laurie Ann[8] Wilson, b. 14 May 1961.

1559. Gaynelle Doris[7] Vanderwall (Myrtle[6], Letitia Mary Jane[5], Elizabeth Levenia[4], Charles G. W.[3], Thomas[2], Charles[1]) was born 11 August 1938 in Columbia, South Carolina, and married on 18 October 1957, Leon Weston Fetner, who was born 24 November 1936 in Columbia. Children:

  1966 i. Leon Weston[8] Fetner, Jr., b. 31 Oct 1958, Columbia, SC.
+ 1967 ii. Marigay[8] Fetner, b. 9 Jan 1961, Columbia, SC.
  1968 iii. Richard Capers[8] Fetner, b. 1 May 1964, Columbia, SC.
  1969 iv. Charlotte Lynn[8] Fetner, b. 23 Jun 1971, Columbia, SC.

1560. Mary Margaret[7] Vanderwall (Myrtle[6], Letitia Mary Jane[5], Elizabeth Levenia[4], Charles G. W.[3], Thomas[2], Charles[1]) was born 17 August 1942 in East Grand Rapids, Michigan, and married on 29 July 1958, in Lexington, South Carolina, William Lewis Browning, who was born 25 April 1940 in Columbia, South Carolina. Children:

+ 1970   i. Sheryl Ann[8] Browning, b. 5 Apr 1959.
  1971 ii. William Lewis[8] Browning, b. 6 Jun 1962, Columbia, SC.
  1972 iii. Nicholas Vanderwall[8] Browning, b. 11 Sept 1963,
       Columbia, SC.
  1973 iv. Robert Bernard[8] Browning, b. 5 Oct 1970, Columbia, SC.

1562. Barbara Ann[7] Wilson (Emerson Edward[6], Letitia Mary Jane[5], Elizabeth Levenia[4], Charles G. W.[3], Thomas[2], Charles[1]) was born 6 November 1939 in Columbia, South Carolina, and married on 29 July 1957, Thomas C. Leitner, II, who was born 6 May 1936. Children:

  1974   i. Thomas C.[8] Leitner, III, b. 19 Apr 1961.
  1975 ii. Brian[8] Leitner, b. 29 Jul 1969.

1563. Catherine[7] (Cathy) Wilson (Emerson Edward[6], Letitia Mary Jane[5], Elizabeth Levenia[4], Charles G. W.[3], Thomas[2], Charles[1]) was born 4 April 1943 in Columbia, South Carolina, and married, first, Troy Cumbee; married, second, Jack Cleary. Children:

  1976   i. Troy[8] Cumbee II, b. 4 Aug 1962.
  1977 ii. Audri[8] Cumbee, b. 20 Aug 1963.
  1978 iii. Sean[8] Cleary, b. 23 Aug 1976.

1564. David Melvin[7] Humphries (Ella Louise[6], Lue Ella[5], Elizabeth Levenia[4], Charles G. W.[3], Thomas[2], Charles[1]) was born 4 August 1923, and died 7 September 1979; he is buried at Black Creek Baptist Church in Darlington County, South Carolina. He married Eva Mae Adams. Children:

+ 1979   i. James Henry[8] Humphries, b. 15 Jul 1947, m. Carol
       Frances[7] Lambert, (for descendants, see #1571).
  1980 ii. Randy David[8] Humphries.
  1981 iii. Thomas Leslie[8] Humphries.

1570. Franklin Harold[7] Lambert (Cecil Edgar[6], Charles Franklin[5], Elizabeth Levenia[4], Charles G. W.[3], Thomas[2], Charles[1]) was born 26 May 1946 in Florence, South Carolina, and married on 23 February 1967, Laura Lee Eason, who was born 4 August 1947 in Florence. Child:

1982 i. Benjamin Charles[8] Lambert, b. 19 Jan 1974, Florence, SC.

1571. Carol Frances[7] Lambert (Cecil Edgar[6], Charles Franklin[5], Elizabeth Levenia[4], Charles G. W.[3], Thomas[2], Charles[1]) was born 9 March 1950 in Darlington, South Carolina, and married on 21 September 1969, James Henry[8] Humphries, #1979. Children:

1983 i. April Michell[8] Humphries, b. 24 Jul 1975, Florence, SC.
1984 ii. Christopher James[8] Humphries, b. 13 Nov 1980, Florence, SC.

1572. Jo Cecile[7] Lambert (Cecil Edgar[6], Charles Franklin[5], Elizabeth Levenia[4], Charles G. W.[3], Thomas[2], Charles[1]) was born 23 December 1956 in Darlington, South Carolina, and married on 24 January 1975, David Glenn Sanderson, who was born 13 February 1956 in Hartsville, South Carolina. Child:

1985 i. Keisha Lynn[8] Sanderson, b. 22 Feb 1978.

1575. Sara Kathleen[7] Cook (Gena Ray[6], Charles Franklin[5], Elizabeth Levenia[4], Charles G. W.[3], Thomas[2], Charles[1]) was born 8 January 1947 in Darlington, South Carolina, and married on 20 February 1971, James Gary Brown, who was born 26 August 1936. Children:

1986 i. James Gary[8] Brown, Jr.
1987 ii. Christine Hilton[8] Brown.

1594. Leslie Drew[7] Peake (Frank Ernell[6], Frank Ernell[5], Isaac Frank[4], Charlotte Frances[3], Charlotte[2], Charles[1]) was born 6 February 1953 in Fairfax, Virginia, and married Donald R. Rickert, of Long Island, New York. Child:

1988 i. Jonathan[8] Rickert, b. 15 Aug 1980, Charlotte, NC.

1598. Derrick Sanders[7] Peake (William Derrick[6], Frank Ernell[5], Isaac Frank[4], Charlotte Frances[3], Charlotte[2], Charles[1]) was born 11 July 1954 in Washington, D. C., and married Melanie Burnette. They currently [1984] live in Columbia, South Carolina. Children:

1989 i. Graeson Derrick[8] Burnette-Peake, b. 17 Sept 1979.
1990 ii. Abigail Loraine[8] Burnette-Peake, b. 22 Dec 1983.

1599. Judith Ann[7] Peake (William Derrick[6], Frank Ernell[5], Isaac Frank[4], Charlotte Frances[3], Charlotte[2], Charles[1]) was born 10 March 1956 and married on 16 September 1978, Paul Martin Marcella. They currently [1984] reside in Waterbury, Connecticut. Children:

1991 i. Kristen[8] Marcella.
1992 ii. Jennifer[8] Marcella.

1604. Evans McMurray[7] Peake (Thomas Hopkins[6], Thomas Hopkins[5], Isaac Frank[4], Charlotte Frances[3], Charlotte[2], Charles[1]) was born 5 October 1961 in Charlotte, North Carolina, and married Bonita Leigh Roberts, who was born 14 November 1961. Child:

1993 i. Jeremy Brandon[8] Peake, b. 16 Jan 1984, Oakland, CA.

1631. Gail Lauren[7] Petit (Muriel Joy[6], Martin Chapin[5], Anne Laura[4], John Wesley[3], Charlotte[2], Charles[1]) was born 16 June 1954 in Coral Gables, Florida, and married on 3 July 1976, Robert Gordon Millson, who was born in 1951, barrister and solicitor, Province of Ontario, Canada. They live [1984] in Windsor, Ontario, Canada. Children:

1994 i. Katherine Ann[8] Millson, b. 19 May 1978, Windsor, Ont.
1995 ii. Douglas Robert[8] Millson, b. 9 Jul 1980, Windsor, Ont.

EIGHTH AND NINTH GENERATIONS

1642. Constance Marian[8] Cooper (Ruth[7], Bernice Gertrude[6], Sarah Glenn[5], Sarah A.[4], Dr. Christopher[3], Sarah[2], Charles[1]) was born 8 October 1923 in Spartanburg, South Carolina, and married on 25 June 1941, Lawrence (Larry) David Breault, who was born 18 March 1922, Hingham, Massachusetts. Children:

1996 i. Ronald David[9] Breault, b. 4 Apr 1942, Weymouth, MA.
1997 ii. Roger Gerald[9] Breault, b. 4 Mar 1944, Wilmington, DE,
   m. 20 Feb 1946, West Palm Beach, FL, Susan Foster, b.
   28 Feb 1946, and they have two children, both born West
   Palm Beach, FL:
   1998 i. Tammy Susan[10] Breault, b. 28 Dec 1965.
   1999 ii. Roger Gerald[10] Breault, Jr., b. 29 May 1967.

1643. Charles DuBose[8] DeLorme, Jr. (Edna Elizabeth[7], Bernice Gertrude[6], Sarah Glenn[5], Sarah A.[4], Dr. Christopher[3], Sarah[2], Charles[1]) was born 2 December 1939 in Spartanburg, South Carolina, and has a BS degree from Wofford College in Spartanburg, a MA degree from USC in Columbia, and Ph. D. from Louisiana State University. He is a professor of economics at the University of Georgia in Athens. He married on 16 June 1962, Betty Rush Tate, who was born 4 September 1940 in Pendleton, South Carolina, a graduate of Limestone College, in Gaffney, South Carolina. Two children:

2000 i. Denise Elizabeth[9] DeLorme, b. 19 May 1968, Alexandria, VA.
2001 ii. Charles DuBose[9] DeLorme, III, b. 28 Mar 1972, Athens, GA.

1644. Daniel Jenkins[8] May (Dan W.[7], Bernice Gertrude[6], Sarah Glenn[5], Sarah A.[4], Dr. Christopher[3], Sarah[2], Charles[1]) was born 30 May 1942 in Hendersonville, North Carolina, and married in Hendersonville on 1 August 1964, Elizabeth Ann Harrelson, who was born 17 April 1941. Children:

2002 i. James Vincent[9] May, b. 1 Jul 1972, Raleigh, NC.
2003 ii. Laurence Jenkins[9] May, b. 7 Jul 1975, Raleigh, NC.

1645. James Franklin[8] Deal, Jr. (Sarah Glenn[7], Bernice Gertrude[6], Sarah Glenn[5], Sarah A.[4], Dr. Christopher[3], Sarah[2], Charles[1]) was born 20 August 1940 in Hickory, North Carolina, and married Edwina Yancey, who was born 18 August

1939 in Hickory. Children, all born in Hickory:

2004 i. Beth Leigh^9 Deal, b. 14 Sept 1962.
2005 ii. Sarah Ann^9 Deal, b. 4 Apr 1965.
2006 iii. James Franklin^9 (Jay) Deal, III, b. 1 Jul 1971.
2007 iv. Allison Edwina^9 Deal, b. 12 Mar 1973.

1647. Edward May^8 Pool (Margaret Helen^7, Bernice Gertrude^6, Sarah Glenn^5, Sarah A.^{4}, Dr. Christopher^3, Sarah^2, Charles^1) was born 16 March 1944 in Spartanburg, South Carolina. A graduate of Clemson University, he married on 28 June 1967 Mary Camille Stokes-Taylor, who was born 30 April 1947 in Greenville, South Carolina. Children, all born Greenville:

2008 i. Thomas^9 Pool, b. 2 Nov 1970.
2009 ii. David^9 Pool, b. 11 Jan 1974.
2010 iii. Maryann^9 Pool, b. 24 Dec 1979.

1648. Margaret Helen^8 Pool (Margaret Helen^7, Bernice Gertrude^6, Sarah Glenn^5, Sarah A.^{4}, Dr. Christopher^3, Sarah^2, Charles^1) was born 28 April 1946 in Greenville, South Carolina. A graduate of Lander College, she married Samuel McClesky, who was born 28 April 1946 in Greenville, an architect in Hilton Head, South Carolina. Children, all born Savannah, Georgia:

2011 i. Jonathan^9 McClesky, b. 17 Dec 1973.
2012 ii. Russell Sims^9 McClesky, b. 29 Dec 1977.
2013 iii. Andrew Pool^9 McClesky, b. 19 Jul 1979.

1649. Kathleen Elizabeth^8 Pool (Margaret Helen^7, Bernice Gertrude^6, Sarah Glenn^5, Sarah A.^{4}, Dr. Christopher^3, Sarah^2, Charles^1) was born in Greenville, South Carolina and married Joe Murphy. Child:

2014 i. Craig^9 Murphy, b. 28 Jan 1967.

1654. Sadie Joyce^8 Hightower (Dorothy^7, Thomas Hancock^6, Sarah Glenn^5, Sarah A.^{4}, Dr. Christopher^3, Sarah^2, Charles^1) married, first, _____ McKee, second, Leroy Hyatt. Children:

2015 i. Cheryle^9 McKee.
2016 ii. Kenny^9 McKee.
2017 iii. Eddie Bruce^9 McKee.

2018 iv. Christopher^9 Hyatt.

1655. Myrtle Jeane^8 Hightower (Dorothy^7, Thomas Hancock^6, Sarah Glenn^5, Sarah A.^{4}, Dr. Christopher^3, Sarah^2, Charles^1) married Carl Eugene Dunn. Children:

2019 i. Susan^9 Dunn.
2020 ii. Stephen^9 Dunn.

1658. Jeannette Suzanne^8 Thomas (Rowland Farr^7, Rowland Farr^6, Martha Elizabeth^5, Sarah A.^{4}, Dr. Christopher^3, Sarah^2, Charles^1) was born 27 June 1956 and married Joseph A. D'Astoli, and lives in Fairfield, California. Child:

2021 i. Andrea^9 D'Astoli.

1659. Jane^8 Wallace (Winter Clough^7, Roberta^6, Jesse Robert^5, Martha Elizabeth^4, Dr. Christopher^3, Sarah^2, Charles^1) married F. D. Brosnan. Children:

2022 i. Sarah^9 Brosnan.
2023 ii. Susan^9 Brosnan.

1681. K. Barron^8 Godshall (Elma^7, Kathleen^6, Jesse Robert^5, Martha Elizabeth^4, Dr. Christopher^3, Sarah^2, Charles^1) married, first, Glenn Toney, and second, Edward Harvey. Children

2024 i. Richard^9 Toney.
2025 ii. Randy^9 Toney.
2026 iii. Lisa^9 Toney.

1683. Rebecca Dianne^8 Gasque (Rebecca Jean^7, Ruth^6, Jesse Robert^5, Martha Elizabeth^4, Dr. Christopher^3, Sarah^2, Charles^1) married Carl C. Long. Children:

2027 i. Kenny^9 Long.
2028 ii. Pixie Ann^9 Long.
2029 iii. Larry^9 Long.

1684. Narcia^8 Buck (Rebecca Jean^7, Ruth^6, Jesse Robert^5, Martha Elizabeth^4, Dr. Christopher^3, Sarah^2, Charles^1) married Curtis Carver. Children:

2030 i. Buddie^9 Carver.
2031 ii. Dani^9 Carver.

1686. Andrea[8] Buck (Rebecca Jean[7], Ruth[6], Jesse Robert[5], Martha Elizabeth[4], Dr. Christopher[3], Sarah[2], Charles[1]) married Mark B. Sullivan. Children:

2032 i. Bonnie[9] Sullivan.
2033 ii. Katie[9] Sullivan.

1687. Alliene[8] Stone (Era[7], Martha Ann[6], John Calhoun[5], Martha Ellen W.[4], Thomas[3], Sarah[2], Charles[1]) married Elmer Barnette. Children:

2034 i. Linda Barnette[9], m. Jimmy Hughes. Children:
    2035 i. Michelle[10] Hughes.
    2036 ii. Shawn[10] Hughes.
    2037 iii. Shannon[10] Hughes.
2038 ii. Larry[9] Barnette.
2039 iii. Lisa[9] Barnette, m. Mark McCurry. Child:
    2040 Amy[10] McCurry.

1688. Shirley[8] Stone (Era[7], Martha Ann[6], John Calhoun[5], Martha Ellen W.[4], Thomas[3], Sarah[2], Charles[1]) married, first, _____ Hurley, second, Ray Oliver Clary. Children:

2041 i. Sherry[9] Hurley, m. Daniel Ray Burns. Child:
    2042 Daniel Ashley[10] Burns.
2043 ii. Teresa[9] Hurley, m. Thomas Martin McGrath.

1689. Sybil Virginia[8] Stone (Era[7], Martha Ann[6], John Calhoun[5], Martha Ellen W.[4], Thomas[3], Sarah[2], Charles[1]) married Charles Johnson. Children:

2044 i. Darlene[9] Johnson, m. David Marlow. Children:
    2045 i. Chad[10] Marlow.
    2046 ii. Todd[10] Marlow.
2047 ii. Kathy[9] Johnson, m. Otis Hightower. Children:
    2048 i. Jennifer[10] Hightower.
    2049 ii. Jessica[10] Hightower.
2050 iii. Eddie[9] Johnson.

1690. Patricia Verbena[8] Harris (Lavare[7], Martha Ann[6], John Calhoun[5], Martha Ellen W.[4], Thomas[3], Sarah[2], Charles[1]) was born on 12 November 1935 and married on 22 December 1956 Augustus Joe Knox, who was born 14 July 1930. They reside [1984] in Spencer, North Carolina. Children:

2051 i. Cynthia Winona[9] Knox, b. 20 Sept 1957.
2052 ii. Larry Wendell[9] Knox, b. 13 Oct 1958.
2053 iii. Tracy Verbena[9] Knox, b. 27 Jul 1960.
2054 iv. Randall Joe[9] Knox, b. 14 Mar 1964.

1691. Melvin Franklin[8] Harris (Lavare[7], Martha Ann[6], John Calhoun[5], Martha Ellen W.[4], Thomas[3], Sarah[2], Charles[1]) was born 4 December 1937 and married on 8 January 1960, Jill Lindsey, who was born 26 July 1942. Children:

2055 i. Lee Allen[9] Harris, b. 2 Jun 1963.
2056 ii. Lindsey Ray[9] Harris, b. 8 May 1965.

1692. Lonnie Darve[8] Littlejohn (Lonnie Vernon[7], Martha Ann[6], John Calhoun[5], Martha Ellen W.[4], Thomas[3], Sarah[2], Charles[1]) was born 27 April 1945 and married on 13 April 1962, Brenda Kay Mason. Children:

2057 i. Darlena Kay[9] Littlejohn, b. 10 Sept 1963.
2058 ii. Darvie James[9] Littlejohn, b. 6 Dec 1968.

1693. Frances Carole[8] Littlejohn (Lonnie Vernon[7], Martha Ann[6], John Calhoun[5], Martha Ellen W.[4], Thomas[3], Sarah[2], Charles[1]) was born 24 September 1947 and married 13 February 1964, Richard Oland Davis, Jr. Children:

2059 i. Richard Todd[9] Davis, b. 22 Jun 1966.
2060 ii. Patrick Carroll[9] Davis, b. 9 Sept 1968.
2061 iii. Frances Nicole[9] Davis, b. 18 Sept 1969.

1694. Edith Brenda[8] Harris (Edisto[7], Martha Ann[6], John Calhoun[5], Martha Ellen W.[4], Thomas[3], Sarah[2], Charles[1]) was born 19 September 1940 and married on 19 April 1958, Herschel Auburn DeVine, who was born 3 August 1933. Children:

2062 i. Michael Auburn[9] DeVine, b. 29 May 1959.
2063 ii. Darryl[9] DeVine, b. 25 Jun 1960.

1700. Robin Marie[8] Auman (Betty[7], William David[6], John Calhoun[5], Martha Ellen W.[4], Thomas[3], Sarah[2], Charles[1]) was born 20 November 1956 and married Fred Clement. Child:

2064 i. Bradley[9] Clement.

1718. Susan Ann^8 Brockman (Sarah Frances^7, George Wesley^6, Mattie^5, Rachel Ann^4, George McCrary^3, Mary^2, Charles^1) was born 16 May 1965 and married 24 May 1980, Richard Keith Lawson. Child:

2065 i. Shannon Michelle^9 Lawson.

1727. Paul Hayward^8 Smith (Rachel^7, Pearl^6, Pearl^5, Rachel Ann^4, George McCrary^3, Mary^2, Charles^1) was born 28 April 1951 in Union, South Carolina, and married on 16 June 1973, Monica Joy Bogan, who was born 1 January 1955. Child:

2066 i. Haley Nicole^9 Smith, b. 23 Aug 1978.

1729. Brenda Kaye^8 Smith (Rachel^7, Pearl^6, Pearl^5, Rachel Ann^4, George McCrary^3, Mary^2, Charles^1) was born 28 June 1953 in Union, South Carolina, and married on 30 October 1976, James Landrum (Lanny) Parker, who was born 4 September 1938. Child:

2067 i. Eric Landrum^9 Parker, b. 9 Nov 1977.

1733. Julie Ann^9 O'Shields (Cornelia^7, Pearl^6, Pearl^5, Rachel Ann^4, George McCrary^3, Mary^2, Charles^1) was born 11 November 1958 and married on 8 December 1978, David Taylor. Child:

2068 i. April Rae^9 Taylor, b. 31 Mar 1981.

1786. Jean Salley^8 Anderson (Eleanor Frances^7, James Louis^6, Sarah Frances^5, James Christopher^4, Sarah^3, Mary^2, Charles^1) married Bruce Williams. Child:

2069 i. Reid Edward^9 Williams.

1800. Donald Ray^8 Sanders (Anita^7, Grover^6, Sarah Ellen^5, Adelade^4, John Thomas^3, William^2, Charles^1) was born 1 June 1937 and married on 22 September 1957, Nancy Elizabeth Gerring. Children:

2070 i. Donald Anthony^9 Sanders, b. 22 Oct 1958.
2071 ii. William Ray^9 Sanders, b. 13 Dec 1960.
2072 iii. Carl Edward^9 Sanders, b. 24 Apr 1969.

1801. Mary Ann^3 Sanders (Anita^7, Grover^6, Sarah Ellen^5, Adelade^4, John Thomas^3, William^2, Charles^1) was born 4 March 1939, married 31 August 1957, Paul Thomas Bell. Children:

2073 i. Paul Thomas^9 Bell, Jr., b. 1 Aug 1958, m. 6 Jul 1979,
    Tammy Brown. Child:
    2074 Kristy Dianne^{10} Bell, b. 21 Feb 1981.
2075 ii. Anita Elaine^9 Bell, b. 13 Feb 1961, m. 9 Jun 1979,
    Melvin Dale Latham. Child:
    2076 Geoffrey Dale^9 Latham, b. 17 Dec 1981.

1815. Richard Thomas^8 Greer, Jr. (Richard Thomas^7, Robert Christopher^6, Louisa^5, Adelade^4, John Thomas^3, William^2, Charles^1) was born 10 August 1953 in Dayton, Ohio, and married on 4 October 1980 at South Lebanon, Ohio, Deborah Kay Bollheimer. Child:

2077 i. Eva Kristin^9 Greer, b. 8 Nov 1980, Cincinnati, OH.

1828. Mary Jeanette^8 Ivey (Lena^7, Sally^6, Bernice^5, Sarah^4, John Thomas^3, William^2, Charles^1) was born 9 February 1931 in Union, South Carolina, and married on 24 August 1948, James Edward Moss, who was born 3 May 1929 in Pineville, North Carolina. Children:

2078 i. James Michael^9 Moss, b. 21 Jun 1950, Union, SC, m.
    10 Jan 1969, Cheryl Holcombe. Children:
    2079 i. Jonathan Michael^{10} Moss, b. 19 Feb 1972.
    2080 ii. Sharon Lindsey O'Neil^{10} Moss, b. 18 Jan 1981.
2081 ii. Frederick Edward^9 Moss, b. 20 Mar 1952, Union, SC,
    m. 1st, 16 Aug 1970, Nancy Brown; m. 2nd, 14 Dec 1972,
    Patricia Peay. Children:
    2082 i. Michelle Lee^{10} Moss, b. 1 Nov 1971.
    2083 ii. Frederick Edward^{10} Moss, b. 1 Jan 1977.
2084 iii. Dennis Carroll^9 Moss, b. 13 Jan 1954, m. 24 Jun 1978,
    Janet Ellis. Child:
    2085 Brandon Lindsey^{10} Moss, b. 8 Dec 1981, Laurinburg, NC.
2086 iv. Timothy Lynn^{10} Moss, b. 12 Dec 1956, m. 30 Dec 1978,
    Lydia Ryan. Child:
    2087 Nakia Dawn^{10} Moss, b. 14 Sept 1979, Union, SC.
2088 v. Pamela Jeanne^9 Moss, b. 24 Jun 1960, m. 1st, 17 Apr 1976,
    Ray Barber; m. 2nd, 23 Nov 1977, Steve Lipsey. Children:
    2089 i. Harold Ray^{10} Barber, Jr., b. 23 Jul 1976.
    2090 ii. Stevie Daniel^{10} Lipsey, b. 8 Jul 1978.
    2091 iii. James Austin^{10} Lipsey, b. & d. 14 Nov 1979.

1830. James Wallace[8] Ivey (Lena[7], Sally[6], Bernice[5], Sarah[4], John Thomas[3], William[2], Charles[1]) was born 18 November 1940, Union, South Carolina, and married on 21 November 1958, Joyce White, who was born 29 December 1939. Child:

2092　James Randolph[9] Ivey, b. 20 Oct 1961, Chester, SC, m.
6 Nov 1981, Union, SC, Laura Jean Collier, b. 1 Jun 1963,
Union, SC. Child:
2093 James Randolph[10] Ivey, Jr., b. 2 Mar 1982.

1831. Charles William[8] Wilson (Nina[7], Sally[6], Bernice[5], Sarah[4], John Thomas[3], William[2], Charles[1]) was born 9 July 1952 in Union, South Carolina, and married on 8 June 1974 at Kelton, South Carolina, Betty Jo Comer, who was born 8 April 1952, Jonesville, South Carolina. Children:

2094　i. Mary Elizabeth[9] Wilson, b. 22 Mar 1977.
2095 ii. Charles William[9] Wilson, III, b. 22 Sept 1980.

1833. Beth Marlene[8] Wilson (Nina[7], Sally[6], Bernice[5], Sarah[4], John Thomas[3], William[2], Charles[1]) was born 14 October 1956 in Union, South Carolina, and married on 1 August 1981 Donald Leach, who was born 20 August 1955 in Charleston, South Carolina. Child:

2096　i. Donald[9] Leach, II, b. 6 Dec 1983, Union, SC.

1848. Larraine Paula[8] Nabors (Rubye Eileen[7], Ida Florence[6], Lucy Smith[5], Medora[4], John Thomas[3], William[2], Charles[1]) was born 29 April 1945 in Tampa, Florida, married 29 August 1965, Leon Graham. Children:

2097　i. Paul Alan[9] Graham, b. 1 Jun 1970.
2098 ii. Phillip Douglas[9] Graham, b. 10 May 1972.

1849. Pamela[8] Nabors (Rubye Eileen[7], Ida Florence[6], Lucy Smith[5], Medora[4], John Thomas[3], William[2], Charles[1]) was born 10 November 1951 in Moultrie, Georgia, and married, first, John Carbone; married, second, George Hodges. Children:

2099 i. Lee Anthony^9 Carbone, b. Oct 1969.
2100 ii. Lane^9 Hodges, b. 1981.

1852. Lewis^8 Frost (Catherine^7, Annie Estelle^6, Lucy Smith^5, Medora^4, John Thomas^3, William^2, Charles^1) married Edna Lee Lennon. Children:

2101 i. Mary Lewis^9 Frost, m. Joab Frederick Johnson, III.
2102 ii. Catherine Karine^9 Frost.

1917. Richard W.^{8} Plowden (Jean^7, Jeannette^6, Della^5, Susan Fair^4, Katherine^3, William^2, Charles^1) had one child:

2103 i. Richard Shane^9 Plowden.

1926. Kathryn Diane^8 Sanders (Patricia^7, Herman^6, James Sanders^5, Susan Fair^4, Katherine^3, William^2, Charles^1) was born 14 November 1958 and married James L. Garner. Children:

2104 i. David Christopher^9 Garner, b. 26 Nov 1977.
2105 ii. Jamie Lee^9 Garner, b. 31 Jan 1980.

1946. Jerry Lynn^8 Edwards (Mary Doris^7, Mary Elizabeth^6, Letitia Mary Jane^5, Elizabeth Levenia^4, Charles G. W.^{3}, Thomas^2, Charles^1) was born 11 July 1943 in Corpus Christi, Texas, and married on 4 August 1961 in Grand Rapids, Michigan, Sharon Kay Elenbaas, who was born 20 October 1941 (divorced 1975). He married, second, Jo Osborne; married, third, Sharron Ann (Peters) Goidich. Children:

2106 i. Robert Todd^9 Edwards, b. 15 Feb 1963, Chicago, IL.
2107 ii. Scott Alan^9 Edwards, b. 22 Feb 1966, East Grand Rapids, MI.
2108 iii. Michael Lynn^9 Edwards, b. 24 Dec 1966, East Grand Rapids, MI.
2109 iv. Bradly Jay^9 Edwards, b. 29 Aug 1971, East Grand Rapids, MI.

1947. Daniel Bryan^8 Edwards (Mary Doris^7, Mary Elizabeth^6, Letitia Mary Jane^5, Elizabeth Levenia^4, Charles G. W.^{3}, Thomas^2, Charles^1) was born 21 August 1948 in Grand Rapids, Michigan, and married on 6 September 1969, Pamela Jo Parker, who was born 7 January 1949. Children:

2110 i. Jay Douglas^9 Edwards, b. 11 Feb 1974, Grand Rapids, MI.
2111 ii. Laura Marie^9 Edwards, b. 27 Jun 1976, Grand Rapids, MI.

1948. Karen Elizabeth[8] Edwards (Mary Doris[7], Mary Elizabeth[6], Letitia Mary Jane[5], Elizabeth Levenia[4], Charles G. W.[3], Thomas[2], Charles[1]) was born 10 August 1953 in Grand Rapids, Michigan, and married on 8 July 1972 in Kentwood, Michigan, Bruce Cernak, who was born 19 February 1951 in South Bend, Indiana. Children:

    2112 i. Christopher Michael[9] Cernak, b. 21 Mar 1974, South Bend, IN.
    2113 ii. Kelly Elizabeth[9] Cernak, b. 26 Sept 1976, South Bend, IN.

1949. James Vinton[8] Edwards (Mary Doris[7], Mary Elizabeth[6], Letitia Mary Jane[5], Elizabeth Levenia[4], Charles G. W.[3], Thomas[2], Charles[1]) was born 23 October 1954 in East Grand Rapids, Michigan, and married on 18 April 1980 in Las Vegas, Nevada, Susan Kay Isaacs, who was born 20 January 1953 in Grand Rapids. Child:

    2114 i. Bryan Vinton[9] Edwards, b. 19 Feb 1981, East Grand Rapids, MI.

1952. Joni[8] Johnson (Betty[7], James Bertram[6], Letitia Mary Jane[5], Elizabeth Levenia[4], Charles G. W.[3], Thomas[2], Charles[1]) married Phillip Thomas. Child:

    2115 i. Mary Ashley[9] Thomas, b. 1 Nov 1980.

1958. Marcia Denise[8] Baldwin (Sybil Joyce[7], Virgil William[6], Letitia Mary Jane[5], Elizabeth Levenia[4], Charles G. W.[3], Thomas[2], Charles[1]) was born 12 January 1961 and married Richard Lewis Miles at Camden, South Carolina. Child:

    2116 i. Meredith Denise[9] Miles, b. 14 Feb 1967.

1967. Marigay[8] Fetner (Gaynelle Doris[7], Myrtle[6], Letitia Mary Jane[5], Elizabeth Levenia[4], Charles G. W.[3], Thomas[2], Charles[1]) was born 9 January 1961 in Columbia, South Carolina, and married on 10 June 1978, Jody McDaniels, who was born 8 March 1958 in Summerville, South Carolina. Child:

    2117 i. Christopher Jody[9] McDaniels, b. 15 Aug 1979.

1970. Sheryl Ann[8] Browning (Mary Margaret[7], Myrtle[6], Letitia Mary Jane[5], Elizabeth Levenia[4], Charles G. W.[3], Thomas[2], Charles[1]) was born 5 April 1959 in

Biloxi, Mississippi, and married on 18 May 1979 at Dunwoody, Georgia, George Demietri Vlass, who was born 16 February 1953. Child:

2118 i.   George Jason[9] Vlass, b. 12 Sept 1980, Atlanta, GA.

"UNCLE DAN" HUMPHRIES

In the cemetery of Sardis United Methodist Church, in Union County, South Carolina, there is a stone which reads as follows:

UNCLE DAN HUMPHRIES

SLAVE OF THE HUMPHRIES FAMILY.

Very little is known about "Uncle Dan." It is not known which Humphries was his master, as several members of the Humphries family owned slaves. However, Uncle Dan does appear on the 1870 census of Union County, South Carolina, in Union Township, page 569, as Daniel Humphries, aged 41, Black. He was apparently unmarried at the time. He is also found on the 1880 census, same county and township, page 42, #417/429, as Daniel Humphries, aged 55, Black, with wife Priscilla, aged 22, and sons Anderson, aged 4, and Wesley, aged 2. Dan does not appear on any subsequent census.

222

Rice continued
  Broddie Riddle 146
  Connie Frances 147
  Cornelia Othela 98,147
  Darlene Annett 146
  David Kenneth 146
  Debra Jean 146
  Donald 98,146
  Donald Paul 146
  Dorothy Nell 146
  Elsie Louise 147
  Harriet Ann 146
  Harriett Lucille 98,147
  Helen 98,145
  James McDowell 98,147
  Iona Mae 98
  Lori Lyn 147
  Louise 98,146
  Mary Alice 98,145
  Mary Susan 147
  Nancy Morris 146
  Renata Nicklus 147
  Shirley Dianne 146
  Mrs. Will vii
  William 98,146
  William Clough Sr. 98
  William Herold 147
  William Stanley 146
Richter, Edwin 38
  Elizabeth 38
  Elizabeth Jane 38
  Martha 38
Rickert, Donald R. 195
  Jonathan 195
  Leslie Drew 195
Riddle, Broddie 146
Rieves, Connie Young 176
  Jami 176
  Jim 176
Riggs, Edward (Ted) 143
  Sara 109
Rippey, Buell 75
  Doris Young Parks 75
Risher, Deborah May 129
  John Wayne 129
Robbins, Clara Pauline 79
  Edgar Allen 78
  Gladys Pettit 79
  Hellen Autapha 79
  Lydia Ophelia 79
  Sarah Esma Maudie 79
  Theodore Monroe 79
  Ulalah (Leila) Young 78
Roberson, Debra Dale 191
  Debra Jean 146
  Melvine Alan 191
  Ronald Wayne 146
Roberts, Bonita Leigh 196
  Edna Lee 185
  Linda Bellwood 114
  T.C. 114
Robinson, Ann 66
  Hazel Betenbaugh 153
  Janet Sue 153
  Ralph 153
  Ralph Douglas 153
Rodelsperger, George 65
  Lillian Humphries 65
Roden, Margaret 5
  William 5
Rodgers, Grace 110
  Thelma 158
Rogers, _____ 131
  John 10
  Martha Ann 131
Rollins, Leila Jesna 65
Ross, Mary Ella 186
Roundtree, James R. 123
  James R. Jr. 123
  John 123
  Judy 123
  Margaret Caldwell 123
Rudisill, Horace F. 43

Russell, Edgar Farr 159
  Edgar Farr Jr. 159
  Edgar Farr III 160
  Frazier Nealy 160
  Ida Rebecca 160
  Jean Neely 159
Ryan, Lydia 203

Salley, Imogene 137
Saltonstall, Katie 96
Sanders, Addie 58
  Amanda Ledbetter 58
  Anita Gregory 179
  Ann Batley 134
  Carl Edward 202
  Carol E. 190
  Carol E. Jr. 190
  Catherine 81,124
  Charles 23
  Clarence Berry 179
  Clarice 58
  Cora Mae 34,52
  Cornelia Pearl 127,172
  Curtis 58
  Dana Maria 172
  Donald Anthony 202
  Donald Ray 180,202
  Elizabeth 34
  Ellen Victoria 111
  Eugene B. 81
  Frances 34,62
  Frances Catherine 61
  Greene 58
  Gus B. 58
  Heyward Berton 127
  James S. 23,34
  Janie 34,63
  J.B. 134
  Jean 81,123
  John 61,78
  John T. 126,142
  John Wallace 127,172
  Johnnie (Jean) 61,99
  Joseph 58
  Josephine Humphries 58
  Julia A. 81
  Katherine 23
  Katherine Humphries 34
  Kathryn Diane 190,205
  Kelly Ledbetter 58
  Katie Louise 142
  Kenneth Wayne 190
  Kimberly Ann 172
  Lori Lyn 147
  Louise 58
  Manly 35
  Mary Ann 127,180,203
  Mattie S. 58
  Merrie Robin 135
  Nancy Elizabeth 202
  Ned Arthur 127
  Patricia Ann 190
  Pearl Frances 126
  Peggy Wood 172
  Pennie 135,178
  Rachel Ann 127,172
  Sabra Renee 172
  Sallie E. 78
  Sallie M. 23,34,49
  Sarah 55
  Sarah Elizabeth 78
  Scaife 58
  Sidney Jackson 35
  Susan Fair 34,63
  Wallace 35
  William 23,34
  William Ray 202
  Wylie 58
Sanderson, David Glenn 195
  Jo Cecile 195
  Keisha Lynn 195
Sannes, John 97
  Martha Jolly 97

Sartor, Adella Frances 53,
    90
  Allie Whitton 136
  Ann J. 32
  Caroline Virginia (Carrie)
    32,54
  Catherine Brandon 32
  C.C. 27
  Christopher Columbus
    (Kit) 32,53
  Clara Eugenia 53
  Claude Christopher 54,90
  Claude Christopher Jr.
    90,136
  Claude Christopher III
    136
  Effie Moore 32
  Effie Pauline 54
  Elizabeth 91
  Elizabeth Catherine 33
  Emma Frances 32,55
  Eoline Brandenburg 54
  Frances Agnes 91
  Irene Fant 54
  James Christopher 32,54
  James Perry 54
  John W. 27,32
  John Young 32
  Julia 32
  Kate 54,91
  Katherine Yazvac 90
  Kathleen 136
  Mary 54,91
  Mary Cornelia 53
  Mary Cornelia (Mamie)
    90,136
  Mary Cornelia (Nellie)
    54
  Mary E. 91
  Mary J. 32,54
  Milton Humphries 90,136
  Pearl Irene 90
  Robert W. 91
  Robert Wallace 54
  Sarah Frances 54,90
  Sarah Young 32
  Theopa Thomason 54
  Thomas 32
  Thomas Bradenburg 90
  Thomas Edwin 53
  Virginia Huntsinger 136
  William Kate 54,91
  William Henry 32
Saunders, Elizabeth 26
  John 31
  John Jr. 26
  Permelia 34
  Permelia (Milly) 26
Saverance, Ella Humphries
    36
  Joseph F. 36
Schanevelt, Pauline 151
Schmidt, Debbie Jolly 176
  Ericka 176
  Gene 176
  Katie 176
Schreyer, Mabel Irene 160
Schurr, Jaime Elizabeth
    183
  Janet Elizabeth 183
  Paul 183
  Paul Benjamin 183
  Susan McDaniel 183
Scott, Callie 94
  Colene Gregory 92
  Luke 92
Sellars, Albert Perry 79
  Guy Calvin 79
  "Inf. Dau." 79
  James Nelson 79
  Julia Young 79
  Lela Bertha 79
  Macnette 79

225

226

Heritage Books by Brent H. Holcomb:

*Ancestors and Descendants of Charles Humphries (d. 1837)
of Union District, South Carolina, 1677–1984
Including Records from Virginia, North Carolina,
South Carolina, Mississippi, and Other States*

Bute County, North Carolina, Land Grant Plats and Land Entries

*CD: Early Records of Fishing Creek Presbyterian Church,
Chester County, South Carolina, 1799–1859*

CD: Kershaw County, South Carolina, Minutes of the County Court, 1791–1799

CD: Marriage and Death Notices from The Charleston *[S.C.] Observer, 1827–1845*

CD: South Carolina, Volume 1

*CD: Winton (Barnwell) County, South Carolina Minutes of
County Court and Will Book 1, 1785–1791*

Charleston District, South Carolina, Journal of the Court of Ordinary, 1812–1830
Caroline T. Moore, Edited by Brent H. Holcomb

*Chester County, South Carolina, Deed Abstracts,
Volume I: 1785–1799 [1768–1799] Deed Books A-F*

Deaths and Obituary Notices from the
Southern Christian Advocate, *1867–1878*

*Early Records of Fishing Creek Presbyterian Church, Chester County,
South Carolina, 1799–1859, with Appendices of the Visitation List of
Rev. John Simpson, 1774–1776 and the Cemetery Roster, 1762–1979*
Brent H. Holcomb and Elmer O. Parker

Kershaw County, South Carolina, Minutes of the County Court, 1791–1799

Laurens County, South Carolina, Minutes of the County Court, 1786–1789

*Lower Fairforest Baptist Church, Union County, South Carolina:
Minutes 1809–1875, Membership Lists through 1906*

*Marriage and Death Notices from Baptist Newspapers of South Carolina,
Volume 2: 1866–1887*

*Marriage and Death Notices from Columbia, South Carolina Newspapers,
1838–1860; Including Legal Notices from Burnt Counties*

Marriage and Death Notices from The Charleston Observer, *1827–1845*

Marriage Notices from the Southern Christian Advocate, *1867–1878*

Memorialized Records of Lexington District, South Carolina, 1814–1825

*Newberry County, South Carolina Deed Abstracts,
Volume I: Deed Books A-B, 1785–1794 [1751–1794]*

*Newberry County, South Carolina Deed Abstracts,
Volume II: Deed Books C, D-2, and D, 1794–1800 [1765–1800]*

*Parish Registers of Prince George Winyah Church,
Georgetown, South Carolina, 1815–1936*

*Record of Deaths in Columbia, South Carolina, and
Elsewhere as Recorded by John Glass, 1859–1877*

South Carolina Deed Abstracts, 1773–1778, Books F-4 through X-4

South Carolina Deed Abstracts, 1776–1783, Books Y-4 through H-5

South Carolina Deed Abstracts, 1783–1788, Books I-5 through Z-5

The Bedenbaugh-Betenbaugh Family:
Descendants of Johann Michael Bidenbach from
Germany to South Carolina, 1752

Tryon County, North Carolina, Minutes of the
Court of Pleas and Quarter Sessions, 1769–1779

Union County, South Carolina Deed Abstracts,
Volume I: Deed Books A-F, 1785–1800 [1752–1800]
Volume II: Deed Books G-K, 1800–1811 [1769–1811]
Volume III: Deed Books L-P, 1811–1820 [1770–1820]

Winton (Barnwell) County, South Carolina Minutes of
County Court and Will Book 1, 1785–1791

York County, South Carolina, Will Abstracts, 1787–1862 [1770–1862]